trained
and trusted
what teenagers can do if you let them

trained
and trusted
what teenagers can do if you let them

The rescue service experiences
of students at Atlantic College
1963–2013

philip green, dagfinn paust, anne perkins

in support of

ATLANTIC
PACIFIC

First published 2022

Published under licence by Brown Dog Books and
The Self-Publishing Partnership Ltd,
10b Greenway Farm, Bath Rd, Wick, nr. Bath BS30 5RL

www.selfpublishingpartnership.co.uk

ISBN printed book: 978-1-83952-400-4
ISBN e-book: 978-1-83952-401-1

Cover design by Ross Slade
Internal design by Tim Jollands

Printed and bound in the UK

This book is printed on FSC certified paper

Dedicated to the memory of David Sutcliffe, 1934–2019

Contents

Contents

List of Illustrations and Photos

HSC = Hoare-Sutcliffe Collection (held by R Slade)

1. David Sutcliffe: the man of action at his desk.

Preface

It was sunny and the first day of spring 2017, as I walked to the Grosvenor Hotel to meet David Sutcliffe. I had a bounce in my step, as if I was still 17 and had received one of the little blue notes from DBS (as we called him) with a positive comment on it, for David has insisted on the meeting, and I did not know why. My wife Louise and I were passing through London to see family while on a European holiday. David arrived punctually at 10 am from the train at Victoria Station.

He was matter-of-fact, friendly but purposeful as we sat down for tea. When the waitress served it, he ordered, more in the military sense of that word than the way it is generally used in a restaurant, croissants and jam for both of us. I was glad to see he had not changed in the 15 years since we last met.

He then pulled out two books from his satchel: his works, *The RIB, The Rigid Hulled Inflatable Boat* and *Kurt Hahn and the United World Colleges*. He inscribed *The RIB* with the words 'To Phil: Canoeists never relied on ILBs. Good for them!' It was not quite true, as the following pages show, but I appreciated the compliment.

I'd read half of it by the time we landed in Toronto, but it took a stormy day on 1 July, at our family cottage, to finish it. I then wrote to him, 'There was one example in the book that I related to personally. It was the May 1978 recovery of the body of a ten-year-old boy who had fallen off a cliff while collecting birds' eggs. I clearly remember the wailing of his distressed father.' My account of that event is included in the stories in this collection. The RIB book listed selected extracts from the college callout logs, with a perfunctory sentence or two for each.

Three days later, David replied, 'I have been giving this some thought. I have come to the conclusion that a collection of sensitive and sensitively edited memories could be a remarkable testament to the early history of Atlantic College and a very appropriate compliment to the account we now have of the rescue boat developments and achievements.'

Thus the idea of this book was born. He wrote:

> My plan would be to consult the lists of successive generations of students, which I have, identify a small number of individuals in each who I know had a rescue experience, and invite them both to write up their own experience

and to alert me to others in the same generation, who, they know, also have stories to tell. Obviously, this would embrace all the services and might (what do you think?) include non-rescue occasions if they were sufficiently remarkable to throw light on the general picture. Staff coaches should also be brought in.

He asked for my guidance and support. He planned to have the book ready by Christmas 2017 – six months away.

Alas, finding students with whom we had not had contact for up to 50 years interfered with that goal. He could not find the official Royal National Lifeboat Institution's list of callouts from the college, so we did not know who to contact for stories. He had used those callout lists for *The RIB*, but returned them after he finished the book. After the RNLI station at the college closed in 2013, the records went missing. We proceeded on a mission to rescue the rescue records. It wasn't until 1 March 2019 that the RNLI found microfiche copies in their Poole headquarters. Privacy protection laws prevented the RNLI from sending us complete copies – we had to make specific requests, and the RNLI had to redact them. It seemed the best course of action was for David to travel to Poole.

In September 2019 I received a shocking email from him:

> I am sorry about the delay in my response. The reason is my medical news, which is not so good. I was put on a course of chemotherapy which has failed dramatically to control the prostate cancer and deprived me of all energy and much of my appetite and has led me to spend much of my day stretched out on a bed or sofa. At the moment I do not have the strength to contemplate a journey to Poole. It is a very great pity it took so long to find the AC records. My approach has always been that we should approach all who took part in rescues on a very personal basis as we are interested in very personal memories. This is why I am against a 'sweep' approach such as Facebook. I think the really important thing is to find a professional and knowledgeable writer who can draw the whole thing together.

He suggested Dagfinn Paust and a few others as allies. We recruited Anne Perkins as the writer. (See 'creative team', page 239).

On 28 September he sent his last email, to me, Dagfinn and several others. He wrote:

> Phil Green described to me many months ago the emotion he went through as a direct result of a very testing experience on an AC callout, e.g., how do

you behave in front of a father who is contemplating the body of his young son lying at the foot of the cliffs? The group stood briefly at attention and removed their helmets. How many fellow students had similar experiences? How did they react, how did they inwardly come to terms to such events? I myself recall a callout on a Sunday afternoon when an elderly man, his wife beside him, had engaged the wrong gear and driven his car clean over the cliff edge. One of the Cliff Rescue team on duty that afternoon was a girl from New Zealand. She was clearly traumatised. How did she express this? By shaving her abundant hair completely and seating herself in the front row at Assembly until it had grown again. It intrigues me, looking back, how we in the college coped with such events. We had no counsellors. Was it the rigour of the overall rescue service training? Was it the intensely close relationship between the student rescue service leaders and their staff coaches? What else?

Phil Green is anxious to emphasize the extraordinary contribution that can be made by teenagers who are trained and trusted. This is all pure Kurt Hahn and should of course receive its due attention.

David gave me altogether too much credit, gentleman that he was. But with that email, a team was launched, and the book moved from conception to development. A few weeks later David Sutcliffe died.

I told a close friend and AC colleague that before David's last email I had promised myself I would never write another book. He quoted Robert Service, 'A man's last need is a thing to heed.' And so it is.

Philip Green, January 2021

Introduction

Boys must be encouraged to achieve physical fitness and to learn the necessary techniques which will permit them to work for others and to do this in situations which can also satisfy their instinct for adventure. To this end we have planned our rescue services: beach rescue, canoe lifeguards, and cliff rescue. Nothing convinces as much as does the saving of life that the common humanity of men is more important than race or colour. The recognition of this by youth ... must, we feel, make some contribution to peace. *Atlantic College (AC) prospectus, 1962.*

If we can plant the germ of new loyalties in mature men [in the NATO college] how much deeper are the roots we could sink in the youth of the Atlantic Community if, at their most impressionable period, we could gather them together in residential colleges. *Kurt Hahn 1955 (Sutcliffe,* Hahn *18).*

Kurt Hahn was the founding father of Atlantic College, and the moving spirit of its rescue services. He brought his life story to establishing the college, his last great adventure in education. Born German and Jewish in 1886, his life was shaped by the tragedies of the twentieth century in Europe, the two world wars

2. Kurt Hahn.

and the Holocaust. By 1955, when he first conceived of what became Atlantic College, catastrophe seemed imminent once again as a bi-polar world teetered on the brink of nuclear war.

Hahn had seen his life in a prosperous, highly cultured Berlin destroyed. Many of his family had been murdered. The country of his birth had been ruined. Like many public figures, for him the great question of the age was how to prevent it happening again.

Hahn was well placed to make an impact. He had devoted his life to education, in particular educating for leadership, and more narrowly still, to inculcating moral leadership as a way of inoculating future generations against the dangers of tyranny and demagoguery. But long before this, he had come to believe that students needed to be educated in a way that enabled them to behave according to an inner moral law. That meant the opportunity to transmute what he called 'noble emotions' through action into a lifelong inheritance (Sutcliffe, *Hahn* 57).

In 1920 he founded his first school, Salem, in what is now Baden-Wurttemberg in Southern Germany. The school is still flourishing and embodies many of the principles of service that came to distinguish Atlantic College. After Hitler came to power in 1933, Hahn, an early target of the Nazi regime for his outspoken criticism as well as his Jewishness, fled to Scotland where he established a second school, Gordonstoun, built on the experience of Salem.

At Salem – which, unlike Gordonstoun and Atlantic College, was coeducational from the start – students were inspired by the ideals of the former Cistercian monastery which housed the school: 'Who can awaken in the morning in the shadow of our minster and become a man without honour or culture?' (Sutcliffe, *Hahn* 95). Over time, Gordonstoun too took local inspiration, in its case from its location beside the sea in Morayshire on Scotland's north-eastern coast, and from the character of the fishermen who lived by it. Long sea voyages became a part of the Gordonstoun experience. Integral to both schools was the idea of trust, with each operating – at least in Hahn's time – on principles of self-reporting and honour.

Hahn believed that every child, regardless of background or academic ability, had the right to and the capacity for personal attainment. Sir John Hunt, conqueror of Everest and pioneer of the Outward Bound schools which promoted adventure as a way of building character, described it like this: 'the essence of [Hahn's] creed was that each boy needed a challenge personal to and attainable by himself, rather than being assessed in competition and comparison with the performance of others' (Sutcliffe, *Hahn* 103–104). The Outward Bound school that Hahn set up at Aberdovey in Wales during the war became a prototype for centres that still play an important role for hundreds of teenagers' development every year.

By 1956 Hahn was in his late 60s. He was sometimes a difficult colleague, and he had been painfully evicted from Gordonstoun after his mental health, often fragile, collapsed. But he remained a tireless networker across Europe and the United States, sustained by a lifetime of contacts and friendships. These were invaluable supports as he continued to dream up and implement schemes of international and outward-bound education. That year, 1956, he was booked to lecture at the NATO

3. Desmond Hoare, always ready to go to sea.

4. Naomi Hoare, friend and mentor to many students.

Defense College in Paris, and it was there that his ideas for a school that would be more academic than Gordonstoun, more international than Salem, offering physical and moral education to pre-university teenagers, finally coalesced.

Hahn had a genius for recruiting supporters and influencing others. Atlantic College would never have happened without the team of eminent public figures that he was able to mobilise, or the deep pockets of his business and philanthropic contacts. But for the character of the college, and its students in the early years, the man who was most significant was Rear Admiral Desmond Hoare.

Desmond Hoare was an Irishman, a career naval officer in the British Royal Navy. He was a veteran of the Second World War's legendary Arctic convoys, the ships that ploughed the perilous northern route in bitter conditions to feed Soviet Russia through the darkest years of the war. In peace he had become actively involved working with troubled boys from west London's slums.

It is a testament to Hoare, and to his wife Naomi, who played a major innovatory role while her husband was headmaster (principal) and later Provost, that he forfeited his Royal Navy pension rights in order to become the founding headmaster (a decision which left him impoverished in retirement). But Hoare was already deeply intellectually involved in the question of the best way of educating young naval recruits to encourage independence, self-reliance and moral judgement, all essential elements in the effective serviceman or woman. Long before they met, to satisfy his own interest, he had tested and found successful Hahn's ideas about the beneficial effects on academic performance of training in non-academic skills.

And like Hahn, Hoare believed the experience of being afloat was an ideal preparation for life itself. 'The human race owes much of its strength to the necessity in earlier generations to battle with nature. Men who now work on the land, those who go fishing at sea in small boats ... develop easily and naturally the qualities of watchfulness, integrity, endurance and resource ...' (Sutcliffe, *Hahn* 205). Atlantic College's rescue services were to develop all of those qualities. In this at least, Hahn and Hoare were a dream team.

In the foreword to David Sutcliffe's *The RIB, the Rigid-hulled Inflatable Lifeboat and its Place of Birth, The Atlantic College*, Naomi Hoare described her husband's belief. 'Understanding between diverse human beings was nurtured most effectively when they were involved in physical activities, especially when participating in the saving of life,' she explained.

So there is some irony in the way Hoare and Hahn nearly fell out over the first major decision: where the new college was to be sited. Hahn loved Scotland and assumed it would be there. He had already been offered Dunrobin Castle in Sutherland, very wild, more than 200 miles north of Edinburgh, and, at 600 miles from London, in British terms very, very remote. Hoare argued that the college would have no hope unless it were within reach of the capital, a university and industry – and also met a genuine demand for rescue services. He compared Dunrobin with another castle that was on the market: St Donat's, in South Wales. The Welsh castle ticked all the boxes. The biggest tick would have gone into the box marked 'danger'.

Another of the eminent men and women who made Atlantic College possible was Tony (Antonin II) Besse, whose father Antonin had been a keen supporter of Hahn's. Antonin had built a vast trading empire in the Middle East in the first half of the 20th century. His son Tony had restored its fortunes after the war, and like his father became a generous supporter of educational causes – perhaps a compensation for the education he missed growing up in wartime France. In 1960 it was his money that secured St Donat's for the college.

His daughter Joy, a student from 1975–77, reflected:

5. *Antonin Besse, whose generosity enabled the*
acquisition of St Donat's, at the helm of his boat 'Ocean Joy'.

Dad never expounded on specific reasons for the UWC involvement, I think he thought very highly of Kurt Hahn and found in the small-knit team of men involved in the foundation of the movement a form of deep shared purpose and trust that fed his soul on lots of levels. Also, Dad was a sort of Don Quixote, he liked to tilt at windmills to show that the impossible could be done. He was right – mostly – but not always, and lost feathers in these battles but they were part of his make-up.

He was physically restless, and happiest at the helm of his sailing boat heading into heavy weather. That is the best metaphor for his life really – sailing his own boat on his own terms into heavy weather, just to come out

6. Joy Besse, Antonin's daughter and a student at AC from 1975–77.

the other side. So the rescue service/physical activity side was very much in keeping with this spirit of actively seeking physical challenge.

The Bristol Channel, with its huge tidal range, fierce Atlantic gales and lethal currents, remains among the most dangerous stretches of water off the British Isles. 'It is not too much to say,' an unattributed quote (very probably Hoare) claims in David Sutcliffe's tribute to the founding fathers of Atlantic College, 'that Inshore Rescue had much to do with the choice of site for the first Atlantic College; first because it is one of the firmest of College rules that students are to stay alive and secondly because the rescue of others is both worthwhile and good fun.' Atlantic College went to St Donat's not in spite of the treacherous inshore beach and sea conditions, but because of them. Readers who are not familiar with the coast of South Wales and the waters off St Donat's should not be fooled by the word 'channel'. Although one may see across the Bristol Channel to the coast of Somerset in England to the south on a very clear day, due west the next stop across the Irish Sea and the Atlantic Ocean is Newfoundland in Canada.

The location meant that Hoare could claim that education would be about more than academic success, the search for which, in his opinion, often came at the expense of developing more important aspects of the human character. As he boasted in 1966, when AC had been running for four years:

Our sailing is conducted in the most dangerous waters in which I have operated small boats. Before we opened the school, all the local experts said we would never sail dinghies off our beach. The Deputy Chief Inspector, RNLI has said that we probably have the most difficult operating conditions of any of their 50 or so Inshore Rescue Boat stations around the coast of Britain (quoted in Sutcliffe, *Hahn* 208).

Clearly, the location posed immediate challenges from the weather and the sea conditions. (Initially, there was not even access to the beach. The sea defences had to be breached to make a slipway from which to launch the boats.) Hoare's imagination and ingenuity found at least partial answers.

Hoare's development of the rigid inflatable boat, which became one of the world's most popular pleasure craft as well as the basis of the RNLI inshore rescue fleet, has its own history. But, as students' memories on the coming pages affirm, the process of design and build carried out by the admiral and those early students in the first decade of the college was integral to the rescue experience.

7. Character-building waves.

8. Educational capsize.

Initially, the boats were primarily to protect sailors in the college's small fleet of Fireball sailboats and single-handed dinghies, as well as the kayaks and surfboats that were a feature of afternoon activities in those years. There was no question that the rescue boats needed to be on hand if other waterborne activities were to take place. The waters, as Hoare had boasted, were indeed treacherous.

But the 'home guard' responsibilities were only ever a start.

Neither Hoare nor Hahn ever intended Atlantic College to stand alone: it was to be the heart and inspiration for a network of coastal rescue services which would be operated, like the college rescue services, by local teenagers. To start with they would be trained at the college, by college students. It was to be, David Sutcliffe later explained, the alma mater of coast rescue training (*Hahn* 211). AC would play 'a leading part in a development affecting the human attitudes of youth at large.'

This was not an entirely novel idea. Hoare was impressed by the way other countries were already moving towards empowering pre-university students in what would nowadays be called active citizenship. Australian beaches, for example, had a well-established surf lifesaving scheme run by teenagers. The US was developing the Peace Corps as a way for young Americans to offer service in the developing world. Britain had the equivalent Voluntary Service Overseas, aimed at that time at pre-university teenagers. Neither Hahn nor Hoare ever imagined that rescue work could only serve and be served by a small, privileged elite.

A college prospectus of 1972 set out the ambition:

> We need to show in a convincing manner that the formal educational needs of modern society do not have to be met at the expense of more important human characteristics. The heart of the matter is the need to demonstrate that self-discipline, devotion, imagination, courage and response to challenge can be developed in materially prosperous societies. Our civilization has many roots. One is that sense of obligation to the community which overrides self-interest when the issue is important.

The project could not have succeeded without the backing of many eminent men and women. But for students at the college, the third in the triumvirate of pioneers was David Sutcliffe (DBS), who had taught at Salem and at Gordonstoun and came to Atlantic College to help launch the new college. In 1969 he became its headmaster, and although he left after a decade, he remained the driving force behind the international United World Colleges movement. (United World Colleges or UWC was the umbrella organisation founded as the movement expanded beyond Atlantic College to colleges around the world.)

9. David Sutcliffe at home in a RIB.

In years to come, he sometimes lost patience with its founding institution, but he never lost contact with the place where it began.

This is not a comprehensive account of the college, and we have not conducted an exhaustive fact check although we have corrected stories where there are errors, for example, of geography, or where a name has been misremembered. Rather, it is an attempt to find out how successful its ideals have been, and how they might be carried on into the future. On the journey, it throws up some tricky questions about the nature of responsibility and trust and where their limits might lie.

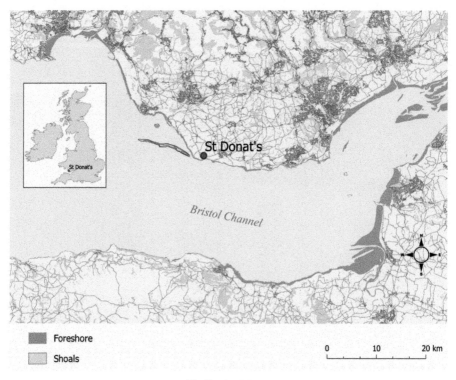

10. Context map.

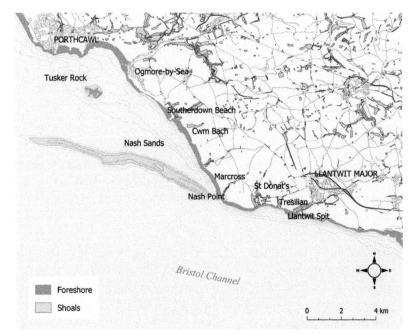

11. The stretch of coast patrolled from the RNLI station at St Donat's.

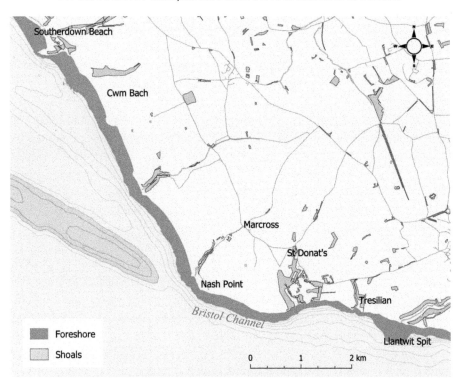

12. The main callout area west and east of St Donat's.

CHAPTER ONE

The Challenge

Did you never realise that the main purpose of the boats was to instil respect for skill of hand in the academically besotted students? *Desmond Hoare, quoted by DBS in his memorial address, 1988.*

In no other aspect of life at St Donat's is it brought home to one so completely that what matters is the quality of a human being when the two of you are suspended from the edge of a cliff at the end of a rope, or out at sea on a rough day. *Desmond Hoare,* A Place in the World *film, 1968.*

Atlantic College's first intake of 59 students arrived at St Donat's in September 1962. The teachers had been recruited, the curriculum set, and there was a place for everyone to sleep. For the students, two intense years lay ahead, culminating for early generations in A-levels, the exams sat by all pre-university school-leavers in England and Wales at the time. In 1971, these were replaced by the International Baccalaureate, a broader curriculum which required students to study sciences, arts and languages. Students aged between 16 and 19, selected by national committees set up in each participating country, came from around the world. Command of the English language was often patchy.

That much was clear. Less clear was that teachers and students together – whether they realised it or not – were about to invent Atlantic College.

Most of all they invented the college rescue services. Rescue was at the heart of the whole purpose of the college, a scheme to weld students into trained teams and then entrust to them the challenging, priceless task of saving life.

It was the right place, and the right time, to launch such an experiment: Europe's growing post-war prosperity was leading to a huge expansion in seaside holidays for which traditional coastal rescue was ill-prepared.

It was easy enough to say what had to be done. Students were to provide protection and rescue for anyone in danger at sea, on the beaches, or on the cliffs. But how? Over the next decade and more, the Admiral, teachers and students were to work that out. How, in particular, to overcome three separate but related challenges: first, how to develop the equipment that would enable them to be as fast and as safe as possible in extraordinarily challenging circumstances; second, how to refine the training that was needed to operate the equipment so that students could learn to be effective in the shortest possible space of time;

and finally, to use that equipment and training to persuade existing lifesaving authorities, as well as the wider public and the casualties themselves, that they knew what they were doing.

In the early 1960s, organised coastal rescue had yet to respond to the new challenge of mass seaside holidaymaking. The Coastguard was an early 19th-century institution that was set up to police Britain's shoreline against smugglers. The role soon expanded to include the rescue of shipwrecked mariners, and the protection of ships' cargoes against looters, a notorious problem not least around St Donat's, long the scene of 'wrecking', where ships were lured by false lights into dangerous waters in order to relieve them of their valuable loads. HM Coastguard developed into a kind of frontier police that kept law and order in coastal waters.

Only in the 1960s, as Atlantic College began to develop Cliff Rescue from techniques developed for the mountains, did HM Coastguard begin to expand its own rescue operations. It invested in all-terrain vehicles and in 1971 the first Search and Rescue helicopter was brought into service. In 1998, the Coastguard merged with the Marine Safety Agency. This was the context in which the College's cliff rescue service developed in close cooperation with the Coastguard.

The even bigger challenge, however, was safety on the beaches. In the early 1960s it was commonplace to talk of a 'Drowning Season', the mid-summer weeks when families went to the seaside often with only the haziest ideas of tides and currents. Around the coast of the UK, more than a hundred deaths by drowning were recorded each summer. Some form of lifesaving service could clearly play an important role. So Beach Rescue was born.

Initially, the College divided beach rescue from canoe rescue: beach rescue operated on the beaches. (Note on terminology: in UK English usage 'canoe' means what the rest of the world calls 'kayak': a one-person canoe with a watertight covering where the paddler uses a double-bladed paddle. The college only ever had kayaks.)

Beach Rescue included surf lifesaving techniques learned from Australia's surf lifesaving associations; these techniques were just beginning to be employed on UK surf beaches. After the two were united under the heading Beach Rescue, kayaking continued to be a major part of the service's programme of boatbuilding and training. From the College's first summer in 1963, students had a serious role guarding the local beaches of Southerndown and Ogmore during the peak holiday period in August.

However, it was the rescue boats that were to become most closely identified with the college's brand.

The rescue boats were initially developed as the safety craft for students sailing and kayaking off the St Donat's beach. But they quickly became part of a novel and much more ambitious venture: that of providing official emergency inshore rescue under the aegis of the RNLI – the Royal National Lifeboat Institution.

The RNLI is one of the pillars of British civil society, a volunteer institution supported entirely by charitable donations that was first set up in 1824 to save life at sea, and today operates over two hundred lifeboat stations along the coast of the British Islands. Atlantic College and Desmond Hoare were to play a big part in changing the face of this venerable institution, designing and testing a new small, inshore rescue craft, cheaper and nippier close to shore than the all-weather unsinkable lifeboats that still come to the aid of those in peril on the sea in conditions too tough for small boats.

The story of the development of the rigid inflatable boat has been recounted by Hoare's successor as headmaster, David Sutcliffe. His book, *The RIB, The Rigid Hulled Inflatable Boat* is the place to go for technical detail, and much else about the early history of Atlantic College. This is the story from a different angle, the story as seen by the students.

For at least the first decade of the college's existence, 1962–72, many of the students who joined the Inshore Rescue Boat (ILB) service were also part of Desmond Hoare's design and build squad. Hoare himself was a naval engineer who relished the experience of designing and refining a boat that was tough enough to cope with the UK's rough inshore weather and nimble enough to operate in shallow, rocky waters. Although a knowledge of the workings of the outboard engines and the structure of the boat remained essential for all crew for the next 50 years, the early years provided unparalleled opportunities for acquiring boatbuilding as well as maintenance skills.

The college's first inflatable was a 13-foot 'RFD' (named after the founder of the company that made it, Reginald Foster Dagnall) which had been bought with a gift of £500 donated by a friend of Admiral Hoare. There were also some French-made Zodiac dinghies. All the boats folded up and were intended to be packed away after use. The only thing that stopped them from folding up in the waves were several pieces of plywood that served to reinforce the rubber floor. These articulated floorboards did not add any linear rigidity to the boat, but they did spread out the weight of the crew to prevent stretching out and possibly

13. Practical boatbuilding.

puncturing the rubberised nylon fabric floor. The boats also had an inflatable keel, which gave them added rigidity when launching through the surf and reasonable directional stability at speeds below 20 knots.

In the first year, the main challenge was keeping the Zodiacs seaworthy and capable of performing their safety boat duties around the college's fleet of Fireball and other sailing dinghies and the squads of kayakers and surfers.

Andreas Schwerdtfeger was among the first students in 1962:

> I had early on in my AC time decided to 'go into' sailing and Rescue
> Boats. At the time our rubber dinghies did not have the wooden under-
> construction that Admiral Hoare developed only at the very end of my time;
> our boats had flat rubber bottoms with wooden grates to be laid inside and
> we were constantly busy repairing them and gluing them back to the side
> tubes. The boats were powered by two outboard engines and the strain
> on the material was fairly high. But we were proud of our material and
> enthused by 'the task' of safeguarding the sailing and canoeing activities of
> the College and the hope of once really doing the great deed. I had gotten a
> RNLI auxiliary coxswain's certificate sometime before and 'my boat,' sailing,
> water-skiing and canoeing were much more in my mind – and are certainly
> more in my memory – than all the academic endeavours to get our A-Levels.

['Coxswain' is an old naval term for a person in charge of a boat, particularly its navigation and steering, mostly used for smaller boats (originally a 'cog'). The RNLI itself uses the title only for the captain of its large seagoing lifeboats, not its inflatables or 'inshore lifeboats'.]

Even though the Zodiacs were not very seaworthy, on a fine day there would be long trips, sometimes even across the Bristol Channel to Somerset. But their flat bottoms meant the boats could not easily navigate the typical waves in the area at any speed. Closer to shore, the height of the surf was often considerable. Nor on a rough day could they get through the turbulence of the rips at Nash Point, a few miles west of the College. Great care had to be paid in this area stretching almost to Porthcawl. The shifting weather and huge tidal differences, and the notoriously fast, dangerous tidal race between the Nash Sands and the shore created large, unpredictable waves. A boat might make it to its destination without difficulty, but the return trip might prove very challenging.

Admiral Hoare was soon in discussions with the RNLI about developing the inflatables as rescue boats and he secured a deal where the college was given a number of different Zodiacs to test. These RNLI boats were prosaically named Zodiac 33 or Zodiac 38. Early boats built by students had exotic names – Freya, Bacchus, Santa Maria and Proteus. Later the designation was either 'X' for experimental, or 'B' for official RNLI inshore lifeboat. The designation 'inshore' was used to distinguish the inflatables from the larger, seagoing vessels that the RNLI had used so far, and continued to use at the majority of its stations. Initially, the College inshore rescue boats were referred to by their acronym IRBs, but AC later adopted the RNLI abbreviation ILB, for Inshore Lifeboats.

Desmond Hoare wanted St Donat's to be one of the RNLI's first generation of inshore rescue stations. But the first objective was to be recognised as part of the Coastguards. One former student from the USA, who arrived in September 1963, recalls that the literature he received from the College in the autumn of 1962 (as an applicant), was already advertising the fact that the Coastguard had assigned a considerable stretch of coastline to the College for patrolling and lifeguarding.

The following year, in October 1963, the College was announced as a trial Inshore Rescue Boat station, one of nine established by the RNLI that year around the coast of the British Isles. However, only the station at St Donat's and two other locations were operational through the subsequent winter season.

Meanwhile, work to improve the resilience and manoeuvrability of the inflatables was continuing. John Grey-Davies was in the workshops between 1966 and 1968:

> I do remember assisting with the construction of the prototype of the
> current Atlantic Class IRB. Desmond Hoare was clearly trying to improve
> on the efficacy of the Zodiac IRB which had a flexible hull making a speedy
> journey rather uncomfortable. One of his first designs became known as X2,
> which is the boat I captained in my second year.

As Hoare liked to explain, the boats were designed as much by the way they handled in the Bristol Channel as by the application of theoretical concepts. John Grey-Davies was at the leading edge of design:

> [The X2] was not an ideal design because it was too long and if it entered
> a tide race, such as that off Aberthaw power station, the bow tended to
> bury itself in a wave thereby flooding the boat with six inches or so of water.
> Other than that, it was very easy to navigate with a steering wheel mounted
> in front of the coxswain's seat in the centre of the boat. It had two outboard
> motors which made it very powerful and potentially very fast. X3 and X4
> had been constructed prior to my arrival at AC with wooden hulls and driven
> using the tiller fitted to the single outboard motor. But Desmond Hoare
> perfected the design and he wished to have a further two constructed.

> During my first year, one was built by a professional boatyard which
> became X6 and the other one, X5, was built in Atlantic College under the
> supervision of Desmond Hoare himself, with assistance from the college
> carpenter and a small number of students which included me. The main
> student was Paul Jeffries who had experience of DIY [do-it-yourself] boat
> construction and was in charge of most of the work we did. I had no such
> experience, but I learnt how to manipulate very basic tools which ever
> since has been extremely valuable to me. We constructed the hull, but
> the inflatable section was built professionally elsewhere. We glued the
> two together and prepared it for the launching which I'm afraid I do not
> remember. X5 and X6 became the main boats used during my second year
> and the design [eventually] became the Atlantic Class IRB.

Everyone involved in the Rescue Boats was also involved in building and maintaining the boats and winches and engines and kayaks, all the equipment needed for the services. It was at the heart of all the activities. For some students like Lis Hostvedt (1967–69) the sense of teamwork and learning new skills became almost more important than going on callouts.

> We did quite a lot of developing the boats ... I was part of the group that
> developed the first one with a fibreglass bottom, built on the principles of

the surfboard. They turned out to be very fragile, especially on that [rocky] coast. We had to do all the preparations and the making of the tube and putting the handles on, in a group of four or six. The timber hulls became really heavy and weren't maintained more than once a year and they absorbed water and became a very different thing to handle. I think the idea was it would be such an easy thing to keep, with fibreglass, but that wasn't the case.

I liked the camaraderie of working in a small group on a project that came to something – it was ours, our project, and I think that was important. And we did launch her and take her to sea. It became apparent before I left that it wasn't going to be a success.

According to David Sutcliffe, one reason for developing the inshore boats was to keep the RNLI in the headlines: as an institution entirely reliant on donations, every life saved was also a rallying cry for fundraising. Admiral Hoare saw that good PR for the RNLI could also be good for the College. That may have been one reason why in 1968 he put forward Lis Hostvedt's name with that year's other candidates for registration as RNLI crew members. No female had ever been recognised as qualified to serve on any RNLI boat.

Desmond Hoare claimed it was all a brilliant coup on his part. Lis Hostvedt says,

Desmond did tell me he was going to do it. He said he didn't see why I shouldn't go forward with the others just because I was a girl. I think he expected it to be rejected – [although] most of the people who stayed on in boats for the second year would have qualified. I do remember him coming up to me later and saying we've had things back and your name went through with everyone else's [submitted as simply 'E. Hostvedt'], so I've now told them you're a girl.

In fact, Hoare was much too canny to risk it going wrong, and he had already received private assurances that her candidacy would be successful. He had also made it clear there would be more female candidates in the future as the college expanded its intake of girls. For public consumption, however, the RNLI was keen to emphasise that this was an exception rather than a new rule. According to Sutcliffe's history of the RIB, the formal response was this:

It is not a practice which we would like to see adopted generally because, although a girl might make just as good a helmsman as a boy, in the majority of cases it is problematic whether she would have the strength and stamina to stand up to a really severe service ... we are prepared to make a special case of Elisabeth Hostvedt provided she can pass the full medical test which is required for IRB crew membership, and that you are in all respects satisfied that she has the physique to stand up to an arduous service.

As it turned out, the RNLI leapt at the opportunity to use Hostvedt's skills – and picture appeal – for publicity purposes. It was at the beginning of the peak in second-wave feminism, and the RNLI was anxious to show it was open to equal opportunity. Hostvedt was sent out to be its female face. She did not get any of the advice about dress and TV appearances and interview technique that nowadays would be routine.

> The RNLI decided rather than make a fuss about women not being suitable, they'd make a thing of it. So I did a TV show where I had to wear my thick RNLI sweater on a hot July day when I had a beautiful stripy T-shirt dress that I had intended to wear.

But it worked. The level of interest showed how Atlantic College and the RNLI had captured public attention:

> I also went on [the national BBC radio show] Jack de Manio, and I went to the Boat Show [the major annual fair for amateur boaters] and met Chay Blythe who'd just rowed across the Atlantic. And I sat on boats and had totally inappropriate low-level shots taken up my legs.

14. Elisabeth Hostvedt, the first female RNLI-registered female crew.

Lis Hostvedt had been one of the first, nine-strong, intake of girls to the College. Sally Stradling arrived two years later, when the number went up to 90, of a total student body of about 300. Going coeducational had taken significant investment in altering accommodation, but in the rescue services, there was no adaptation to the arrival of girls. Seagoing rescue services in particular favoured the big and the strong and although there were often excellent swimmers among the girls, few of the female students could match the males for sheer physical strength. There is no record of it ever becoming an issue among the students, but at least in those early years, coeducation was not the same as gender equality.

Another of the girls who arrived in 1969, Penny Sutton, was actually awarded the boy's scholarship by her county education authority, Cheshire. (Local education authorities in England and Wales were important providers of scholarships until cuts to their budgets in the 1980s made backing less well-off students unaffordable. Without such support, Atlantic College lost an important social dimension.) In Sutton's words:

> Having obtained the Cheshire boy's scholarship for that year I found myself
> in all-male double maths classes and mainly male physical science classes. Of
> course, the rescue service I chose was also mainly male dominated – I had
> the feeling girls were tolerated but should not expect too much. I remember
> very few specifics of our first year training. I remember rushing through
> lunch in order to be down at the seafront as soon as possible. I remember
> gluing our wetsuits together looking forward to the day when we could
> use them. We went out in exciting weather conditions, presumably mostly
> in the cold, although I do not remember being cold. We practised rolling
> [uprighting] an IRB which was a great deal harder than rolling a Fireball. If
> you had not capsized when out sailing a Fireball you were considered not to
> have tried to test the boat and crew to the limit.

Sutton, like other girls, found a champion in Admiral Hoare's wife:

> Naomi Hoare was my mentor down at the seafront. She taught us girls to
> sail, she encouraged me when things seemed to be too much. I vaguely
> remember being part of an IRB crew in my first year, but the second year
> boys were mostly not interested in a female first year IRB crew member.
> I was not as strong, fast or tall as the boys, all of which were very useful
> attributes in IRB. I spent as much of my time down at the seafront as
> possible, in other words when I was not studying. Having been top of my
> class until then, I found A levels a very different matter and had to work

hard to keep up with the work. It did not help when the bottom half of my maths classes dropped out and I found myself at the bottom [of the class].

Admiral Hoare had already championed the introduction of girls to the college. Now he decided it was time for an all-female ILB (Rescue Boat) crew.

'Des [Hoare] was keen to have an all-girl rescue boat,' remembers Sally Stradling, who became a crew member:

> [He wanted] the first RNLI craft to be built and crewed entirely by females. A number of us put our names forward and the crew of X16 finally comprised Penny Sutton (Captain), Sian Owen, Marnie Drummond and me. We all worked hard on the construction of the hull with hours of endless sanding, painting layers of varnish and finally the attachment of the tube and seat. Anticipation of the launch date mounted which finally took place with Des and Naomi and a small crowd of fellow students on the foreshore. Short speeches, the cracking open of a bottle of champagne over the bow and the boat was duly launched. The excitement of this ground-breaking event was short lived as the X16 was for some inexplicable reason doomed to engine failure.

Penny Sutton, like Lis Hostvedt, cherishes the memories of the teamwork of boatbuilding as much as the challenge of going to sea.

> We painted X16 (Atlanta) yellow and green. This was perhaps not the best combination of colours as someone kindly pointed out, but then I am certainly not an artist. We spent hours scraping the rubber on the tube so that we could glue it to the wooden hull.

Dave Nockels, a contemporary of Penny Sutton's, was also hard at work on his boat.

> For some Rescue-Boaters, usually just a few, the building and maintenance was a major task. Usually carried out in addition to seagoing, this pretty much involved out of hours working, and even some missing of classes. For me, it was an essential part of the experience.

The level of expertise that the really keen rescue boaters acquired was remarkable. Dave Nockels had an experience that could have been catastrophic, had he not already learned enough about engines to anticipate it. The lesson stayed with him for the rest of his life:

> X9 was 'my' boat. Of course, the best boat in the fleet. She was essentially a longer version of other contemporary boats, such as X11. Reflecting the

extra length and weight, X9 had a 65 hp outboard which was a different design; the others were fitted with 50hp.

We began to hear a 'tinkle' from the engine, most notable at idle. Upon investigation, we found that the flywheel (located on the top of the engine) had become cracked. The flywheel has several purposes but basically it helps to make the engine run more smoothly. It spins at very high speed (engine speed). On X9, it was constructed of various pieces of steel. The main part of the flywheel was a plate with drilled holes to allow it to be connected to the crankshaft. It was bolted to the engine crankshaft with about 8 bolts. The flywheel had cracked between the holes. These involve a well-known engineering phenomenon called stress concentration, where the holes form the starting point for the crack and its propagation.

Such a cracked flywheel is extremely dangerous. To make sure we understood that, a couple of students were shown a harrowing film of the consequences of a flywheel bursting on a Mercury test boat on a lake in the USA. As the burst happened, it was like a grenade exploding, with shrapnel bursting from the engine and killing the boat driver. I never forgot that lesson. Many years later I used the knowledge gained to investigate a funny vibration and subsequently identify a crack in the tail rotor drive of a helicopter. Such a crack would probably have proved fatal, had it propagated.

Looking back over his decade at Atlantic College and the extraordinary achievement of developing a prototype that transformed inshore rescue, Desmond Hoare claimed he was merely responding to necessity. He declared that it was only the 'maintenance burden which in 1965 sent us looking for a new solution that would preserve the rescue qualities of the inflatable at a lower cost in time, labour and money.' This was what he called the 'discipline of the moment'.

Among the early models was Atalanta, 'united by glue with a tube and a flat piece of ply', according to Hoare. But even though she was not very seaworthy, she won a 40-mile powerboat race in Porthcawl.

The admiral was always keen to test the boats the college designed against the RNLI boats, although, as John de Blocq van Kuffeler remembers, not invariably with the result he wanted:

Desmond Hoare was of course keen to demonstrate that X1 was superior to the other inflatables, including our Freya, the official canvas bottomed RNLI boat. He therefore organised a race between all the boats and offered the sum of £10 as a prize for a meal for the crew at a local restaurant of their choice. The race was round a series of buoys. My fellow crew members and I were very competitive and serviced Freya's 40 HP Evinrude with new plugs and a new propeller before the race. The starting gun fired and X1 raced into an early lead upwind with us in Freya in second place close behind. On rounding the final buoy, the coxswain of X1 took the turn at too great a speed resulting in their propeller coming out of the water and it temporarily slowed them down. We took the turn inside them to lead the race home and win. This was not the result Desmond Hoare was looking for, but he gracefully presented the prize to us in Assembly together with a signed photograph of Freya and crew. The three of us had a great dinner that weekend at the smart restaurant on Sully Island – £10 then bought the best dinner for three people in South Wales!

To underscore how seaworthy the RIBs had become, in 1969, at three weeks' notice, two students built 'Psychedelic Surfer' to take part in the gruelling 1,700 nautical mile Round Britain Powerboat Race. She came in 19th place out of over 60 entrants. Just 24 boats completed the entire course.

There was one more experimental concept to be tried before the final design was settled in 1973. Peter Williamson and Angus Matthews, both students from 1969 to 1971, were her builders. Angus Matthews has written an account of their adventures:

15. Psychedelic Surfer.

Through the winter and spring of 1970 Peter Williamson and I were responsible for construction of a new rigid hull inflatable boat (X-15) built at Atlantic College under the intense supervision of Admiral Hoare. Her unofficial name was Jemima Puddleduck to emulate the esteemed names given to the RNLI's larger lifeboats. The concept was a midsized inshore rescue boat for use inside the surf line. Unlike the previous mini boats, designed to be launched from patrolled beaches, X15 was intended to sweep in from the sea to conduct a rescue inside the surf break with the ability to return to sea with the casualty. The layout was unusual with two seats positioned side by side well aft in the boat. This was done to move the weight aft to provide more lift when riding down a steep wave and to salvage enough space for a prone casualty. The traditional centre console would have used most of the space as she was narrower in the beam as well. The bow had additional dead-rise to improve performance in surf. The transom was angled more sharply than other X boats to allow the engine to be set to lowest tilt adjustment to hold the bow down for open ocean use and tilted up to give more bow lift in the surf. (This was well before the existence of the power trim option.)

The first engine on the boat was a 40hp Evinrude outboard equipped with an experimental Hamilton Jet pump in place of the traditional lower unit and prop. It was great in shallow water and for a standing start from the sand at Southerndown as a wave rolled in and floated the boat. It was also very effective for towing as we could overpower a larger IRB with more horsepower like X11 when tied stern to stern with both boats powering away from each other. The Admiral loved tests like this. The prop-equipped engine would cavitate [over-rev] and slip; the jet provided steady thrust. The jet was also fantastic for soaking Beach Rescue teams with its discharge blast. The engine had a lot of problems: over-revving resulting in cracked fly-wheels and scored piston rings due to the high RPM. The Admiral determined there was a loss of some 25% of efficiency at the high end, reducing the boat's speed considerably. The boat was then equipped with a conventional 40hp Mercury and performed very well.

At the end of term in the Spring of 1970, Peter and I convinced the Admiral that we should show the flag by a journey down the Thames from near the headwaters at Lechlade to Chertsey where I had a summer job at Penton Hook Marina. The Admiral was very keen on this because he appreciated the value of both an adventure and promotion.

Peter Williamson recalls in particular the controversy over side-by-side seats:

There was considerable opposition to having seats side-by-side. One of the problems was how to deal with issues at the rear of the boat. This was solved by ingenious innovation and theft. The Tythe Barn had a number of plastic chairs with conveniently shaped plastic orange backs and seats. We purloined a couple of them and removed their legs. The crew seat swivelled from front to back on a couple of bolts and the driving seat was fixed.

Problem solved.

In 1973 Desmond Hoare was granted the patent rights for the RIB design. Famously, he sold them to the RNLI for £1. Little did he know of the tremendous commercial success that his revolutionary design was to have. Neither he, personally, nor the College itself benefited financially.

Psychedelic Surfer and Jemima Puddleduck (X15) were predecessor variants of the X17 hull. After RNLI assessment, a new class of inshore lifeboat, the 'Atlantic 21', was named after the College, in recognition of the development work it had done. In 1973 the College took delivery of B-508, one of the first of the Atlantic 21s to go into service. B-508 was built from wood but was then used to make a mould so that all future Atlantic 21s could be built from glass-fibre. Because of its speed and seaworthiness, soon only this College boat was used for callouts.

The design developed quickly. Easy-to-see orange-coloured tubes were added, and a 'roll bar' above the engines, with an inflatable bag that the crew members could engage if the boat should flip and help bring the boat upright again. The difficulty of righting the boats, and the unpopularity of training to learn how to do it, becomes clear in the next chapter.

For the next 30 years, Atlantic College operated Atlantic-21s from St Donat's. Only in 2000, when the last RNLI boat, the Colin James Daniel, arrived at the college, was there an upgrade to the Atlantic 75. Atlantic 21s had been phased out entirely at AC by 2008, but together with their successors, the Atlantic 75 and 85, they are still to be found all around the coast of Britain.

Boatbuilding did not stop at the college just because the design for the RNLI had been finalised. In 1978, David Sutcliffe reintroduced wood – which had largely been replaced by fibreglass – and the S series was launched, student-built training boats. Only in the 1990s did boatbuilding cease – briefly revitalized around 2000–2001 when several boats were built, in fibreglass, moulded on a previous AC boat. The first one was called the Phoenix, progenitor of a series of 'P-boats'. In 2015, Robin Jenkins, an ex-student and former rescue boater and boatbuilder, started a charity called Atlantic Pacific at St Donat's, building mini RIBs (a concept called 'Lifeboat in a Box') to be exported to disaster areas around

*16. An AtlanticPacific RIB: a new version of the original
concept of training young people to save lives.*

the world, accompanied by suitable training. They were modelled on one of the very first RIBs, X6. All proceeds from the sale of this book will go to Atlantic Pacific.

The boats were not the only area of innovation. Establishing a cliff rescue service required a similar level of adaptation, a response to what Desmond Hoare liked to call 'the discipline of the situation.'

Many of the local beaches lay at the foot of cliffs 30–60m high, made of the crumbly local mix of sandstone and shale: very unstable. They were to be one of the most constant sources of casualties. Holidaymakers took unthinking risks and fell, or they were hit by falling rocks, or trapped and cut off by the huge rise and fall of the tides. Suicides leapt. Rock climbers misjudged an ascent.

Even for properly trained and equipped climbers these cliffs were dangerous. Worse, the basics of cliff rescue – being able to descend the cliff safely and come

17. Character-building cliffs.

back with a casualty – were made almost impossible because of the difficulty of anchoring ropes in the shallow soil and unstable rock at the top of the cliffs.

The first head of Cliff Rescue was Peter Jolley, a chemistry teacher. He was backed by the head of maths, Peter Dean and Graham Lovelock, head of chemistry. Later, Jolley summed up the situation he found on arrival:

> I can well remember how terrified I was of the damp rubble of these cliffs compared with the good sound rock on which I had previously climbed … we also surveyed the clifftops for belaying points and were dismayed to find that, apart from two small stretches, there was precious little to tie a rope to along nine miles of cliff … there were numerous vertical faults even in the coastal bays, and the headland points were so unstable as to be suicidal to the climber. For about thirty feet at the base of the cliff the rock was weathered by the sea and was smooth and firm, but the top twenty feet of any cliff is very unstable indeed. Water draining from the land makes this section wet and very loose. In wet and frosty weather large sections break away from the top and in dry seasons the shale bands become powdery and produce a rain of smaller stones when disturbed. Because of wave action at the base, this kind of cliff is always overhanging …

Jolley came up with three guiding principles: avoid headlands if at all possible (most people get into trouble in the bays, caught by the incoming tide). Place no strain on the lip of the cliff. Keep both rescuer and casualty away from the cliff face.

Jolley set out to overcome the challenges. Consulting widely, he learned of the Molex ground anchor, a long metal rod literally screwed into the ground by two people using a bar. Three of these screws in a triangle, experiments showed, provided the necessary security. Then he heard of the Tirfor Hoist (a lifting device developed to free victims of fallen masonry), which he adapted. Finally, he and the various engineers that he persuaded to help developed a crane with a swinging boom to carry the cable and support both rescuer and victim while suspending them away from the face of the cliff and out of danger of falling debris. The crane had a lifting capacity of 15 cwt or 762 kg. In a news report, the *South Wales Echo* announced that it had been constructed by a Newport engineering firm for £52.10s (about £1,000 in today's money).

But that was only the start. The first version of Jolley's crane was so heavy that in his words, 'over longish distances the rescue team was in need of revival itself on arrival at the cliff.' It was decided that the safety factor was too large, and the crane was made to less demanding specifications.

18. The crane – an innovative solution to safe climbing on unstable cliffs.

Another problem was the painful burns inflicted by rope sling and carabiner abseils, which was solved by adapting a parachute harness. A third was communication between rescuer and the top of the cliff. VHF radios helped, but they were cumbersome and difficult to use. Jolley correctly called for a helmet-fitted radio integral ear and microphone of the sort later used by the RNLI.

In its third year, 1965 – as that early publicity material had envisaged – Cliff Rescue applied to become an Auxiliary Coastguard unit. Training at Swansea and

Llantwit Major ensued, and the status was conferred.

Even so, when Ivar Lund Mathiesen – who had extensive expedition experience – started teaching at AC in 1974, he found the crane redundant and the whole operation a little quaint.

> During the AC term weeks, the unit would receive callouts for the occasional incidents, and the unit had at that stage established rescue techniques known from the British climbing scene, rather than using Coastguard equipment and techniques. There was a complete Breeches Buoy kit at the college, but that was dumped in a store somewhere, together with the remnants of the crane, which seemed to have been decommissioned before my time. [A Breeches buoy was a 19th-century device where a lifebuoy was attached, literally, to a pair of breeches (pants). The buoy and its accompanying line were fired by a rocket out to shipwrecked sailors who

19. Keeping up to date with 19th-century techniques: the Breeches buoy.

secured the rope at their end and then, stepping through the lifebelt into
the breeches, slid down it or were hauled to safety.]

Even after St Donat's had replaced Llantwit Major as the area's Auxiliary
Coastguard station, the Breeches buoy was still on the equipment list. According
to Lund Mathiesen:

> When the new Llantwit Major Coastguard Station was opened on the
> college ground, next door to the carpenters' hut on the road down
> to the seafront, it consisted of two buildings, one for the college Cliff
> Rescue equipment, camp store etc, and a neighbouring hut exclusive for
> Coastguard equipment – store, office, radio equipment etc. In addition,
> we had two Land Rovers, both equipped with capstan [winch]: one short
> wheelbase for regular patrols and callouts, and one long wheelbase, which
> carried most of the technical Cliff Rescue – gear, rope bags, stretcher etc, in
> addition to having passenger carrying capacity up to 8 team members. There
> was also a horsebox type of trailer, fully equipped with the breeches buoy
> equipment, rocket launchers etc.
>
> Once every two years or so, the company was drilled in the use of the
> breeches buoy equipment, normally watched over by a senior Coastguard
> Officer from Swansea. The culmination of the drill was the launching of the
> heavy rocket from its launching pad. A lot of noise and smoke! On one such
> drill on the field next door to the academic buildings the rocket narrowly
> avoided penetrating the college farm's sheep shed. A present civilian
> spectator was so impressed that he immediately baptized his little dog Cliff
> (Rescue).
>
> Occasionally, these rocket drills were organized as a competition with
> neighbouring Coastguard companies – those competitions were normally
> won by the college team; it proved very difficult to beat those strong, fit and
> motivated AC students!

The Land Rover played a significantly more important role in rescue.

> If we had vehicle access to the cliffs, we could use our Land Rovers, which
> had capstan fitted, powered by the vehicle engines. There was some implicit
> danger in these operations as the stretcher/crew members could get stuck
> under an overhang with disastrous results. Good communication and signal
> procedure were essential. During bad weather with rain and high winds,
> radio communication could be difficult, and we had to rely on whistle
> signals. The stretcher could be raised horizontally, with 2 rescuers 'walking'
> it up.
>
> To deal with incidents away from vehicle access, we had prepared packs

20. Technology supporting muscle power – using the Land Rover capstan.

21. Cliff Rescue training.

with light equipment and could within minutes establish a rope recovery system using climbing pulleys and prussic (rope) brakes attached to a number of small (30–40 cm long) steel stakes, a system well known from the mountaineering/alpine scenes.

When staff member David Cope took over Coastguards in 1987, little changed:

For rescuing people who had been cut off by the tide and were mobile we would use a variety of techniques which basically involved hauling the rescuer and the casualty up the cliff on two ropes. The capstan was part of one method used and because we were a large company, we sometimes just pulled people up by hand (8–10 people sitting on the ground in a row with ropes running over pulleys – 20 yards back from edge). It was one of the recognized techniques that the Coastguard insisted that we use. Where there wasn't room to sit people or we couldn't get the Land Rover into position we would haul using a series of Z Pulleys. The rescuer would descend to the base of the cliff on one rope and take with them a second rope which would then be attached to the casualty via a Rescue Strop. The rescuer & casualty would both be attached together & then hauled up. We also used a piece of equipment called a Tragesitz, whereby the rescuer would put the casualty in the Tragesitz and then piggyback the casualty off the cliff. The rescuer had to have real strength in their legs. We adapted a couple of things from mountain rescue – a bell stretcher to get people off rocky faces. Coastguard insisted we use a stretcher that wrapped around you and flexed (great in a mine or a ship but not much good if you had a spinal injury).

One answer to the icy and treacherous waters off St Donat's that Hoare introduced was the wetsuit. Now they are so commonplace it is hard to imagine a time without them. But in the 1960s they were not available off the peg at an affordable price, and Hoare decided the students should make their own.

The idea was refined by Naomi, who designed a pattern for a one-piece, which for the next decade was made by every new student involved in any of the seagoing activities or services. It was a rite of passage, and – painfully for some – a test of application and dexterity. For the first few years, each one was cut out from large rolls of neoprene and glued together, with offcuts of neoprene to back up the seams on the inside, by the students themselves. It was the first task of the first term.

For the next two years, peeled off at the end of the afternoon of seafront activities (no one went in or on the Bristol Channel without one), flesh that was already mottled by the cold was also left with the lingering imprint of each seam. But it is hard to imagine how cold the first generation of students must have become, going out with no wetsuits at all. Andreas Schwerdtfeger was one of that hardy number:

> In our first year we still went out in jeans, sweaters and anoraks; then we acquired neoprene suits – but not already tailored ones that you can buy off the hook today. At our time the College bought sheets of neoprene and cutting papers, so we cut the different parts of a suit out of the neoprene and then glued them together. Glue was important in our Rescue Boat times!

The process rapidly grew more professional, and more ambitious. By 1969, those with more than the most basic craft skills, like Sally Stradling, personalised their wetsuits:

> In the first year, on joining Rescue Boats one of the first tasks was to make our own wetsuits. A full-length wetsuit with collar, arms, legs, neoprene bootees and gloves. This was accomplished in one of the boat sheds under the supervision of an external seamstress who guided us through taking measurements, cutting patterns and then cutting out the neoprene pieces which were carefully glued together. We cut out bright orange identifier

22. Tailoring in neoprene – the all-in-one wetsuit.

emblems to stick on the back – mine was a 'stag courant' or running stag – the emblem of the Stradling family I had seen on a roundel on the Lady Ann Tower.

Phil Green's diary from nearly a decade later shows a similar level of enthusiasm, although not necessarily expertise:

Monday Sept 27. I started my skin suit. There weren't enough scissors to go around. There was no English class, so I worked till supper.

Sept 28. Bea finished her skin suit in two 1400–1600 sessions. Bet it will fall apart sooner or later. Probably sooner. [Note: it did not.]

Sept 29. I stayed all afternoon making my wetsuit and finished the taping all over.

Sept 30. After lunch I designed something for my wetsuit. Then I went and stuck a sperm whale on wetsuit and started sewing it.

October 1. Finished wetsuit. Put it on and in company of Reinard and Stephan I did some [kayak] rolling. Afternoon I sewed up my wetsuit. [Note: my wetsuit fell apart!]

October 2. Sewed wetsuit.

* * * * *

Paul Belcher, who joined the staff at AC in 1975, regarded DIY as an important part of the non-academic curriculum.

When I arrived [wetsuit making] had gone over to buying in kits that were pre-marked. These had to be cut out, glued together, and tried on, adjustments made and finally taped and stitched. You had the satisfaction (or not!) of knowing that you had created something for yourself that you were going to be wearing a lot. Eventually this moved to buying in ready-made suits as they became more commercially available. These were certainly warmer but the skill of making something for yourself was lost. The earlier students were certainly more adept at being able to mend their wetsuit if it developed a hole as they knew how they constructed it.

Boats, wetsuits – and kayaks and other surf-worthy devices – were all produced in the college workshops.

The decision to allow students to build their own kayaks, despite the noxious chemicals involved, was taken early. John David had joined the staff in 1963 and was at the heart first of Beach Rescue and later of the IRBs. The college had decided on a kayak, the KW7, as best suited for the college's activities. But they would need repairing and that meant resin and fibreglass. It was a short step from repairs to building from scratch as John David recalls:

> In 1973 we had Alan Byde working at the seafront and he was a canoeist and canoe builder. Also Eric Williams [housemaster and teacher] attended a canoe-building course at that time. I built my own canoe, complete with Welsh flag on the bow, in 1973–74 when I returned from Singapore. From then on, all Beach Rescue keenies took the opportunity to build their own canoes using the KW7 mould.

John David also remembers other bought-in equipment:

> We bought in two surf skis from Keith Slocombe in St Ives. In 1968 Erik Osvold and Mike Code won the GB title on the double at the GB Championships at St Ives and Erik won the title on the single. Then John Welch, over the summer vacation, built a single racing ski out of wood to an Australian design, a beautiful craft on which Kurt Arens won the single ski title in 1970.

When he arrived, Paul Belcher got involved in kayak making:

> When I started there was Alan Byde at the seafront who was a specialist in constructing fibreglass kayaks and passed his skills onto the students. It was a labour of love for many students to create their own kayak. Many hours were spent in the initial stages of creating the design in coloured gelcoat that they wanted. When Alan Byde left, the skill was transferred from student to student. You helped someone build theirs and then someone helped you with yours. The students did this in their own time in the evenings and on the weekends. There was staff coach input to advise on the techniques e.g. to cut round the edge on the mould just before the resin was due to go off. This was done initially in a lean-to, part of which went under the east seafront tower, and then in a wooden shack on the end of the jousting field. We did eventually get a better workshop built with extractor fans but ironically this was just before plastic kayaks started to become available.

> I started buying plastic kayaks for the Service. They were certainly more resilient and required less maintenance but again a skill of working with your hands and producing your own creation was lost. With the fibreglass kayaks, after a few sessions of seagoing, then especially if you had been attempting pop-outs in surf, you needed to have a session mending the pressure cracks. The plastic kayaks also changed the mentality of what you could attempt.

23. Surf ski competition in the 1977 SLSA championships on an unusually calm day. Phil Green (front) and Harald Heiene (76–78).

When rock hopping in a plastic kayak it did not matter so much if you hit a rock but with the fibreglass ones you had to be more precise or you knew you were in for a session of maintenance.

Thinking back, it is interesting to consider the amount of chemicals that were being used (some of them nasty ones) and how there were much less rules and supervision than in the chemistry lab where much smaller quantities of chemicals were being used. It was almost impossible to build a fibreglass kayak without your clothes becoming coloured and even your hair when you had your head inside trying to lay the strips to join the two halves together and contending with the fumes. It was a delight and a worry to eventually see if your kayak would release from the mould and that you did not have any air bubbles in the layers. Students naturally tried to experiment but not all experiments turned out as hoped for. An example was Mark Wolsey's (76–78) green kayak which was certainly very light indeed but would develop a pressure crack as soon as you even breathed on it. There was something good about paddling in a craft that you had created for yourself.

Phil Green spent hours in the workshops in his first year constructing his kayak.

Feb 6 (letter home). Yesterday I started building a kayak. [The design] represents some kind of marine carnivore, perhaps it could be a killer whale if you really use your imagination. Today I will spend up to eight hours in the BR workshop working on it.

February 10. Took kayak out of the mold.

Feb 12. (letter home). This week I finished building the body of my kayak: it really looks sharp with those killer-whale teeth and bloodshot eyes, and a great big PTO on the bottom with letters one foot tall.

Feb 18. Spent the whole afternoon in the workshop building my canoe, i.e. laminating the seat and putting the ropes on it.

Feb 21. Christened canoe. Two friends of mine pulled me into the water after a Dutch girl friend of mine smashed a bag of orange juice over the nose. Paddled out backwards. Had a lovely surf on long steep waves (50 m surf).

24. Phil Green's kayak in action.

The standout bit of kit for Beach Rescue in the early years was the Australian surfboat, Cabbage Tree II, which was owed to John David.

John David had won a Churchill scholarship to study surf lifesaving techniques in Australia and spotted the potential of a surfboat for getting students out to sea and building confidence and enthusiasm.

> Cabbage II Tree was gifted to the college in 1968 by an Australian surf lifesaving team known as the Palm Beach crew, at the end of their GB tour. The Palm Beach tour in 1968 followed on from my time in Australia in 1966–67. She came over as deck cargo and Chris Branson, a crew member studying at Oxford at the time, came with me to Liverpool docks to pick her up from the dock side. We had built a trolley to the required specifications. She was presented to us on the beach at St. Ives after we had won the 1968 SLSA of GB Championships. There were two Canadians in the crew we put together, Mike Code and Tim Milligan. I remember we had her in the workshop for a month or more for a strip down and re-varnish. It was worth it. Easter project week we took on Perranporth at Falmouth and walloped them!

Tim Milligan remembers the surfboat well:

> As you probably know we picked up Cabbage Tree II after winning the 1968 SLSA championships in St Ives. John David had us row a lot from the foreshore, miles along the coast with asses burning, and then, as often as we could, at Southerndown when there was some surf running. This was the lead up to the first GB race held during the 1969 project week. It was during that week that we actually learnt to surf big waves thanks to some random Australian that happened by and offered to help us. We were a bit hesitant about going out in waves considerably larger than what we had experienced at Southerndown. He curled up under the quarter bar, dressed in pants and a woolly grey sweater and off we went. We made it out fairly easily and then caught what I remember was an awfully big wave. We shot oars, grabbed John's feet just as everything went white and we started to broach and fill with water. I suspect we were as white as the spray until a head popped up from the bottom with a big smile and a big cheer and shouted, 'let's go crack another!' From that point we were confident we could handle anything. We had a very strong crew led by the late Eric Oswald at stroke. Eric had rowed in Norway so taught us both technique and the Norwegian boat calls to set the stroke. Behind Eric was Dave Polya, with me at 2 and Mike Code in the bow. We had a great week of surfing leading up to the race against Perranporth but unfortunately the weather got really rough, so we had to move the race across to Falmouth Harbour

25. The surfboat Cabbage Tree II at sea.

where they set out probably a 2 km course around 2 buoys. We won easily, thanks to the calloused asses we had acquired with John driving us up and down the coast. I took the second crew out and we won that race by open water as well.

Leading up to the end of term, and leaving, I spent a lot of time sanding and varnishing Cabbage Tree as by that time she was starting to show some wear. Suspect my time might have been better spent studying but the lure of that fabulous boat was too much.

But the idea that Cabbage Tree II was any kind of rescue boat, despite the reel and line, was a fiction.

It was never part of our regular training. We did it a few times and gave up. It was certainly not practical compared to a rescue canoe. Same as the reel and line, lots of training but more for competition than rescue. Don't think anyone would run for a reel and line when boards and torpedo buoys are available. Coming over the side of the boat wasn't much fun for a patient.

In its way, the surfboat was an omen of things to come. It had once played a genuine role in Australian surf lifesaving. But despite the vestigial reel and line that in theory allowed a rescue swimmer to be rowed out beyond the surf and then put over the side to swim back in for a rescue, in fact it was already principally a competition boat, an opportunity for teams of lifesavers to have a different kind of fun. John David doubts they were ever seriously seen as rescue craft:

The Australians never saw the surfboats as rescue craft – they were ideal for their sporting use which meant that they had a strong recruiting potential.

26. Cabbage Tree II in heavy seas off Newquay.

We used them in the same sense in the college. The boat's retention of the mini reel and line was, I suppose, symbolic.

During my time the surfboat was part of Beach Rescue's equipment. Giving it a home, as it were, ensured there would be a regular maintenance programme. It also made the trip to Cornwall for the Easter Project week as part of the Beach Rescue 'convoy'.

Competition was an essential part of building and maintaining kayaks, canoes and skis, as well as the surfboat. It played an important role too in training for Beach Rescue, as Paul Belcher recalled:

AC took part in the Surf Lifesaving Society Welsh and British championships. In the early days we often won them. There is the famous occasion during the apartheid era [in 1969] when the College who had a good chance of winning the British championships, but the student captain decided to march [his crew] off the beach and not compete as a protest to the [all White] South African team being allowed to take part in the championships. We were usually strong in the running and swimming events but were eventually overtaken in the board and ski events by competitors who had trained on them for many more years. The introduction of an Intermediate Age group which the students fitted into, had us back into winning ways. I can remember Babsy Baddacky winning the Ladies Ski. She was well in the lead on her way into shore when a huge wave from behind her caught up with her and front looped the whole long ski quite dramatically. Babsy rolled it back up again and came in across the finish line. Officials tried to disqualify her because whilst underwater her helmet had been wrenched from her head. Pleasingly, Charles Thomson the head of the SLSA stepped in and reversed the decision saying that it was the most impressive piece of female ski paddling that he had ever seen.

We also took part in still water Lifeguard competitions in pools, Corps of Canoe Lifeguard Championships, long distance ski races, down river kayak races, swimming competitions and canoe polo matches, on one occasion getting through to the British Championships in London. I recall a kayak race on the sea where first of all you had to run to your kayak, pull it into the water and launch in surf. I had had the idea of putting zips into the spray-decks and having them already on the boats so that you could just slide in and zip up rather than taking the time to fit it on all the way round. This together with his explosive paddling allowed Mark Wolsey to be about half a metre in front of the other competitors going up the face of a particularly large wave. He just made it over the top whereas everyone else was back looped and pushed back to the shore. The race was essentially won at that point. Ramon Buencha and I and Titia Hedema and Karen Wood competed in 2 person kayaks in the famous and gruelling Devizes to Westminster canoe race.

Under the auspices of the RNLI, we provided the lifeguard cover on rescue boards for the swim of the Tenby Ironman Triathlon for several years. Of all the Triathlons that I have been to this was the one with the best organised and professional lifeguard cover that I have seen.

On occasions when the sea was rough at the start of the first lap there were many pool swimmers who had problems and had to be picked up by the boards and then moved to the ILBs to be transported back to the start.

We even on one occasion provided the kayak round up cover for a duck race!

But as Paul admits, in the end engines replaced muscle power, even for the lifeguards:

There was always the good-natured rivalry between Lifeguards and ILBs and it was satisfying to tow one of the boats back with kayaks if their engine failed. It was also reassuring to know that they were around if assistance was required in getting someone back to the slipway quickly. It was also good to be towed along leaning back in your kayak with a rope wrapped round your paddle, telling them to put the throttle down. Starting in the

27. Leslie Crawford competing at the SLSA
(surf life-saving association) championships 1977.

1980s, lifeguards did use engines. For several years we had our own 2 person Arancia ILB (a small inshore boat developed in New Zealand) which was very nimble in the surf. The Lifeguard Staff gained their qualifications on this boat and gave first year students a trip out in it though the surf at Whitesands during 1st year camp, using them as patients to be picked up from the water. We also used a Jet Ski for a couple of years with a sled behind it. One person drove the Ski and the other lifeguard on the sled quickly got the patient onto the sled with them between waves.

Over the generations from 1962, canoes and kayaks and skis were all to migrate from being indispensable in surf rescue to mere showcases for skill and muscle – while the rescuing was done either off the beach or by these New Zealand-made Arancia-class inflatables, powered by outboard engines.

*****

SOCIAL SERVICE

There was one more challenge to meet: what should students who either didn't want or were not able to participate in one of the three 'rescue' services do instead? As David Sutcliffe realised, many students wanted to make a very direct contribution to the community in which the college was based, and not necessarily with the drama and emergency that was such a draw in the other services. So the Social Service, also known as the 'tea-drinking service', was born, with a mission to visit the housebound and bring opportunity to the deprived communities which were all too common in the South Wales county of Glamorgan.

Julie McDonald was involved in the service between 1977 and 1979.

> While the Beach Rescue, ILB and Cliff Rescue Toughies were carrying out their high profile training on the cold and craggy seafront, flexing their muscles, going through their pitch perfect paces, preparing to face rare but sometimes serious incidents with superhuman efficiency, other services were toiling away in the background, hiding their powerful lights under the nearest bushel. The Estate Service took care of the beautiful and functional AC grounds, in August period the Extra-Mural Service provided therapeutic and fun craft and outward-bound activities for local children, and the Swimming Teachers reached out to a local community with limited access to lessons in the necessary aquatic skills.

> But all year, day in day out, and many evenings, another service was carrying out essential work without any fanfare – the unsung heroes of what was – affectionately? Unfairly? – dubbed 'the tea-drinking service'. In between adrenaline hits, the other services, shivering on the shore, watched enviously as we piled into a van to indulge tea and homemade Welsh cakes beside a roaring fire with a sweet old lady, entertaining us with stories of the war … or did we? The reality of Social Service was somewhat harsher. Certainly, tea was drunk – gallons of it – but there was so much more to it than that.

> A key feature of the UWC curriculum is service to the local community, and Social Service provided just that. Unlike Beach, ILBs and Cliff Rescue who were subjected to rigorous safety drills, we ventured out into the homes of the elderly, the local psychiatric hospital, a school for the visually impaired, or a club for children with disabilities … all with no training whatsoever.

> We were on a steep learning curve – we witnessed poverty, struggles with mental and physical health issues, and loneliness at close quarters. Twice a week, we clambered into the rickety van, unequipped with such luxuries as

seat belts, put our lives into the hands of whichever dedicated and kindly teacher was accompanying us that day, and off we went. One day we would visit homes of those deemed needy in Barry Island, or Llantwit Major, another we would be at The Blind School in St Donat's, or in the evening, the (now long gone) Bridgend Mental Hospital.

With nothing but the support and example of those committed teachers, we attempted to make conversation with and entertain sometimes sad, lonely and troubled people. Overall, we were greeted with enthusiasm and warmth, but occasionally bewilderment and suspicion. Memories of Ellen from Denmark elegantly and kindly fending off advances from a young psychiatric patient spring to mind; Martin from Germany having to clean windows and wash dishes before earning his cuppa, and several of our number coping with (largely unintentional) racism and xenophobia. When August Period came, we could be found painting and decorating crumbling homes in the slums of Cardiff, Project Week spent with a probation officer in Birmingham. It never crossed our minds to say no – we didn't question, we just got on with it. We didn't love it, we just did it. It was not the most photogenic of services; these were not occasions where we pulled out our camera for a memorable action shot.

But we learned much. Farzin from Iran, inspired by our work with the blind, learned braille, and was nominated for an award for developing a computer programme in the Computing Group to print braille on paper/punch tape – in 1977! And this while mastering macramé in order to teach it. We may not have realized at the time, but these life lessons were far-reaching, and many of us went into caring professions. Brigid from Melbourne, the esteemed president of AC Social Service, became a world-renowned professor in paediatric social work, Martin from Munich graduated from teaching kayak rolls to young blind kids to consultant psychology, Mirai from India is now Director of Self Employed Women's Association in Ahmedabad.

Thrown in the deep end ourselves, did we rescue anyone? Perhaps one another, as we came to understand and empathize with each other in the face of the challenges of growing up under such extraordinary conditions. Having tea with old ladies in Llantwit Major was a fast track route to establishing international and intercultural understanding for those of us who joined the service from beyond the shores of the British Isles. Today, in the current climate of strict health and safety has meant that the 'left-over' service has come into its own. As far as what is now termed co-curricular experience at Atlantic College, the sea and cliff rescue services have been transformed into activities, and services are a much-expanded version of the local outreach service us Social Service Toughies pioneered.

CHAPTER TWO

Training

> The vital areas of student responsibility are in the rescue and social services
> and the academic programme, in all of which the students are given fairly
> demanding tasks and left to get on with it by themselves ... not watched
> over like children. *Michael Code, AC 1966–68 (quoted in Sutcliffe, Hahn 26).*

The guiding principle for all the services was to train the students and then trust
them to make the right decision in action. In Desmond Hoare's words, 'They are
to be taken seriously and given serious tasks, and proper training, and the best
equipment.' He added confidently, 'and they will never let you down.'

Students were to sample all of the services – cliff, boat, beach and canoe (kayak) –
almost as soon as they started, in what was called activities week. On the basis of
an hour or two's experience, they were then to commit to one service or another.

Rhodri Bradley-Jones started at the college in its second year, 1963. The principle had
already been established that second-year students would instruct the first years.

> I joined the Canoe Rescue Service probably because David Sutcliffe was my
> housemaster and he was also in charge of the Canoe Rescue Service. The
> only training that we had was from the year above us and took place in the
> swimming pool. Nothing written!

One of the first decisions was that there should be a core curriculum of
competences that would be compulsory for every student regardless of rescue
service. These were to learn to swim – a college prerequisite for RNLI registration
even though not required by the RNLI itself – and not just learn to swim, but swim
to a standard where students could pass the gold survival test of the Amateur
Swimming Association, and in addition learn enough lifesaving skills to earn the
award of merit of the Royal Life Saving Society. Students also had to train for the
Higher Award in first aid of the St John Ambulance Brigade.

In the early years, Desmond Hoare also taught some theory of boat handling,
tides, waves and weather as well as navigation and some local knowledge. He
collected his ideas and experiences together in a 30-page manual of key skills,
issued in 1974. It was based on his assumption that while practical skills can only
be learned by doing, any thoughtful student needs to understand the theory.
There are nine pages on waves and tides (with diagrams) and a single sheet on
boat handling. That was learned not from theory but by 'bashing the Bristol
Channel'. Hoare wrote:

Training as an ILB coxswain comprises some theory and much practice. Seamanship cannot be learnt ashore and there is no alternative to spending hours and hours at sea if one is going to be safe in boat handling and competent in rescue. Nevertheless, intelligent people usually like to understand some of the theory which underlies their experience. The theory enriches the experience.

Many students, like Sally Stradling (1969–71) remember 'Des's lectures':

I remember sitting in the sunshine at the seafront in a group of first year Rescue Boaters being lectured by Des on extreme tidal ranges in the Bristol channel, neap and spring tides, etiquette at sea and how to handle an RIB – always think about the engine cutting out – NOW! Keep the bow pointing into the waves to avoid breaching and be aware of anyone in the water. To come alongside another RIB, you had to put your hand up, wait for the coxswain of the other boat to put their hand up and then go alongside. (This resulted in a number of hands going up simultaneously when HRH Prince Charles was at sea on a training session with us in the Bristol Channel on one of his visits to AC, as everyone wanted to meet him!)

[Prince Charles made several visits to the college, encouraged by his godfather Earl Mountbatten of Burma who had become president of the new United World Colleges. Charles's visits were good for publicity but not always as entertaining as Sally Stradling found them. Mathew Goodman remembers one nearly a decade later, in 1978:

Prince Charles wanted to go out on an ILB, so someone in their wisdom decided to put on a show, launching not only the B-Boat but every craft the College owned, as I recall – all the other ILBs, canoes, sailboats, and possibly even the surfboat. The ILB boat captains drew straws to see who would have to stay behind to serve as beachmaster. Naturally I drew the short straw and had to spend the next several hours waist-deep in the freezing waters of the Bristol Channel. When the B-Boat finally pulled in with Prince Charles aboard, he said, 'Bloody cold out there' – to which I responded, 'You should try standing down here for a while.' This may explain why you haven't seen me on the New Year's Honours List ...]

The cold, as Sally Stradling recalls, was always a feature of the AC training experience:

RIB training was taken very seriously, and everyone was expected to take part in regular drills such as rescuing a swimmer from choppy waters. I remember one February in icy waters, taking it in turns to go overboard and practice being the rescuer secured by a line, reaching a swimmer and bringing them to the side of the RIB and being hauled back into a bobbing boat . The cups of hot tea and biscuits prepared by Naomi in the sailing tower, that we consumed shivering in our wetsuits after this training, never tasted so good.

Sutcliffe and Des gave us training to prepare us for sitting the coxswain exams' written papers including boat handling, navigation, tides, weather reports and rescue scenarios. The BBC weather reports from coastal stations always even now reminds me of this – Shetland, Faroe, German Bight …

The admiral wrote his manual on inshore rescue boat training in 1974, after 12 years of experience. He had by that time joined the RNLI management board and was a recognised authority on safety, according to David Sutcliffe's portrait of him in his book *Kurt Hahn and the United World Colleges with Other Founding Figures*, self-published in 2013 (Sutcliffe never got to grips with the catchy title). Some of the admiral's early students, however, found his training techniques at the least challenging, and occasionally actually frightening.

* * * * *

On the water, on the beach and on the cliff, the pattern of training was by practice. After the first year, the main trainers were the students themselves, with the first years led by second years and staff members maintaining only a discreet presence. This practice continued throughout the life of the rescue services as Paul Belcher, who joined the college staff in 1975, recalls:

28. A second-year passing on signal know-how to a first year.

To qualify to patrol on the beach you had to pass the relevant Surf Lifesaving exam. Initially much training was done with the line and reel and belt swims and this was a major part of the exam. This caused students to have to work together as a team, you could be a superb swimmer but if the brake-man had left the brake on, then the whole reel would be rolling along the beach behind you and you were not going to get anywhere. As it was realised that few rescues in Britain were actually carried out using the line and reel, the training moved to using rescue boards and torpedo buoys as well as free swims. The exams involved theory, including first aid and most importantly resuscitation, swimming/running, timed fitness tests, and a wide variety of different rescues.

One major problem that AC had was that for the first years the term ended in May and the second years had their IB exams in May. Thus the SLSA exams had to be taken at the end of April or the very start of May. The sea was not really warmed up at this time and the other clubs sensibly waited until, say, July to take their exams. As it took a great deal of training to prepare for these exams, this training had to happen over the winter months. It was certainly cold even with a good wetsuit and this provided character building training for the students. Some students had not even seen the sea before arrival at AC and it took time to be able to handle a rescue board in rough surf conditions and to gain the techniques to swim out through surf. Lifeguard students will probably remember being exhorted by me to swim head down and duck dive under waves. So the training had to be done whatever the weather conditions were. Southerndown beach, when the tide was low and coming in, could have a particularly strong drift down towards Witch's Point which many students experienced.

29. Witch's Point. The line of broken water beyond is the tidal race off Nash Sands.

30. Training with a belt and reel. Blue sky did not necessarily indicate a warm day.

The philosophy of AC and the UWCs placed an importance on giving students real responsibilities. One aspect of the training of Lifeguard Service students that I greatly valued was entrusting 2nd years to provide part of the training for the 1st years. 1st years were trained in groups of about six by two appointed 2nd year Group Instructors. The Group Instructors ran the pool sessions (the Staff Coaches were present at the seagoing sessions) and were responsible for preparing their group for first the Pool Lifeguard Award and then the SLSA Beach Lifeguard award. Being a Group Instructor was always a coveted job and excellent skills and dedication to their group was shown by these individuals. They continued their instruction right up to the Lifeguard exams even though their own IB exams were imminent. In many cases you can see how being given this trust and responsibility early in life has been the first steps in what they have gone on to achieve.

*****

For most students, despite the constant cold, the frequent knocks from the unruly seas, the unintended duckings and the unstable cliffs, it was fun. Having been encouraged to join Canoe Rescue by his then housemaster David Sutcliffe, Rhodri Bradley-Jones recalls a rugged introduction:

> This was the first rescue service set up by David Sutcliffe and he took a keen and direct interest. Emphasis was on learning to Eskimo roll and by 1964 a few of us were amongst the first in the country to perfect rolling the canoes with hands only. We only had a few of the heavy wooden Eskimo kayaks and rather more of the resin slalom canoes. The Eskimo kayaks fitted like a glove and were really

unstable. Rolling skills were absolutely vital as it wasn't easy to slip out of them under water. They had a slim triangular cross section and getting into and out of them involved a certain amount of flexibility and contortion!

Much to David Sutcliffe's delight, we could take the Eskimo kayaks out into the Bristol Channel in sea conditions that made it impossible for any other craft to take to the water. In hindsight, we sometimes found ourselves in the sea in quite dangerous conditions, but I think we grew enormously in confidence from overcoming our fears and coping with the conditions.

We were expected to use our common sense much of the time and I would say we (and the teaching staff) were pretty gung-ho. I remember within a few days of arriving, our year was lined up above the slipway and asked who had sailed a boat before. As a few said that they had, they were paired with a nearby boat. I half put my hand up to say that I had crewed on a sailing boat a couple of times. Before I could say anything, I too was allocated a boat and in a matter of a minutes, I found myself launching a one-man sailing boat into the Bristol Channel and working out for myself how to manoeuvre it. I sailed reasonably successfully for the first month or so without understanding the difference between going about and gybing. In the process, I became expert at righting a capsized sailing boat. I don't remember receiving any training, but I probably did have a brief introduction to the sailing boat.

31. The importance of the roll – David Sutcliffe instructing.

32. Clearing the airways – resuscitation training.

The merging of beach and kayak rescue services did not end the role for kayaks in rescue. David Ross was a student from 1967 to 1969:

> We were all trained to do a rescue in kayaks and do mouth-to-mouth while in a kayak. We all competed to try and get the two young women teachers who were training with us to be our patients. Never happened.

Phil Green kept a diary through his first year, 1976–77, which gives an idea of how hard the enthusiast could train. These are just a few extracts:

> September 8, 1976. DAY ONE. test (incredibly easy). Discovered my watch was not waterproof.

> September 11 [From a letter home]: We were issued with spare wetsuits. The waves were gigantic. When one came, I would start to paddle, it would catch me and wow! Would I ever move fast. I just lay on the board and didn't stand up, but the waves would take me to the water four inches deep from several hundred meters out. It was fun paddling out there. Every time a wave came it would break all over my face, go up my nose and ears. Then when it passed, I would slap down onto the other side and continue paddling. It was very tiring. This is what made me decide to join Beach Rescue, although there is more involved in it than just that. Lots of swimming to do as well.

September 13. Pool: swam 4 lengths with PJs on in 2:45 minutes. Tread water, inflate PJs [as a make-shift life jacket]. (Very difficult). I then swam 13 laps. Very boring.

Sept 23. Woodwork lecture (Beach Rescue). We learned how to screw and how to lubricate.

Sept 24. Another boring lecture about Beach Rescue repairs.

Sunday Sept 26. in a letter home this day: This week I learned to do an Eskimo roll in a kayak. I consider that a big achievement because for two summers [in Canada] I have been trying to learn and never did.

Oct 7. Went to Southerndown. The waves were really big and the surf was messy. I capsized several times but only managed to roll up twice. This makes me realize I need a lot more practicing in rolling. Every time I capsized, I lost my paddle, but when I did manage to surf in it was quite fun.

Oct 8. Swam in the pool with my wetsuit. That was quite exhilarating. Then I practiced my rolling in the bats [short kayaks] and then in the 'Flying Dutchman'. It sure is difficult in these proper canoes compared to the bats.

Nov 3. Right after breakfast first aid classes began. We saw a few really gory movies, with people spewing and bleeding, and one being stabbed by a spear gun.

Nov 4. I didn't have much free time with this bloody intensive first aid course.

Nov 5. Early morning we had a practical work with first aid. Ecch! What a mess. Blood everywhere (not real blood of course).

Eboo Versi (1969–71), like most enthusiastic kayakers, had arrived at the college with no experience. But he soon acclimatised.

It would not have been possible to become competent as a rescuer without exposure to risk. Personally, I can only recall one experience which I can say was life threatening. Six us of us were surfing in kayaks off the seafront as the waves were, unusually, quite spectacularly ideal. We all knew that there were superficial rocks and boulders as the water was not that deep near the shore so it was not possible to surf all the way in to shore after the wave had broken (white water wave surfing) as one could on a beach. Therefore, it was critical that we left the wave before it broke.

There was one particular wave that was largest in the set of waves that, unsurprisingly, all six of us in our excitement, caught. In retrospect we would accept that was foolish and dangerous for so many people to be on the same wave. I was positioned 4th from the right and this was relevant as the wave was breaking from the right. Before it broke, the first two kayaks on the right turned off to the right and so left the wave. I followed suit but the 3rd person was still surfing perpendicular to the wave front so I collided with him causing his kayak to turn right and therefore come off the wave – leaving me continuing down the wave front.

The two on my left back-paddled and so left the wave. I was too far down the wave to back-paddle, so I again turned right to try to leave the wave but was too late and the wave broke on me.

We had been trained to not capsize in such a situation by leaning into the wave with our paddle but given the size of the wave, it took all my strength to be able to ride it and not capsize. I was acutely aware of the danger of the large boulders that I needed to ride over and that if I had capsized, I could have suffered a broken neck or a severe head injury. I saw and heard the teacher on the slipway shouting, 'Ride it! Ride it!' Riding a white-water wave is quite exhilarating and fun in that it is extremely bumpy, much like being in an airplane in turbulence, but at that point it was not fun.

I survived the main force of the wave and felt relieved as I felt that I was slowing down, when I hit a rock and the kayak was lifted out of the water but then I continued to glide into shore. As soon as I felt the bottom of the kayak scrape on the sand, I quickly pulled off my spray over and went to examine my kayak. To my surprise, there was not a scratch to be seen so I went to inspect the other side and there was hardly any kayak left. It was a complete write off.

33. Too many kayakers catch a wave.

In retrospect we did many things wrong and we should have had rules in place to avoid dangerous situations like this one. That said, there will always be circumstances, no matter how many checks and balances are instituted, when accidents will happen. That is the nature of rescue services. [33]

Under Paul Belcher, canoe and kayak activities were developed as much as a sport as a rescue vehicle.

Kayaking was an integral part of Beach Rescue. It taught understanding of the sea and tidal currents. A kayak group should be self-sufficient in terms of safety techniques when out at sea. Kayak Instructors were appointed to work alongside the Group Instructors when a first year group had a kayaking session. The ability to roll your kayak back up was a great skill to learn and made the sessions much more enjoyable. This could be learned together with the hand roll in the indoor or outdoor pool, but the real test was could you reliably perform it under pressure in the cold sea in rough surf conditions. For the year that we had the tank on the jousting field, paddles were not allowed as they might damage the lining at the bottom of the pool. So I had students rolling their kayaks back up with table tennis bats. That cohort of students was very good at hand-rolling but needed to improve their paddle rolling.

Students who chose to, took and gained the British Canoe Union Sea Proficiency Award after they had done the required three-day trips first. They also took the Corps of Canoe Lifeguards award. We were very lucky that we had the director of the BCU, Oliver Cock, and the president of the WCU, Sandy Buckle, as the examiners for this award. The incidents that they thought up were always interesting and exciting, however at times they became more real life than was originally intended!

Kayaks allowed you to get to places and explore, that you could not really do any other way. The sea to the right of the slipway on an incoming tide with the right surf conditions was an excellent point break that was perfectly suited to kayak surfing. If you rode the wave well, you were rewarded with a very long ride and could then circle round and repeat the trip.

I was pleased to introduce ideas that had not been tested before. Several times I took a group of students by kayak over to Porlock Weir on the other side of the Bristol Channel, camped out for the night and then paddled back the next day. It was an excellent exercise in working out how to allow for the tides and being committed so that you had to keep paddling. Night paddles to Llantwit were a great success and showed how your balance in a kayak comes from feel as much as from sight. The students delighted in taking their glow sticks up to the SOCH [social centre] with them at the end of the trip in their wetsuits. Kayaking happened less as the SLSA exams approached and also less in my latter years as other craft, e.g. Stand-up Paddle Boards, were used. I did run a kayaking activity some terms that was open to any student at the College and used Lifeguard students as instructors. A Challenge Camp was introduced for 2nd years in the woods by the river Wye, this included a variety of activities as well as encouraging the students to be self-sufficient in their open-air cooking. Canadian canoes were used for a day trip down the Wye [River] through Symonds Yat rapids. It was a loss when this Challenge Camp was dispensed with.

*****

Once the college became an RNLI Inshore Rescue Boat station in early 1964, students had to be officially qualified by sitting RNLI exams. Desmond Hoare was colour-blind, officially a bar to naval service, yet despite this he had had a successful naval career, and his readiness to bend rules was illustrated by his advice to short-sighted candidates for RNLI registration to memorise the number plate on the doctor's car before the medical examination, as that was the only sight test they would have.

Later, the experience the admiral had of training students at the college fed through to his involvement in standardising national skill levels for the RNLI. But John Grey-Davies, who started at AC in 1966, vividly remembers the unorthodox approach that Hoare's training took at the time:

> The training to be a coxswain was very basic, but generally good fun.
> We had first aid training, we had to achieve the advanced swimming
> qualification, tie complex knots such as a bowline behind our backs,
> understand and make detailed copies of the radio fishing forecast. But of
> course the most fundamental was how to handle the boats and deal with
> emergencies such as if one was capsized and how safely to tow other boats
> such as sailing dinghies. And of course we had to become very familiar with
> the nearby coastline up to ten miles in either direction. I also remember
> in August at the beginning of my second year leading a flotilla of IRBs
> across the Bristol Channel to Minehead where a sea mist descended and
> I had to lead them back using the compass permanently mounted next to
> the steering wheel on X2, taking into account the very rapid speed of the
> tide. Fortunately, we emerged from the mist just off the Atlantic College
> slipway. That could have been a disaster! We were also used as a community
> service for things such as surfing and lifesaving competitions. I remember
> accompanying a boat by road on a trolley to Porthcawl, launching it to be
> the rescue boat for a surf lifesaving competition. We remained at anchor

beyond the point of breaking waves and sat there for a couple of hours or so. No swimmers needed any assistance at all. The only problem was that one of our crew became seasick due to the motion of the boat in the waves!

With hindsight, one of John Grey-Davies' contemporaries, Pelham Allen, believes Hoare kept a close eye on the competence of every crew member.

Training was very much second years teaching first years. In our first year most of those of us who were reasonably keen would have gone out more than once a week on average for a couple of hours. So by the end of first year, we would have been involved in launching and recovering boats 50 or 60 times. We were just going out into the Bristol Channel and banging the boats about. In early days we wouldn't have driven them ourselves and we would have spent a humongous amount of time hanging on to trolleys on the foreshore etc. …

A lot of time would have been with the sailing dinghies, towing boats, transferring passengers. It was a very active time. We did all of that in the first year – then we came back in August and there would be no second years anymore, so you just got on with it. There was some degree of assessment: probably DBS would sign off individuals as putting enough hours in and reaching a level of competence. Some people would sail through that because they'd been messing about in boats all their lives; for others it was a bigger hurdle.

Cox'n was an AC term, not an RNLI one. It meant you could take a boat out in charge. Not everyone would have been allowed to do that, they might have continued in the crew. Some people took to it like a duck to water and some people didn't, but like a lot of these things it was mainly a function of the hours you put in.

Training would have been bringing a boat in on your own, in easy conditions, in more difficult conditions, and recovering and towing a Fireball, man overboard drill, starting a stopped engine – the basic rules of the road. I don't recall a check list or a tick box but there would have been a broad sense of the skills you had to have. Within the ranks of cox'n some were more serious than others. I wouldn't have been allowed to be the lead person on something like the Tusker Rock rescue – although it would have been fudged – I hadn't got the depth of experience. There was a degree of awareness of that.

Dave Nockels came to AC in 1969 with no seagoing experience at all and became one of the most proficient coxswains and boatbuilders that the college produced.

34. Challenging boathandling for helm and crew.

The remarkable thing was the speed at which it all happened, from rank landlubber to coxswain, in just over a year. [In my day, the RNLI allowed us to be called coxswains of Inshore Rescue Boats – only later being demoted/ changed to helmsman of inshore lifeboats.]

The early period at AC was a blur. The only choice of rescue service for me was obviously the boats: never occurred to me do anything else. Much excitement at all the strange new things, totally absorbing and being involved in quite extraordinary activities. After a period, it all settled down.

An important aspect of everything done in the Rescue Boats was the essential teamwork. As I recall, it was not much discussed nor the subject of formal or explicit training. However, it was absolutely key and simply unavoidably necessary to carry out the Rescue Boat operations and other activities off the slipway. The most obvious aspect would be the teamwork needed in each boat's crew (typically three people). However, it also was integral to the everyday routine of going to sea and then returning, moving all the boats from their parked area down the slipway to the water, and then returning them to the parking area after seagoing. This all happened before the formal concepts of 'human factors' and 'crew resource management' had ever been invented.

The core of the practical training centred around looking after the sailors (whether they liked it or not). In fact, this was a fantastic way for Rescue Boaters to learn so well and so quickly. It also gave us the opportunity to legitimately whiz around when a sailing boat capsized or drifted too far away from the slipway.

35. Messing about in boats.

Weather was a key issue, forming the start of every afternoon's activity, everyone listening to the Shipping Weather forecast on the BBC, and one of us recording the forecast and actual report for each sea area on a blackboard. A short discussion of the underlying weather followed, in order to decide whether to go to sea or not.

One of the most important transitions, emphasised as much by students as by instructors, was from first year to second year, from learner to teacher. Dave Nockels' experience would have been familiar to many other students:

August period [the six-week period when only students returning for a second year were in residence] involved some more formal training but also was the time we got used to being in charge. There were a few trips away, e.g. across the Channel to England. An interesting feature of the rescue services was that the student heads of each service and boat captains were elected by the students in that service. In my year in Rescue Boats certain people had become quite high profile and I imagine expected to become one of those heads. In the event, other people were elected, who were better in dealing with people.

In my second year, I found myself spending a lot of time and effort training our first years. It was the first time I had done anything like that and found it fascinating and extremely rewarding to be able to pass on knowledge. Not all training was so entirely positive. I recall spending what turned out to be an extremely cold afternoon in February in the Bristol Channel, teaching a series of first years how to right a capsized RIB manually, using ropes and our own body weight to turn the boat the right way up. It taught me about hypothermia, and I took some long while to warm up, once back ashore.

That was as true for other services, including Beach Rescue. Paul Belcher wrote:

August Period was a special time and a rite of passage for Atlantic College students. Service happened every afternoon and was four hours long rather than the usual two hours. It gave an opportunity for students to be given responsibilities and transform from 1st years to 2nd years. It culminated in the infamous August Review where Staff performed for the students and at least one Lifeguard sketch was always present.

* * * * *

But training is about more than acquiring skills. It is a state of mind. Malcolm Dixelius, a Swedish student from 1963 to 1965, recalls an episode from those early days:

Although a weak swimmer, the Atlantic College experience left me with one serious passion: the Beach Rescue service. I couldn't get enough after my first experience of patrolling Southerndown beach in 1964. When I left AC in 1965, I decided to come back the same summer to work and train with the new crop of students. I was even back for a third turn in 1966. I competed for St Donat's SLSC (Surf Life Saving Club) in two British championships, 1964 in Torquay and 1965 in Woolacombe.

Some of my best days in 1964–65 were spent on arduous trips to Cornwall in a cramped van, sharing a trailer with the other boys in the Beach Rescue unit, living on corn flakes and milk, soggy sandwiches and the occasional pint of cider in the evenings. We learnt from hardened surfers with a background or experience from Australia or South Africa. We grew to respect high waves, dangerous tidal conditions and treacherous currents. We learnt how to save others from being too foolhardy in rough conditions. Or what would be sometimes more difficult, warning people from taking risks in seemingly calm conditions.

That was basically what we did at Southerndown beach. We passed on that knowledge. We gave information. We knew how to judge if the conditions were safe for swimming, surfing or strolling along the cliffs. It was up to us to monitor those who ventured beyond the surf. We were on surfboards, surf skis and kayaks. We walked up and down the beach, monotonously moving our flags back and forth as the tide rose or fell. Vigilance was our most important quality and I am convinced that we prevented many people from getting into trouble. I am equally convinced that we also saved lives. Many holidaymakers were shockingly naïve and unaware of the dangers on the Bristol Channel. Far too many people didn't even know how to swim in those days.

All this said, in my three seasons with the Beach Rescue unit, I cannot recall a single really serious incident where we were called upon to send out a swimmer on a belt to rescue a person in distress or drowning. We trained regularly for it, we learnt the drills with the reel, we knew how to drain and resuscitate a person, who had been under water. Every year I was there we put together a team to represent St Donat's at the national championships. That was a strong inspiration to perfect our skills, as we would be judged both for speed and precision. But it seems that our mere presence at Southerndown was enough to avoid drowning incidents. Yet, there is a moment I will never forget, when our training sessions unexpectedly turned into a real lifesaving situation. Thanks to the quick thinking of swimmer Dan Larsen.

In the summer of 1965, Leif Carlsson, a fellow Swede from the same year, borrowed his parents' car and drove all the way from the small city of Luleå, near the Arctic circle, to St Donat's. I didn't have a driving licence, so my job was to guide Leif through a European road system that was only spottily equipped with road signs. Our goal was to be the first Atlantic College students to become qualified Beach Rescue instructors. Two teachers, who had been with us the year before, were our trainers: Roger Haslam and John David. In a short period of time, we were supposed to put together a new team for the championships. Our skills as instructors would be judged by representatives from the Surf Life Saving Association of Great Britain, the same people in fact who would referee at the championships.

The class of 64–66 had some exceptionally good swimmers, topped by Dan Larsen, who had represented the Danish national team in the 1500 metres freestyle event. Dan had an economic, yet powerful stroke, ideal for a rescue swimmer. So when it came to showing our prowess to the examiners, Dan was our obvious choice as number one, the swimmer with the belt. The day of the test performance, buoys had been placed on the perimeter of the surf. The waves were high, it was difficult to see heads sticking up in the surf. First of all, we sent out another strong swimmer to a buoy as 'the victim'. My recollection is that it was Leif. At least, he doesn't seem to remember this story, which is so vivid in my memory. I guess he missed it because of what happens next.

When the victim reaches the buoy, he will raise an arm to show that he has completed the swim. That is the signal for the rescue squad to start running towards the water, swimmer first and three linesmen behind. The surf is now so high that it is difficult to follow where our swimmer is and after a short while we cannot see him anymore. But as long as he is pulling the line, the squad on land keep feeding him more. Suddenly there is a slack on the line. We begin to worry. Where is Dan? Nowhere to be seen in the vicinity of the buoy and the victim. Suddenly we see an arm raised in the water, totally off course. It looks like Dan's. Either he has completely lost his sense of direction, or he is in trouble, maybe caught by an unexpected rip current. We decide to pull him in.

As Dan gets into the shallow water it seems that there is nothing wrong with him. But suddenly he stands up, holding a young girl in his arms. When they get up on dry land, we can see that the girl is totally exhausted, but well enough to stand up and walk by herself. Dan has reacted with a rescuer's instinct. As he was making his way out to the victim, he spotted the girl struggling hard against a current pulling her further and further from land. That's when he abandoned his 'examination rescue' and decided to swim to her assistance. Once he caught up with her, he immediately decided not to leave her battling the current alone. The obvious choice was to hold her head above water and let the two of them be pulled back by the linesmen.

Leif and I got our instructor's awards anyway, despite the aborted test. In fact, Dan's good judgement may even have contributed to that. I've had reason to repeat the story many times in my life as an example of moral courage and the kind of spirit we were supposed to learn at Atlantic College. As I write this, 55 years after it happened, the image of Dan in knee-high water with the girl in his arms still brings tears of emotion to my eyes.

Moral courage, and the importance of training to the point where it triumphs over fear, were points made by several students, like Simon Daman Willems who was at AC from 1974 to 1976:

I recall throughout my life, including in my years in post-conflict Iraq, the training we had and how it had brought us (in my case aged 15!) to understand that usually there is no clear 'best' course of action, and that practicing safety procedures is vital. The rigorous training (yes, and the fun too) helped me later when in a 'sticky situation': remain calm, evaluate unemotionally, act decisively. It also taught me the value of teams and team leadership: we had to work as a team to succeed, trust our teammates with our lives, at the same time there was no room for democracy on a callout, and we understood it. Democracy could play out in the changing rooms after recovery of the boat.

This would have been the kind of response that both Hahn and Hoare would have hoped for.

In parallel with increasingly professional skill training for boats and on the beach, Cliff Rescue now took a great leap forward under the leadership of Ivar Lund Mathiesen, already a highly experienced expedition leader. Under Jolley, Cliff Rescue's first head, five areas of expertise had been identified: basic rock and rope work, first aid training, cliff rescue techniques, shore to ship rescues (the Breeches buoy!) and equipment maintenance and design. Ivar Lund Mathiesen set about broadening the service's ambition.

> When I arrived in 1974 the service was known as Cliff Rescue, but it seemed to me more like a mountaineering/climbing club, with a loose connection to Llantwit Major Coastguard, who occasionally would call upon the College to assist with tasks along the cliffs when the rather unfit local coastguard needed help pulling up climbers at Ogmore, etc.
>
> I was surprised to learn that climbing trips during the weekends meant that the unit stood down its callout responsibility completely. I was not impressed by this and understood that to be accepted as a professional rescue unit, things had to change.
>
> My task became eventually to help develop the unit into an efficient, modern and professional search and rescue unit, using the most modern rope techniques and rescue/self-rescue techniques known from the European and British climbing scene, including the Tragsitz, the (split) Bell stretcher etc. Modern mountaineering first aid was introduced and practiced under the instruction of national experts. Eventually we had created a unit fit for 24-hour callout duty, 24/7/365, officially included in HM Coastguard's organization.

Etienne Grall, AC 1976–78, would echo Ivar Lund Mathiesen's confidence in the training they received which stood the rescue service in good stead whatever the challenge:

> As members of the Cliff Rescue unit, we spent many hours practicing drills to get casualties up or down cliffs, using techniques and gear that were designed to be portable, be deployed rapidly and suited for the shallow soil on top of the rugged Welsh cliffs. Week after week we became more familiar with the techniques but above all, more capable of operating as a team, where roles are clear and communication is efficient. It involved a mix of discipline – respecting the decisions of those in charge (and we took turns at all roles) – and initiative – being able to identify problems and

36. Cliff Rescue teamwork.

troubleshoot them. All drills involved trusting the equipment and trusting your teammates: even at training, a mistake could mean serious injury or worse.

As we entered our second year, aged 17 and with the sense of now being in charge, we felt eager to demonstrate that we were up to the challenge.

There were many false alarms, but actual callouts were rare. And one day in October 1977, it happened: the siren, rushing down to Cliff Rescue shed for instructions. This time it was for real: report from Coastguard was that two climbers from Cardiff University were in difficulties on the Southerndown cliffs, one with 'sustained injuries of broken ribs and a broken arm after falling 15 feet'.

Sitting in the Land Rover rushing to the scene, we were running scenarios through our heads, all involving some form of acrobatic use of the rope techniques we'd been practicing so much. There was excitement and nerves. It almost came as a disappointment when we realized that, being low tide, we could access the climbers along the base of the cliffs, a few hundred meters from the nearest access point.

Yet, it was a true emergency and the adrenaline kept pumping. It all happened in a blur: grabbing the gear, running to the location, meeting the 2 climbers. We loaded the casualty onto a stretcher and carried him back to the road access. No fancy rope work and yet, carrying an adult in a stretcher over uneven rocks at low tide is not easy. We took turns as our hands got sore, trying to keep as even a pace as possible and avoiding slipping. Those not carrying acted as spotters to find the best route or stood near to carriers to support as needed.

We made it back in good time and delivered the casualty to a waiting ambulance.

Strangely, although we were all very close, I do not remember who else was in the rescue party. I believe that in the end, since we all trained together, it was just the team that mattered over the individuals.

When David Cope took over from Ivar Lund Mathiesen in 1985, he inherited this well-rehearsed system of training, although training events did not always pass off as smoothly as intended.

Coastguards had to train once a month officially, 7–9 pm first Monday of the month … We had this big dummy stuffed with sand called Roger, weighed about 16 stone [100 kg]. We couldn't strap a live person to the stretcher for training, so we used Roger. So one Monday night in the mid-90s, Peter Furlong, our Sector Officer, and I drove to Nash Point, and manhandled Roger out of the Land Rover. He had the arms and I had the legs and we were swinging the body to throw it over the cliff (so students could practice bringing it up) and as we're swinging it a car pulled up with a couple in it, obviously seeking a bit of peace and quiet for a kiss and a cuddle. They caught us in the headlights, and they just turned around and shot off. We were expecting the police to arrive to investigate a possible murder but fortunately they didn't show up.

The Breeches Buoy practice that happened periodically was normally prior to the annual Breeches Buoy Competition that used to take place every September and where Coastguard teams from around South Wales competed to see who could set up a rescue in the quickest and neatest time! The setting up involved firing a rocket out of a gun. The responsibility for this always fell to Les Beckwith, a local man from Llantwit Major, who had been one of the few who transferred when the Coastguard station moved from Llantwit Major. So the scene was set, on the sports field we had all the equipment laid out and people in position and I gave the order for Les to fire the rocket! Off it went, not in the nice parabolic arc over the imaginary ship's mast 100 m away that it was supposed to do ... But 1 m off the ground and was seen to veer off to the right into a field of sheep! Fortunately, no sheep were hurt and no student witnessing it will forget the incident!

*****

Tim Haney, a student at AC between 1979 and 1981, was involved in a series of traumatic callouts as an official member of the Coastguard squad. Yet like many recruits to the rescue services, he came to the college with little experience in or on the water, or the cliffs. He had joined Cliff Rescue to overcome a fear of heights.

'The sea is crashing in below you,' he told the climbing magazine *Highwire* later, 'and you have to change over the equipment ... You get used to it after a while, so you're not frightened all the time. You build a trust for the system. You feel that if everything is done properly – these knots are right, the stakes are in at the right angle – you are safe. You don't worry at all about falling.'

This sense of mutual trust allied with instinct was felt across all three services. Simon Daman Willems recalls a particular moment when his training became critical to preventing one of the college boats being wrecked.

One day when that reflex training played out was not a callout, though the B-boat was at sea on exercise. I was not on the boats; I was doing something in the Sea Area in normal clothes. The tide was high, and seas medium to heavy, so waves would dump at the last minute on the steep slipway. This made landing an ILB very tricky. Timing is critical: you had to be on the back of a wave and cut the engine just as you reached the trolley. Cut the engine too soon and you missed the trolley, too late or ahead of a wave and you surfed up the slipway.

My colleague coxswain came in to land X-11, and mis-timed the landing for whatever reason. The boat, probably weighing 500–600 kg, surfed over the trolley and then off the east side of the slipway, scattering the landing party before it. The coxswain got in and tried to restart the engine (X-11 had an electric start) without success. The boat was now broadside on to the seas, hitting the rocks with each wave and about to be lost. In danger of being crushed by the boat, people swam away. I don't know why, but I ran into the water, angry the waves would take our boat! I leapt into X-11, and the reflex kicked in: engine down – check, fuel primed – check, stop switch (the lanyard that cut the ignition) reset – OOPS! In the melee the coxswain had left the stop switch 'OFF'. Click switch – 'ON'. Throttle in neutral – check, raise idle – check. Turn key and crank. The engine started on the first attempt. There was, though, no way to go forwards, the stern on an ILB

37. Preparing for a landing.

moves into the turn, in this case to shore, and the bow was already on the rocks. Going forwards would pivot the stern to shore and the prop would smash on the rocks. I checked no one was behind, and probably did the first ever reverse 'jump' over waves in an ILB, clearing the rocks and heading out to sea. Coming alongside the B-boat (Luke Celt was aboard and I recall his jaw hanging down) my first words were 'Please give me a life jacket before John David sees me!' (We lived in fear of the Deputy Headmaster JOD. John did actually come up to find me later that day and thanked me.) The boat was punctured in several compartments, but that tube that makes a RIB what it is gives massive buoyancy and we stayed afloat. Another ILB-er from the B-boat transferred to X-11 to lift the engine on landing, and together we successfully landed her despite the tonne of water in her ruptured hull. I think the trolley collapsed under the weight!

What stuck with me (after I had warmed up!) was that the whole engine restart which ultimately saved X-11 was done without thinking, it was a reflex. There was no time to look up the procedure or think about it, the boat would certainly have been lost only seconds later. I learnt that there are situations to stop and reflect, and others where reflex training saves you.

38. Beached – a landing that went wrong.

Sue Harris, née Parker, who was a student from 1976 to 1978, also remembers the importance of a training so intensive it produced a reflex in challenging circumstances. Late one afternoon in April 1978, she went on a callout to search for a boat that had been reported missing.

> The water was choppy but not particularly rough. It was pretty cold and it started to rain at some point. It soon became dark. We went back and forth over the search area several times following instructions from the Coastguard but there were no sightings of the boat. The waves seemed bigger and I remember it was a real effort to hold on as we were bounced around by them. Eventually we were told to return to the college, which was a relief to me as by then I was very cold and wet from the spray.

> When we were just getting round to making our approach to the trolley, Winand [Moonan] turned to me and asked me to do the landing – his glasses were covered with sea spray and I thought he probably couldn't see the trolley clearly. I had done surf landings before but only in daylight. I didn't have much time to think, but I do remember looking through the darkness at the people holding the trolley in the waves and thinking, I have got to do this right so no one gets hurt. We caught the wave, the engines were cut and the boat plopped onto the trolley first time. I think all the training we did just kicked in, we had practiced everything so often and were used to working as a team.

> The other thing which has stayed with me was how calm everyone was, there was no sense of drama, rather a strong feeling of being part of a team. I've always felt grateful to Deon Glover and John David for bringing home to me through the ILB service just how important thorough training and preparation are in order to deal with such challenging situations.

Ian Paley arrived at the college in 1977 already set on joining the British Royal Navy. An uncle and two cousins were RNLI crew members in the north east of England.

> A good thing about Rescue Service training is that it was mainly practical and taught by your second years. From learning how to record and interpret the shipping forecast, through keeping safe whilst taking half a ton of boat down/up the slipway and launching/recovering, to swimming from the boat, swimming under the boat, lifting engines etc. etc. nothing was left out. Sure, there was more academic training, e.g. chart work, during August period, but largely you learned by doing. We got cold and wet, which taught us that you should keep your wetsuit in a good state of repair (and some of us added to it by fashioning neoprene bootees inside oversize

39. An afternoon at sea, with the giant Fireball the 'Mama Ollo'.

plimsolls, making neoprene balaclavas and gloves).

We had some structured training in that the RNLI defined a large number of things we had to get signed off before we could have an RNLI jersey and a coxswain's knife. This included sailing, first aid, knots, splicing ropes, weather, navigation, swimming (to ASA Gold Standard) and lifesaving to RLSS bronze standard. We learned a huge amount about small boat handling, in all weathers. We learnt how to handle a Fireball sailing boat in high winds ... and all at the tender age of 17/18. Some also mastered kayaking, including how to roll. Not me, but my younger son can do it.

Of course, our skills and experience grew more once our second years had gone and we had the place to ourselves during August period. Then, our first years arrived in September and we taught them. We also learned together how the boats were constructed and how to fix them, in and out of the water.

The training is all about being able to operate an inshore lifeboat service in a challenging environment safely and effectively. My view here is that we learned everything about how to control an ILB and look after our crew members during our first year. Sure, our first callout in August 1978 was a bit ragged, but we got to sea safely and could have been effective if we hadn't been recalled. The learning continued throughout August and our

40. Safe landing – followed by the haul up the slipway.

skills, knowledge and experience were passed on to our first years. We also built increasing confidence, and competence, by going to sea at least twice per week and doing shore training and maintenance when it was clearly not safe to go to sea. For some of us, it was an obsession and it detracted from our academic studies.

Emotionally, it was all about the adrenalin rush, from the time the klaxon and siren sounded to the point at which the RNLI ILB launched on service. Once you were in the boat, the thought process was about what you might be called on to do when you arrived on scene. It could be as simple as fixing a line to another boat and towing it to a safe place, or in one case transferring an injured climber from A to B. At the age of 17/18, being selected to go out in a powerful boat to perform a rescue, is a huge ask, but we did it about ten times during the August 1978 to May 1979 period.

But year-round immersion in the Bristol Channel was never an easy experience and it was not for the faint-hearted. In 1984 Morgyn Warner finally secured the coveted RNLI jersey and the college coxswain's knife after a year of hard-won experience that had had its inspiration thousands of miles away.

I first heard about Atlantic College from Steve Griffiths (AC 81), whose brother was in my class at high school in Zimbabwe. His accounts of his experiences, friendships and his time in ILBs at the college inspired me to apply. ILBs sounded amazing, combining community service with outdoor physical challenges. It also sounded fun – from making your own wetsuits, helping with boatbuilding, learning navigation, boat-handling, first aid, and being a member of a crew. Steve also told me about the legendary Deon Glover, a fellow southern African who was the teacher heading ILBs at the time. Deon was a remarkable person, who mixed authority with humour calm and kindness and he was also one of the reasons that ILBs was my first choice of service.

But a commitment to the cause couldn't warm up the sea for a Zimbabwean.

I would never have missed an ILB session for anything, but it was not always easy. Winter could be challenging – getting wet launching boats in February and then driving around in choppy and windy conditions doing navigations drills on the Bristol channel was cold and a bit miserable.

Nevertheless, the camaraderie of the crew was great and we were learning useful skills. One of the things that we were all working towards was to become a registered crew member. This meant that you had to pass a number of tests in boat-handling, navigation, first aid and radio. To go out on an official callout, you had to have passed these tests and be deemed suitable to be a crew member by the staff.

Not all ILB-ers were registered with the RNLI, but all were involved in launching boats, training and supporting the RNLI station. I was fortunate to be registered as a crew member in my second year.

In its way, every afternoon spent on rescue service activities was a form of training. Sometimes it was intended as a training exercise, like this one Simon Daman Willems remembers from the mid-1970s, a time when a national economic crisis was making Britain an angry and divided country – but not so angry that people failed to respond to basic challenges to their humanity:

The emergency services were on strike then for better pay & conditions and only attending emergencies. We were carrying out a training drill, recovering a team of actors from the sea, made-up as if they had horrific injuries. This had all been shared throughout the emergency services, and we were preceding communications with 'DRILL!'. Somehow though the good people of the local ambulance service and a local journalist picked up our radio communications and arrived in the Sea Area. Sirens blaring, blue lights flashing, just as we landed the 'casualties'. I don't know if we thought to remind them it was a drill or thought they were part of the drill so leave them to get on with it, in any case we carried on. The actors were wonderful, up to the moment when one with a truly horrendous head injury couldn't contain himself any longer and sat up and started laughing. This set off the whole group of actors, and made the local papers – to the chagrin of the ambulance corps.

But drills had a way of going wrong. Neill Patterson was one of the early students, at AC from 1963 to 1965.

> [I] was asked to go down to the jetty [seafront] in my rubber suit as I had been chosen to participate in a rescue exercise. I had no idea what this involved until I was straddling the side of the boat and was informed by the German crew that I was to be dropped off half a mile out to sea and the other boats would then rescue me. In my black suit, boots, gloves and peaked hood I was like a seal and virtually undetectable in the water. Over the side I went and I listened to the sound of the boat's engine receding.
>
> I am a bad swimmer. I swim like an injured crab and do a poor breaststroke and a plausible back float. So I lay on my back, thinking. The sea was relatively calm and I rose and fell in the swell, briefly having some visibility and then sinking down into the trough of the waves. It was remarkably quiet and time seemed to stand still. My flotation system seemed to be working and I thought – don't panic. It'll be over before too long!
>
> After a while I thought, there are other things in this water apart from myself; and I became a little less reassured. Each time I was lifted up on the swell I looked around and listened, but my hood blocked out distant noise. Then I thought: 'How did I get chosen for this exercise'? Was this Hoare's notion to get rid of me? I had lost track of time and cannot say how long I was out there. Probably rather frighteningly long. So fortunately, as I rose again in the swell a rescue boat appeared and I was hauled on board rather bemused by the whole event.
>
> Forty plus years later I met a colleague at Dartmouth, USA and the first thing he said to me was, 'Did you know about that scandal about you when you were at AC! It was all hushed up.' I wondered which scandal he was thinking of! I learnt soon enough that it was about me being thrown into the Bristol Channel. A significant error had been made by the boat crews. Hoare had said 'Chuck a buoy into the sea as a rescue exercise.' – not a boy! It was a case of lost in translation.

More than 50 years later, we could find no one else who remembered the incident. But intended or accidental, Neill Patterson's experience was not the last time a supposed 'victim' spent a disconcertingly long time in the water. In 1977, Doug Hamilton was asked to help out in an exam session for the Corps of Canoe Lifeguards.

James Mendelssohn, who was the head of the Marine Science service at Atlantic College, approached me and suggested that I be the 'victim' since I was a strong swimmer and experienced SCUBA diver.

The plan was for me to swim offshore, pretend to be in distress and that a group of paddlers in kayaks would come to my assistance and help to return me safely back to shore.

I was well prepared with my wetsuit, fins, buoyancy compensator (which would double as a life jacket), and an old empty disused SCUBA tank. I recall wading into the water and swimming off into the rough waters of the Bristol Channel and waiting for my would-be rescuers to come to my assistance. It turned out to be a particularly rough day with strong winds and large swell. I swam a good distance from the shore, not wanting to drift back onto the rocky shoreline. I waited for some time and was puzzled that I had seen no sign of the kayakers.

After a while I started to kick my fins vigorously to try to propel myself off the crest of the waves in order to better see my surroundings and locate the kayakers. I was surprised to spot several capsized kayaks with students swimming beside them. I soon realized that they would not be rescuing me.

I felt safe, and I felt calm. I was warm, and I was very familiar with the coastline. I concluded that I was on my own and would need to come up with my own plan to get safely to shore. Swimming to the rocky shoreline and cliffs adjacent to Atlantic College was not an option as the waves would likely dash me onto the rocks. I knew that 2 miles to the east was a nice sandy beach, known as Llantwit Beach. The wind and the swell were tending to push me in that direction. I decided that the safest thing for me to do was to swim with the current toward Llantwit Beach. I preferred the idea of landing on a sandy beach to being tossed onto the rocks by the big swell.

As I started to swim away from the college and towards the beach, I could see a large crowd gathered along the cliffs adjacent to my position. Someone was using a long paddle to give signals. I assumed that the signals were meant for me, not realizing that an Inshore Lifeboat (ILB) was en route and trying to locate me. The signals indicated to come closer to shore, so I swam closer to shore, not realizing that in so doing I was swimming away from the boat which was approaching me from behind. Suddenly I spotted the boat which was now quite close to me. I recognized my roommate Gary Price at the helm of the boat. As the boat approached me, I remember taking off my SCUBA tank and passing it up to the people in the boat. This is what I naturally would have done when returning to a boat after a dive. The people in the boat told me to forget the gear and to grab their hand and get into the boat. I was quickly brought into the boat and was soon safely ashore.

I returned to my dorm and showered and changed in time for afternoon class.

When I look back on this experience it seems odd that I did not feel afraid or distressed with my situation. I felt safe and in control despite the hazardous conditions. I don't remember having a formal debrief or discussion with anyone about what had happened, what went wrong, and what we could learn from this.

I was naively unaware of the distress and concern that my prolonged swim had caused for James Mendelssohn and the other staff members at the college. I also did not appreciate the danger that the crew of the ILB had faced as they came to my aid. In fact, I remember this experience with a sense of exhilaration and have shared this story with friends and family over the years with a feeling of excitement and nostalgia. It is only now, as I reflect on this incident that I realize that it may have had a bigger impact on those involved in planning the exercise, and those involved in my rescue, than it did on me.

The view from one of the Rescue Boat crew, Matthew Goodman, illustrates in what difficult conditions Doug Hamilton had stayed so calm.

The ILB note is about our latest 'callout', the sixth and most exciting thus far. It was on Wednesday, when I was supposed to go out in activity time anyway. We actually stayed on shore to do maintenance on the boats because it was too rough to go out for a normal day's seagoing. However, Beach Rescue (the canoeing and lifesaving service at the College) was sending out about five canoeists to pick up a supposedly tired swimmer for a canoe life-guarding exam. The canoeists couldn't find the swimmer (who is luckily a very hardy Canadian) and eventually all capsized and fell out of their canoes. So we were called out in what turned out to be the roughest day I had ever been to sea in, to pick up the swimmer and to make sure the canoeists got in alright. Some of the waves were 12 or 15 feet high and at one point, we almost capsized the twin-engine 21-foot Rescue Boat, which would have been very dangerous. Anyway, we survived and managed to rescue the swimmer and get the canoes to safety.

Unintended consequences dogged training sessions. Dimitrios Sotiropoulos (1969–71) had had very little experience of the sea when he began his ILB training.

I had joined the Rescue Boats and one day went out with the captain of my boat who was a 2nd year blond boy from Scandinavia (I think from Norway but I can't remember his name). It was quite rough with medium size waves.

Sailboats had also gone out. The weather being what it was, gave us, the Rescue Boats, the job of towing back the sailboats that had gone far.

On one of these occasions, the Scandinavian wanting to train me asked me to drive the rescue boat and approach a sailboat in order to throw it a rope and tow it. I approached the sailboat but I was about 3–4 metres away from it to avoid hitting it. Then the Scandinavian insisted that I drive the boat closer and closer. When my boat was about to touch the sailboat with a wave trying to push my boat hard against it, I got scared that my boat would crush the sailboat, and I turned the steering wheel abruptly away from the sailboat.

I did not have experience driving boats and I thought I was driving a car. What a result! My rescue boat's left back corner (and perhaps engine) hit hard the right front part of the sailboat, smashing it and opening a hole a bit higher than the sea level.

The Scandinavian was very polite, did not say anything, he just took over the steering wheel and towed the sailboat back. I was very embarrassed, especially seeing David watching with his binoculars what was happening. To my surprise, no one ever said anything to me during that day or afterwards. That was the spirit of Atlantic College!

A much scarier encounter with the dangers of sea activities occurred at the end of the March project week in 1978. A group of students had gone to Newquay to improve their surfing and surf lifesaving skills.

The week was nearly over when Luigi Boscarelli found himself in grave difficulties.

It is the end of March 1978, we have arrived on the last day of our Project Week in Newquay; it was the third time that I came to Cornwall with the Beach Rescue Unit of Atlantic College, this wonderful beach has once again given us an extraordinary welcome.

The combination of a full moon aided by strong winds were magnificent throughout the week, with waves at least 10 feet tall, if not more, and this helped to make for an unforgettable holiday. For me it will be that without any doubt.

I'm the last on patrol, and it is just past noon. We will be back soon, but there is still a first year in the water, about 50 metres from the shore, a German boy, he still wants to taste the euphoria of catching the last crashing wave. He is very good, but the crashing force of the wave overwhelms him to the extent that he cannot control his Eskimo roll, and he gets out of his kayak which is lost in the foam of the waves. I'm in my kayak and worried about him, so I

41. The surfyak (or surfshoe) in action at Newquay..

paddle towards him. He's a very good swimmer and he quickly reaches the shore. I want to find out where his kayak has ended up, because with the polystyrene bars inside it cannot completely sink. I had just started reflecting on this when I see a series of big waves which are about to strike me.

I'm confident on how to deal with them, as I have learnt this in the past two years, and I also am not afraid of surfing this massive wave. I start paddling towards the beach, and the wave behind me grows ever higher, and when it's almost about to break over me, I lean towards the right resting my paddle on the crest of this magnificently high wave. Miraculously, I start to slide inside the curve of the wave. I sense the curve taking shape behind me, I'm happy, certain that I can remember always this incomparable feeling of freedom. A happiness which lasts sadly for only a split second.

All of a sudden from within the wave the first-year's kayak appears swamped with water and heads straight towards me. Instinctively I push my hands in front to protect myself, but the kayak's path is unstoppable. It tears into my spray deck and literally sticks there penetrating my wetsuit on my left thigh. The wetsuit is 5 mm and stretchy and gives me some protection, but still the kayak cuts 3 cm deep into my thigh and tears my muscles.

I sense that I'm wounded but the roar of the wave deafens my cry of pain, and in the confusion of the moment, I let go of my paddle and find myself outside my kayak but a long way from the shore.

The rough waves continue to hit me, and I ask myself whether I can manage to get to the shore. I feel the sea floor at the point of my right foot, and I'm heartened by that, but when I try to support my left foot, my leg gives way and I can't control it. I feel helpless, and I'm on the point of fainting. My companions finally reach me and pick me up under the arms to support me and bring me to shore. Out of the corner of my eye I see a small tear on my wetsuit my left thigh, in the shape of a figure 7, and around 4 cm wide. From there spurts a powerful flow of blood, straight – unstoppable. I notice the faces of my friends look grey, perhaps because of the overcast day, and extremely worried. They are unable to speak. They lay me down on the ground, pad the wound and elevate my leg. My throat's dry and I can't speak.

Mark Wolsey who is close by asks me 'Luigi, if in English foot is the singular, what is the plural?' I look at him sarcastically, and reply, 'Don't be stupid, obviously it's feet'.

I see a broad smile across his face, and then happily he says to me 'you're not going to die!' I guess that his concern, like the others, was that my femoral artery was severed and that I wouldn't have much longer to live.

The ambulance arrives quickly – and I am taken to Truro hospital. There is no one from the AC with me, I'm alone in the Casualty department. The doctors want to cut my wetsuit, but I told them not to do it, as I want to wear it again. So they peel it off me. When they reach my thigh a bloody mass, a portion of my thigh muscle literally jumps out, and I throw back my head and say, 'oh my God!'

The kayak has cut clean through the vastus medialis and sartorius muscles. I will be operated on during the night, when they will reattach the cut muscles. When I wake up, no one from AC is next to me, as the team has gone back to college the same day. I ask the doctors whether I could also go back to college. They ask me to lift my leg, and if I can manage that, then I can go back. I manage it – 'bravo', and I can go.

However, they keep me in hospital for a whole week to recuperate. They discharge me – and I am able to walk with crutches, although they say that I will remain a cripple for the rest of my life. In my own mind I can't accept that. I reach Cardiff station with a nurse, where an ambulance takes me to Atlantic College where many of my friends come to find me. The college did not do an investigation of the accident afterwards as far as I remember.

The consequences of this bad injury have minimally affected my functional abilities on a physical level. Until the end of the 90s, I ran half and full marathons and took part in cycling competitions. I have been a Boxing Referee since 1989, conducting and judging more than 15,000 matches. I joined the WBA in 2014, I have been assigned 42 times, nine of which were

World Titles. Only in recent years have I experienced some cramps at night while sleeping ... but nothing more.

It goes without saying that the memory of that bad day has never stopped me from going back to canoeing, indeed as soon as I returned to Italy, I founded a Kayak Club with five dear friends, together we took part in white water canoeing, and participated several times at VOGALONGA – a 35 km long-distance race in Venice.

I am still a kayak enthusiast, and especially in the summer I can't wait to go back to Elba Island.

Despite the risks taken almost every day, Luigi Boscarelli's injuries were among the gravest ever suffered by a student. But safety was always a work in progress. For the first few years, for example, there was no polystyrene ballast in the front and back of a kayak. But after a student crashed through the footrest and got stuck, unable to use his arms, in the front of his kayak while doing a loop on a wave, it was hastily retrofitted everywhere.

One common feature of the experience of getting it wrong in training is the stoicism of those involved. Anna Margareta Sundberg arrived at AC from Sweden in 1973 with only a hazy idea of what she was letting herself in for. She coped with everything that came her way with a cool that should make her a legend.

Before our first stormy day at sea, I had been training in canoes. We used the paddle to turn the canoe and ourselves from an upside-down underwater position and back up for air. It seems silly to be so pleased with something so simple in the safety of a pool, but my teenage self was.

Our second-year instructor explained that this rolling technique could be used to surf or go under the waves. He might have been looking for a reaction when he told us it was possible to roll straight through the waves when they were too big for boats. He said this technique was useful for rescue work. We listened regardless of if this was done or not. In the pool that day we wanted to do anything hands-on and real, something like real work, not schoolwork.

To me all activities seemed easier than volunteering as a helmsman for our headmaster in a stormy sailing competition a few weeks earlier. Out at sea with Mr Sutcliffe was very far from the headmaster's office. There he was altogether another person and owned everything about sailing with furious perfection. He was not pleased with my sailing experience. Never had I seen anyone take competing so seriously. I was shaken.

Finding something new to participate in seemed wise. Beach Rescue, RNLI and diving were some of the options.

They all involved the sea. The Bristol Channel's high tides in late autumn were nothing like the balmy Baltic in summer. The Channel was a place that absolutely needed life rescue, even sheep needed rescuing here. [This is a reference to an occasion when some sheep had strayed into tidal marshes and rescue boats were sent to help.]

It was fun paddling a canoe out to sea, it was freedom before the rain turned icy and waves got big. A swell turned me upside down and a current grabbed the paddle. I was without paddle, out at sea with my teenage hips and wetsuit firmly stuck in an upside-down canoe. I was a girl in a beautiful yellow canoe possibly built by skinny college boys?

The power of the waves pushed the canoe with each swell. It was enough to get air between the waves. In a strange way the sea felt like a friend. I got air with each rocking and was drifting towards land. But after a while my 16-year-old self understood this was not a good place to be. It was getting cold and the cliffs came closer. Between gasps for air and big waves and just before crashing onto land, my hands could feel the sand on the bottom of the beach. It was enough to push upwards. The canoe helped by the surf turned around. With a loud bang it was thrown onto a slice of beach the size of the canoe itself under the cliffs.

There I sat. My big hips and wetsuit glued to the bottom of the canoe and no one in sight.

Don't know how much time passed but I knew we had been a group at sea and I had gotten lost. Sometime later, I don't know how long it took, a tall boy in a black wetsuit came running. For some reason I said nothing. Maybe I was ashamed? Without speaking he grabbed my arms and tried to pull me out. The inside of the water-filled canoe held me firmly and made noises each time he pulled. I pushed too while feeling embarrassed. Not a word was shared between us until this college boy, better described as a man, got me out. He was calm and silent as if this is what he did routinely every day. I was not proud needing rescue myself. Although in retrospect maybe I should have been?

My first words were 'thank you.' I could have said it many more times. His words were 'where is the paddle?' We returned to AC without talking as if this was any day. It was dinner time. We walked into the dining hall wearing wetsuits. Later someone said this young man was in Beach Rescue and so strong he was called 'Frankenstein'. Afterwards I joined the divers and stayed safely under the waves.

CHAPTER THREE

Klaxon!

In early 1969, a promotional film called *A Place in the World*, was released. It shows the headmaster David Sutcliffe – who had just taken over from Admiral Hoare – sprinting out of the staff room to pick up the emergency phone which sits in an alcove just off the outer courtyard. He takes the details of the 'rescue' and then reaches up on the wall to push the button that sounds the klaxon. The scene, palpitating with urgency, cuts to a breathtaking aerial view of the whole castle and its surroundings, every stone ringing with the demands of an emergency.

In the earliest days, the bell of the church in the grounds below the castle was rung to signal an emergency. But soon the emergency telephone with an amplified ring tone was installed. If the emergency was real (i.e. not a wrong number), a klaxon sounded. Later generations learned what the alert meant from their second years. For the college's first students, like John Smalley, there was no gradual introduction to the sound of the klaxon and the responsibilities it demanded.

42. The castle and the seafront, the rescue service 'racetrack'.

It was a weekday morning at St Donat's, and lessons were in progress as normal. Another day in the second term of Atlantic College's second year. The sounding of the siren took everyone, I think, completely by surprise. After all, we knew it was there and what it sounded like, but we had never heard it as an interruption to lessons. Once the first few seconds of realisation had happened, the teaching staff instructed everyone to 'turn out' in their rescue service 'gear' as soon as possible. Almost without exception, those same teachers were also our guides and instructors in the four rescue service teams which now scrambled back to the dorms (all in those days within the castle itself) and out into the yard in front of the portcullis gate to be briefed on what was to happen.

All the rescue services, including Cliff Rescue, were based on or near the seafront. Teaching, eating, socialising and sleeping took place several hundred feet higher up the hillside, in and around the castle itself. It was in the heart of the castle that the callout telephone was based, in what was known as the Gun Room, just outside the staff common room and the Director of Studies' office.

The telephone had a loud and distinctive bell and whoever was nearest to it was obliged to answer it. That was usually, but not invariably, a member of staff. Dave Nockels (1969–71) was in Suart House, right above the staff room.

> The phone was red (of course) and the phone ringing set off the intermittent klaxon. There was a mushroom button on the wall beside it to set the callout siren off. As I recall that was very like the air raid sirens and could be heard throughout the estate. Don't know who turned it off. I was never there for that!
>
> I was fortunate (on numerous grounds) to be based in Suart House in the Castle, half a dozen steps from the callout phone. I got to answer quite a few calls due to my location (when not down at the seafront or at sea).
>
> Many were wrong numbers.
>
> The klaxon phone has figured large in my subsequent career, reappearing at regular intervals. To this day, now long retired from emergency responses, an autonomic adrenaline rush and racing heartbeat is built into my innate reaction to a klaxon.

Dagfinn Paust, a near contemporary, recalls it as 'living over the shop':

> I felt that it was as if we were living at a 'fire station', always on the alert for the klaxon to sound the alarm for callout by one or all of the rescue services.
>
> It was cool to sit in Economics lectures in the Marion Davies room and hear

the phone just across the courtyard. Had the windows not been so small (and had they been on the ground floor) we would have jumped out!

I remember that the phone had a very loud, special sound. I guess that unless a designated staff member picked up the phone, then anyone in the vicinity could pick it up and take down all the pertinent details such as the nature of the distress and the presumed location e.g. 'two people may be trapped by the tide East of Tresilian', trying to get as much detail as possible. Then when someone pressed the alarm button, the klaxon's wailing sound would be heard all over the castle and the school grounds as far as the rugby fields.

Those students who were in a rescue service, maybe half the student body, would run down to the seafront area, rushing from all directions, some happily escaping dreary lectures for the promise of adventure. Many of the members of the boat and canoe rescue services would often be observed running down from the castle undressing on the way to prepare to get into the wetsuits hanging in the changing rooms.

Only when we arrived at the seafront would we learn what sort of callout it was, and quite often there might not be a need for all three services.

Meg Westley was at AC between 1970 and 1972. She was a member of Cliff Rescue.

The telephone rings in the castle, in a small room off the courtyard. The telephone is entirely reserved for one purpose: to receive distress calls. The ring is distinctive, unlike any other. Whoever is nearest – student, teacher or staff –must answer it.

I am near enough to hear and recognise it, but too far away to possibly be the closest person. I am in class, in the Marion Davies Room. I'm slightly more terrified than excited by the idea of having to answer this vital telephone. The person who does bears a great responsibility. They must take down the information and follow a procedure which alerts everyone to the emergency, if in fact there is one. The phone rings very rarely.

The students around me – dozing at their desks, pondering a lost Bridge game, or dreaming about the next visit to the local pub – sit up abruptly. The air is electrified. We wait. Just as we are ready to assume it is a false alarm, and the teacher begins to speak again, we hear the blast of the klaxon. It's almost deafening within the castle, designed to reach even students sleeping up the hill in the dormitories. It is the most thrilling sound in the world. Suddenly we are important people.

The College transforms from a school full of slouching multinational teenagers into a full-scale emergency scene. Without a word, almost everyone leaps up, dropping whatever they are doing, and we run out into the pouring rain. Many race to the seafront, to the rescue boats and canoes.

I run to the Cliff Rescue equipment depot. No one speaks during the initial mad dash. No one walks calmly, but neither do we bump into each other. We rush into the depot and start pulling on our gear: climbing boots, anoraks, helmets, harnesses, carabiners. It's a lot of gear but we have had it drilled into us over and over again that this equipment can save our lives. And our lives could well be at risk if we have to abseil down a cliff to rescue someone.

Mr Grant-Wood, Mr Agerbak and Mr Loveluck [three teachers] are in charge, issuing orders. No one fools around; everyone is tense, serious, wound up. We do not yet know if our service will even be required. Often it is not, as there are far more accidents at sea than on the cliffs. We proceed as though it is our call, and pile into the Land Rovers. My heart is pounding; I desperately hope this will be a call for Cliff Rescue.

Mr Grant-Wood is on a radio or walkie talkie, getting information. There is some confusion about which rescue service is required, so we are all heading out, just in case. The Land Rovers bump and rattle as we roar along the winding Welsh roads, jouncing us mercilessly against the metal seats. Pumped with adrenalin, the students are now talking, speculating, passing overheard snippets of information around the Land Rover.

As so often, Cliff Rescue was not required.

From the other side of the fence, Jonathan Lipscomb grew up at Atlantic College where his father, John, was a maths teacher. Jonathan was a student himself from 1977 to 1979, but his earliest memories are of the significance of callouts in the private life of a small boy.

From memory, callouts at that time were signalled by a klaxon and it was only later that the klaxon became attached to the telephone and a siren followed if a callout was confirmed.

At that time, the klaxon would send me running to the gate at East Drive to see the beige Cliff Rescue Land Rover depart, always with two students perched precariously on stands and hanging on to the back of the vehicle (imagine that being allowed today!) Again, if memory serves, amber roof lights were then in operation for non-mainstream emergency services and blue lights came later. (On the subject of blue lights, my father, by then Hon. Sec [and therefore in charge of overseeing ILB launches] was later offered one for our car. He declined, having an eye to the effect on resale value of four redundant screw-holes in the roof. My brother and I were bitterly disappointed!)

Late Spring was always the time when, with the weather improving and the safety lessons of the previous year forgotten, a certain apprehension could sometimes be felt, particularly at the weekend if the weather was fine. As children, the perils of both the incoming tide and the instability of the cliffs were drummed into us, as is evidenced by early written work. Inevitably some of the more unfortunate details of accidents would slip through the parental firewall and the consequences of falling from those cliffs did not require any explanation, even to a child.

Nevertheless, at the age of ten, it is the disruption to my routine, from bedtime stories to birthday parties, that seems to have been uppermost in my mind. My primary school 'news' book from 1971 contains two relevant entries (spelling corrected!):

'17th May – Last night at a quarter to eight our 9th callout of the year. Dad was halfway through a chapter of *Peter Duck* [a sailing thriller for children by Arthur Ransome].

'24th May – Yesterday was my birthday. I was 10 and [there follows a list of party guests] after tea we were going down to the beach and I heard the callout telephone. There had apparently been two at identical times, so it was difficult.'

The adrenalin rush triggered by the sound of the klaxon never faded: Ian Paley (1977–79), remembers going on at least a dozen callouts.

> The klaxon would blare in the castle courtyard and we would all drop what we were doing and dash down to the seafront, into the changing rooms, put on our wetsuits, jackets and life vests and start getting the boat ready. If we had enough people, we would walk the boat down the slipway for launch. Otherwise, we would attach the boat to the winch and guide it down to the water. The Bristol Channel has a huge variation in water height between high and low tide, so each launch was different, each with its own challenges.

And competence was always closely monitored, as Ian Paley recalls:

> I remember our first callout on 14 August 1978. JOD (John David) chose the crew and there were five of us onboard. Before returning to the college [for the August period], I had completed a 14-day communications training course with the Royal Navy Reserves in Plymouth … so if I couldn't drive,

I was going to be on the radio, wasn't I? We went to Southerndown and back but were not needed in the end. Sadly, there was one fatality. Being the first callout, adrenalin had very much kicked in and although I thought my radio protocol was OK, I was singled out for a mention by JOD as I was clearly too excited and not really intelligible. Strangely, I only ever got one other opportunity to sit in the seat behind the coxswain!

John Lipscomb, Jonathan's teacher father, remembers that the routine did not necessarily produce ideal results in terms of a calm and collected group of potential crew members.

In the early years, Peter Jolley or David Sutcliffe would have been nearby during the working day if no one else had managed to get there more quickly. If the call was genuine (i.e. not a wrong number!) the person receiving the call would push the button on the wall above to start the klaxon sounding and then everyone would start running! In those early days, most teaching was in progress within the Castle area.

The combination of the urgency of the callout signals and the heart-stopping race down the dozen or so flights of stone steps that linked the castle's elaborate Tudor terraces to one another meant that adrenalin could easily overwhelm rational decision-making on the seafront.

On one occasion, teacher Tim Agerbak remembers, even the staff got carried away:

John Grant-Wood [and I] each drove a Land Rover full of students. [But we] went off in opposite directions. I'm not sure who got it wrong, but we roared off, one going up, the other down Bristol Channel. Then we both twigged – someone in the van must have said 'you got it wrong' – we both thought we were on the wrong course, and both turned around – all to support some sort of Beach or IRB rescue. We were driving at full speed blaring our horns, and on the same road. We met, pulled off into a field, got out and both doubled up in laughter. In fact, we weren't needed anyway.

Another teacher, Andrew Maclehose, recalls two different alarms.

I have an idea that the klaxon was high up on the outer wall of the Bradenstoke or Lady Anne Tower but I have no idea who would set it off, or how. The fire alarm was different – a rather lugubrious air raid warning sound. The sound and the excitement would be familiar even now.

But trying to persuade his students to learn enough history and economics to get into university, Maclehose – who by then was Director of Studies – sometimes found it hard to keep the balance between responsibility for the rescue services and the need to do the academic work. He was once reprimanded by Desmond Hoare for being late to the early morning swim because he had been marking students' work, an occupation the admiral thought significantly less important than the discipline of the early swim (a daily requirement for all male students). Maclehose's reaction to the klaxon reflects the dilemma:

> I will add a slightly different perspective – that of desperately insisting that those taking actual A-level or IB exams should not leave them (though mock or internal exams were a different case).

However traumatic or frightening what came next, for many the sound of the klaxon was the biggest thrill of the term. Simon Daman Willems noted:

> Callouts are adrenalin rich, the sirens, people running, you have little time to reflect, you just do it. Like soldiers, we were drilled repeatedly to carry out tasks until we could do them in the dark and when very cold. And when adrenalin was coursing through your blood, caution (which equals safety) fell away as well. In my later career in engineering, I would remind people this was why we would practice lifeboat drills offshore, practice emergency escape, practice the correct way to attack a fire. When an emergency happens and sirens are sounding everywhere, people shouting, it is vital that reflex kicks in and while it may not save you, it certainly means you won't be injured or worse because you are trying to figure out how your life jacket works.

Once the college became an official inshore RNLI station in 1964, it was charged with keeping detailed records of every callout, and it became necessary to have a launching officer who would also be Honorary Secretary, the de facto head of the station. This role was initially filled by Admiral Hoare, followed by John Lipscomb, then David Sutcliffe and others before the role evolved into that of the Lifeboat Operations Manager. Over the years, other 'launching officers' were enrolled to deputise when necessary to meet the onerous obligation of 24/7 cover, every day of the year.

When the callout siren sounded, the Honorary Secretary, or one of his launching officers, would be in charge at the seafront when boats were launched and when they got back later. This senior person would often listen in to any radio communication with the boats, and sometimes quite informally debrief the crews after callouts.

Accidents, and sometimes fatalities as a result of people falling or even jumping off cliffs, were a common reason for callouts for the AC rescue services. Small craft were also vulnerable in the perilous waters between Barry and Porthcawl, where in a strong wind, the tide-driven surf could come rolling in at a speed of up to 18 knots (more than 30 km/hr). Although assisting boats and mariners would be a key area for the lifeboats, at the College 'people trapped by the tide' was to become possibly the most common cause of callouts for the Rescue Boats in the ensuing decades.

But for the students who had raced to the seafront, what mattered was whether their service was needed, and if it was, whether they would be selected to go. There was always great excitement, and often disappointment, when the Honorary Secretary or his deputy would announce who would captain the boat or boats that were to go out to sea, and it was decided who would be selected to be the other crew members.

It was widely recognised that the adrenalin rush of a callout undermined sensible decision-making. Phil Green, a senior member of the Beach Rescue squad in 1977–78, issued this stern note to his team:

> If there is a callout, move quickly but QUIETLY AND EFFICIENTLY. The ILBs are our first line of rescue where speed to the scene is required. Our major contribution is as an efficient, organised back-up rescue and search force. Speed to the scene is important, but quiet discipline and preparedness are absolutely essential.

> A callout party will be designated from those present and ready at the seafront. Typically it will consist of six canoeists, a First Aider and four shore party. Lack of footwear, torn skinsuit etc. endangers a prolonged operation Only those properly attired will go. In the event of a number of prepared people, defer to the most able.

There were almost invariably more willing crew than there were spaces on the boats. The process of selection was Darwinian in its ruthless lack of respect for the feelings of those vying to be chosen.

It was especially harsh in Beach Rescue, where callouts were almost vanishingly unusual.

According to Paul Belcher, the instructor,

> The decision of who went on the callout was the responsibility of the

Staff Coach who would be driving the van. They would look at who had assembled and make a decision based on who was reliable and could handle a kayak in the prevailing conditions.

Unsurprisingly, some of those who were overlooked felt it was a matter of favouritism and sometimes straightforward discrimination. The problem was made worse by the existence of a competition squad of the best swimmers and kayakers.

In 1977 Phil Green was sufficiently worried about it to address the issue head-on in a newsletter.

> Any split-ups of this presently close-knit group will occur when the competitive element comes in. Who will fight to get on the elite team, who will be allowed to go on callouts etc. ... however it must be seen and clearly understood that the aim of this Service is NOT to train an elitist, highly skilled callout committee but that a selection is inevitable and if one is not chosen there is no room for negative criticism and dissatisfaction but instead a devotion and enthusiasm from each and every member towards his/her Rescue Service and a striving for generally high standards for everyone.

Occasionally staff knew there was a traumatic experience ahead and picked students they thought most able to cope, as Phil Green's own experiences showed. But sometimes in the Rescue Boats, the boat captain may have picked their friends. Once the college was fully coeducational, there were further tensions. Whichever service was needed – and often it began as all three – staff had a considerable say in who went out. As the college's Coastguard obligations evolved, a core group of members were designated official Coastguard Auxiliaries with their own uniform while the others, who trained as hard, were members of the Cliff and Mountaineering Service. There was a callout roster for the qualified, but there was no certainty that those on it would be the ones who went out in an emergency.

Lis Hostvedt, the first woman to be qualified by the College as coxswain in 1968, resided, with eight others, in the Vicarage, just outside the college grounds. So she was usually too late to get to the seafront in time to go out.

> I went out once on a callout after two boys who'd disappeared. I think the tide had come in and cut them off. It was late afternoon. It wasn't very nice because every time you saw seaweed you thought it might have been a head. And in fact the Coastguard found both boys the following morning on the beach, both drowned.

43. Elisabeth Hostvedt at the helm.

*44. Penny Sutton, officially the first woman
to go out on an RNLI callout.*

I remember going down to the seafront fast. The first aider always took
'their' boat, and it just happened that our first aider had been working
down on the seafront. So I got to go out.

But for some reason this episode was not officially recorded by the RNLI. Two
years later, Lis' sister Kristin and Penny Sutton also qualified as coxswains.

It is the latter, Penny Sutton, who is recorded in the annals of the RNLI as the first
woman crew member to go out on a rescue. In her memory, although it was a
fight for everyone to be considered for callout duty, it was much more of a fight
for the girls, however well qualified.

I do not remember being assigned a place on the callout duty roster.
However, when the siren went, I would go down to the beach in the hopes
of being included on a boat being put to sea but mostly I was part of the
launching and recovery crew. This was actually quite exciting in itself as
quite often the launches were done in inclement weather with big waves
pounding up the slipway. I was disappointed not to be included as part of a
boat crew, but that was just par for the course.

I think I remember my only callout as being in good weather to investigate
a small Swedish sailing boat flying the British courtesy flag upside down – a

recognised sign of distress. It turned out that the crew were not in trouble and had not intended flying the flag upside down.

When the siren went there was always a general air of excitement, wondering what the problem was. We knew we were well trained and had the confidence that we could cope with whatever we had to do. If the weather was too bad to launch on our slipway, we would tow the boat behind the school van round to the next beach. I remember one such occasion when this was done. The surf was so high that we had a lot of trouble launching the boat and were knocked off our feet more than once.

I think I held my own in IRB and earned the grudging respect of staff and (male) students for sticking it out.

But there was a strong sense that only the best went on a callout: it was the premium way of giving service. Sally Stradling noted:

Normally the crews comprised the toughest, fittest students whilst the others made up the launch and landing parties handling the boats to and from the sea on trolleys and keeping radio contact. Responsibility for self and others was assumed, to take care of others as well as being aware of what you could give in the circumstances.

In the light of the pumped-up teenagers arriving breathless at the seafront, and the likely impact on their ability to make calm judgements about risky choices, Simon Daman Willems looks back with admiration at the trust placed in the students by the staff.

Regarding DBS [David Sutcliffe], I can only recall his calm and professional demeanour. A callout brings out adrenaline and machismo (that wailing siren on the castle), which had no place on a safe callout. You could feel his trust in us, he did what he could to get us on our way without micromanaging. He consulted with us as equals. Yes, in spite of the awe he inspired, and the ticking off you might get later, at those moments we were equals. Had he shown doubts in our skills or sought to control our actions from shore we would not have been effective, and he knew it. It was a skill I tried in later years always to apply myself, not always with success. Empower your team, let them get on with their work, help them learn afterwards from any mistakes. I owe much to this remarkable man.

The sound of the klaxon occasionally meant comedy rather than drama, as Rhodri Bradley-Jones discovered early on in AC history.

One sunny, blue-skied Sunday afternoon in the summer of 1964, the callout alarms sounded. We'd taken a message from the police that there was a very large group (a family of four generations) trapped under the cliffs at one of the Southerndown coves. The police were very concerned because there were babies and children as well as adults and it was clear that they were unaware that it was a very high spring tide and they were all likely to drown.

As Canoe Service captain, I gathered my team of canoeists together and we shot off through the narrow lanes to Southerndown in our long-wheel-based Land Rover, with the emergency light flashing. As we launched into a good swell at Southerndown, we noticed that there was an enormous crowd of onlookers on top of the cliffs who had gathered to watch the tragedy unfold. We paddled round to the next bay where the family was entirely cut off and about to drown. I was the first to arrive but only just, as the Cliff Rescue boys were abseiling down the cliff above them and the first rescue boat was just hoving into view around the headland.

'Don't worry!' I said to the cut-off and bedraggled group. 'We've come to rescue you.'

To my surprise, the response was a very ungrateful, 'Fuck off!'

Remaining calm, I said, 'You clearly don't understand that there is an exceptionally high tide and if you remain here, I'm afraid you will drown. But don't worry, we will get you safely back to dry land.

'Fuck off! We're on dry land and we don't need rescuing.'

'Oh yes you do,' I said. 'The exceptionally high tide is about to engulf you.'

'No, it isn't, the tide turned 10 minutes ago. We do this every Sunday!'

Sure enough, they were right. The tide had turned. Tails between our legs, we retreated. The Cliff Rescue boys hauled themselves back up the cliffs. The Rescue Boats returned to sea.

On our way back to the main beach, I was knocked over by a decent-sized wave and as I hung beneath the canoe, I realised that I hadn't fastened my spray sheet carefully enough and the canoe was filling with water making a roll impossible. Thankfully, one of the rescue boats came to my aid and the sight of me and my canoe being rescued gave rise to a huge cheer from the crowds on the clifftop.

There was a rescue after all! The crowd had its entertainment!

CHAPTER FOUR

The First Rescues

August 1963 was the first ever 'August period', the weeks when only second years were in the college. AC had taken responsibility for lifeguard duties on the popular local beaches at Ogmore and Southerndown. The Director of Activities, Charles 'Chick' Thomson, told a Western Mail reporter that the school was 'contracted' to look after 10 miles of coast and that they had had their first callout, a false alarm, in June (*Western Mail*, 2 August 1963).

Towards the end of that first August period, two rescue boats were called out to the sea off Ogmore Beach in a search for a missing local man. Neither they nor the Llantwit Major coastguard found anything (*South Wales Echo*, 21 September 1963). The missing man's wife and children returned home distraught. But happily he had not after all been drowned or caught in a rip current. Instead, the man – a local personality known as Uncle Bill who ran the Palladium cinema in Aberdare – turned up three weeks later in Blackpool, safe and sound and having suffered memory loss.

In October the RNLI paid its first visit to the college (Sutcliffe, *RIB*). To what was said to be the 'respectful astonishment' of Desmond Hoare and his boatbuilding team, they requested advice. The RNLI then sent a series of inflatables for the students to test and adapt to the rugged conditions on the Bristol Channel. That winter, with the tests continuing, St Donat's was informed it was to be one of just nine experimental inshore rescue stations around the United Kingdom.

Less than six months later, on 15 March 1964, two boats, the RNLI boat Freya and the college-adapted inflatable Aphrodite, launched in earnest – although not from the foreshore at St Donat's, but the beach at Southerndown because the surf conditions at St Donat's were unsuitable – and recorded the first lives saved by the new rescue service. Andreas Schwerdtfeger tells the story:

> I think my crew and I were the first in the history of the College to save lives.
> It happened in March 1964, when we were called out on a stormy day after
> a coastguard helicopter had sighted a sailing dinghy in distress. We always
> had two boats loaded on trailers and so we hooked them onto the Land
> Rovers and drove to Southerndown Beach. There had always been a huge
> competition about who would be first and which boat would be quicker and
> we were the lucky ones, arriving first and getting the boat off the trailer and
> into and through the quite large waves [7 foot, according to a newspaper

report] on the beach. My crew consisted of two co-students (Hans-Christoph Schwab and Helge Petersen) and we were accompanied by the Headmaster, Admiral Desmond Hoare.

I must say, looking back, that the Admiral never once interfered in the handling of the boat and the rescue operation which with hindsight I find absolutely miraculous and which shows how serious the rules of the College to train students towards responsibility and leadership were taken.

The sailing dinghy with two men on board had capsized; both men – two brothers – were frozen and unable to upright the boat. They just wanted to get aboard our boat and, I think, abandon their dinghy but that, of course, was against our pride. We took them aboard, then secured the sailing dinghy to our boat with a line and after that two of us got into the water to right the boat, take down the mast and take it in tow. All of this took us quite a while in the rough sea and I am quite sure the rescued sailors were not too happy. The Admiral watched stoically.

In the end we managed and set off for 'home', the Southerndown Beach, where, to my shame, I must admit that I capsized our own boat when I miscalculated the speed we could make between the breaking waves. We had always got to our AC landing slip safely by accelerating full blast before a breaking wave – but with a sailing dinghy in tow this technique didn't work and we were too slow. So the wave hit us from behind, washed over the boat, capsized it, and put us unceremoniously on the beach. But we were all soaked and cold anyway and this mishap did not dampen our enthusiasm and joy of achievement even if a heroic deed ended rather humbly – a good lesson perhaps for us youngsters. The Admiral, anyway, was not amused with this end.

Hans-Christoph Schwab was also on the crew:

It was not only reported in the local press, but also in the German press, as in addition to the Admiral we were three Germans in the boat to aid the forlorn brothers. [In the long aftermath of the Second World War, the nationality of the crew would have been cheered as further proof of a remade Europe.] Getting back ashore we felt good about the rescue service having been able to help in a real live situation versus just guarding our own sailing outings.

Despite his lack of amusement, for Hoare this must have been an important development in the real-time experiment in training and rescue. Certainly he drew some significant conclusions, according to David Sutcliffe's account (*RIB*). This account misses out some of the detail of the official report (for example, that the RNLI boat was held up by a mechanical failure with the trailer and put to sea later). Compared with Andreas Schwerdtfeger's account, it verges on the poetic:

> The afternoon's sailing activities were over and most people were in the
> shower when the call came ... Because of the surf and tidal conditions,
> the boats were moved round to Southerndown Beach by road. Aphrodite
> launched first into 8-foot surf at 17.10 with the RNLI Zodiac inflatable
> following soon after. The Zodiac almost immediately fractured its floorboards
> and spray deck support [this was one of the most serious design flaws that
> had to be corrected] and was at reduced speed. A helicopter heard overhead
> had gone home because of poor visibility. The dinghy had capsized several
> times. Its occupants were lying exhausted in the bilges and did not see their
> rescuers until they had come alongside. Their chances of survival without
> rescue were nil. During the landing through surf, one of the casualties was
> separated from the boat but was quickly recovered ... This rescue clearly
> demonstrated the fragility of the standard RNLI inflatable in surf at that time,
> the value of the skin suit in entering the water to assist, and the importance
> of familiarity in handling sailing dinghies. In his official report Desmond
> Hoare also stressed his view that crews of two were insufficient for inshore
> rescue boats – three was the safe minimum.

For another student, Jim Buckheit, a first year who started in 1963 and who
was part of the beach party helping with launch and landing, it had all gone
according to plan:

> A disabled sailboat was reported drifting with the outgoing tide west of
> Nash Point. We towed two rescue boats behind vans and launched them
> near Monknash Beach. I served on the beach crew. The senior boys on the
> rescue boats, along with Adm. Hoare, made quick work of catching up to
> the sailboat and towing it, along with its crew, back to the beach where an
> ambulance was waiting.

The rescue was reported in all the local papers, giving the college some admiring
publicity – particularly useful as it came only days after its inauguration as one
of the new style of inshore rescue stations. 'The surf was so rough,' Admiral
Hoare told the reporter from the *Western Mail*, 'that it capsized us all as we
were beaching. We are used to these conditions,' he added, 'and everything was
under control.'

* * * * *

In June 1964, as the first generation of students prepared to hand over to the second, the callout siren went again. John Smalley, one of AC's first students, heard the klaxon:

> All 52 (I think) students were members of whatever rescue service they had elected to join after the first few weeks of trials and 'activity sampling'. Those of us in the Cliff Rescue team were mainly united in our dislike of the prospect of unexpected introduction to the chill Bristol Channel waters in the depths of a Welsh winter (or spring, for that matter). We had all selected a service and subsequently trained for the possibility of a callout, but never actually contemplated the possibility of having to put newly acquired skills into operation. Now, it seemed, those skills were out to be put to the test in a real-life situation for the very first time.
>
> Mr Thomson ('Chick' Thomson to all and sundry), Director of Activities, was an ex- Royal Navy senior member of staff and was the person, I think, who gave the first ever callout briefing. I remember little of the detail, but the salient facts were that a small party of holidaymakers were reported to have been trapped in a bay on the southern end of Southerndown Beach by an incoming tide. Cliffs on the point to the west of them prevented safe passage to the broader expanses of beach, and the cliffs behind them were steep and unstable, and could not be scaled. The rescue services were tasked to effect a retrieval of this small party of people to prevent the possibility of a tragedy should they panic and be swept out to sea (or whatever else may befall them).
>
> As soon as the four rescue teams were dispatched, it became a competition as to who could arrive at the scene first. (The rescue services were nothing if not competitive in this regard.) Clearly, the Canoe Rescue crew would be pressed to get their canoes to the scene and launched in time to be of any practical benefit, and the Surf Rescue team were hardly likely to be involved since there was no prospect of them being able to 'deploy' to do their thing in the circumstances which had been described to us. And so it was more or less a two-horse race between the Rescue Boats, on the one hand, and our merry band in the Cliff Rescue squad on the other. Since we had a Land Rover ready with the appropriate gear stowed and a second to ferry the labour force, we were odds on to beat the Rescue Boats. They would have to be launched off St Donat's slipway and driven against the prevailing wind (and probably the tide and Nash Point currents) to Southerndown.
>
> As we had hoped and expected, when we arrived on the cliffs at the southern end of Southerndown Beach and began to off-load equipment and set up for an abseil descent to the beach, there was still no sign of the Rescue Boats on the sea below. Just as we were completing the preparations

for the descent of two crew members, with harnesses and a stretcher for the purposes of winching up unsuspecting holidaymakers from down below, two developments transpired. The first was a sighting of the first of two rescue boats off the point to our east. The second was the arrival of a TV Wales news crew complete with reporters and a mobile outside broadcast camera crew. I have a clear recollection of David Jolly, chemistry teacher and one of the mainstays of the staff who ran the Cliff Rescue unit, [Editor's note: probably Peter Jolley, head of CR. David Jolly was Director of Studies.] saying loudly to one and all, 'You'll have to do a good job today, lads. It looks like you're going to be recorded in action for posterity by the TV newsmen who have just shown up!' … or words to that effect.

And then the most unexpected, and anticlimactic turn of all. A police car drew up and an officer emerged to report to all of us on the clifftop that the 'situation commander' had just received news that the tide was on the turn, the holidaymakers merely had to wait for an hour or two to be able to make their own way, unassisted, back to their car and that any attempt to effect a rescue would be more dangerous that simply leaving events to evolve. There was no immediate or foreseen threat to the people down below, and they were being advised (I am not quite sure how) to be patient and wait for the now receding tide to allow them safe return to the place from which they had come.

Mutterings of mixed frustration and relief from all and sundry were interrupted by an approach from the TV news crew. They were keen to take some footage back to their news editor and were all set up for filming. We were set up and ready to make an abseil descent from the clifftop. Would we mind turning this occasion into a training exercise which could be filmed for possible airing on the evening local news broadcast that night? we were asked. Well, no, we wouldn't, we replied. And that is what happened. That is the reason why Ieuan Edwards and I were to be seen on the local TV news that evening abseiling from a clifftop in Southerndown to 'rescue' (allegedly) 'trapped' holidaymakers (who in fact were not trapped at all). That 'almost-rescue' was the one and only time in my two years at AC that I was involved in a callout. At least we returned to the castle that afternoon feeling that it had not been completely for nothing that our lessons had been interrupted. It had all been rather exciting: the Cliff Rescue team HAD been the first to arrive at the scene of potential rescue … and we were all looking forward to the chance of seeing ourselves 'on the telly' before dinner that evening (which I think we did).

CHAPTER FIVE

Wins

Building and maintaining equipment, hours and hours of training at sea, on the beach, in the pool and on the cliffs, all of these went into developing mutual confidence and effective teamwork. But nothing really counted until it had been tested for real. After those first years, callouts continued to be infrequent, except during the summer period, and places on the rescue crews hard-won. They could also be dangerous. Yet the satisfaction of accomplishing a successful rescue overwhelmed the unpredictability and uncertainty of an emergency that put the rescuers themselves in jeopardy.

Many rescues were challenging, demanding quick thinking and sometimes innovation from the teenagers at the scene. The students were effectively on their own, even if a teacher had driven them to the callout. There was no one apart from each other to look to for advice, no one to offer reassurance that they'd taken the right decision. Some of these rescues have lingered in the memories for decades, like this rescue where climbers had to be plucked, literally, from the cliff face on the coast between Southerndown and Ogmore. It was a Sunday afternoon, 22 April 1979, when for the second time that day the klaxon sounded.

Erik Borg was in the Cliff Rescue team:

> On an April day in my second year at Atlantic College, the sirens rang out at
> the College. We ran to our rescue units to respond to the callout. As I was
> in Cliff Rescue, I ran to the rescue barracks halfway down to the slipway
> and pool area. We got our gear ready and put on our anoraks, helmets and
> harnesses and got into the Land Rover that was going to take us to the
> scene of the accident. In Cliff Rescue, at that time, we had designated roles
> as rescuers depending on who arrived first. These roles had specific numbers
> from one to three. Number one was in charge at the top of the cliff, number
> two and three abseiled down the cliff. Rescuer number two was in charge of
> the rescue at the cliff face and was assisted by number three. On that day, I
> was in the second position and in charge of the rescue down the cliff.

A Coastguard official was already at the scene, radioing frantically for progress reports – as another member of the group, Tomas Kåberger, remembers:

> The Coastguard officer who was at the place before us radioing to us,
> 'To Atlantic Mobile: Where are you? Where are you?!!' 'This is Atlantic
> Mobile 2 … We are passing through St Brides!' [A village about a mile

before Southerndown.] Answer: 'Step on it! For God's sake, step on it!!' I remember that his apparent desperation made me, sitting in the middle of the car on the bumpy ride trying to get my gear on and knowing I would have the responsibility in charge on top of the cliff, absolutely calm and focused.

Meanwhile, the inshore rescue boats were on their way too. Colin Harrison was on the crew:

Having had a callout on the afternoon of Sunday 22 April, it was a surprise when the klaxon sounded again just before the evening meal.

The College's rescue services were tasked to [aid] an injured climber on the cliffs between Southerndown and Ogmore. The College's lifeboat, B508, was launched with a crew of four. In addition to myself, the crew was Jeremy Jose (captain X9), John Gocek (captain X11) and Ian Paley (captain X24).

One advantage of having a boat in the water at the scene of a cliff rescue is that the crew can see more than those at the top of the cliffs peering over the edge.

Arriving on scene we saw two climbers on the lower part of the cliffs, where there was an overhang. The injured climber was perched on a very narrow ledge and appeared unable to manoeuvre himself because of a damaged ankle. It was apparent that the climbers had to be rescued by being taken back up the cliffs – difficult for the injured one because of the overhang – or lowered into the lifeboat if we could get the boat in there.

45. B-508, the College's first official ILB.

The Cliff Rescuers had been warned of the extreme difficulty of the rescue, as Erik Borg describes:

> On our way to the accident, we were radioed that there were two climbers stuck on the cliff face, and that they were unable to climb up. They could neither descend down the cliff, as the tide was coming in and the water was deep below them. As I approached the climbers, I realized that they were stuck under an overhang and that I would not be able to reach them to put on the extra harnesses I had brought down with me. However, the climbers had their own harnesses on. I radioed up to Tomas Kåberger who was in charge on the top of the cliff and asked if I could snap the ropes into the climbers' harnesses. After a short discussion and some clarification of the situation, we decided to use the climbers' own harnesses to haul them up.

As well as managing the situation he faced while hanging 100 feet below the lip of a cliff, Erik had to maintain contact with the ILB which had just arrived:

> Halfway through the rescue, the ILB joined the scene of the accident. I was in radio contact with Jeremy Jose on the boat, and he suggested lowering the climbers into their boat. I conveyed my concern that the waters were choppy and the boat was moving both vertically and horizontally. Cliff Rescue was determined to complete the rescue mission we had started and haul the climbers up the cliff to safety.

Colin Harrison, from the boat, naturally recalls that the ILB was in charge, and had come up with an innovative solution to the problem that Erik had identified:

> With the sea rolling in and breaking against the foot of the cliffs we could not attempt a beach landing. The only alternative was to deploy the anchor and then veer in, i.e. using the anchor as a fixed point and feeding out the anchor warp to control our progress towards the shore. We had practised veering the ILBs at College. This entailed passing the anchor warp [rope] through the bow fairlead and around the bow cleat and feeding out the warp as the boat engines were operated in reverse. The problem we had in this instance was that the engines would be dashed against the cliff face or the propellers damaged on any underwater rocks that we could not see.

> We decided that by veering in bow first the engines would be protected and the rubber tube would bounce us off the cliff. This was not a manoeuvre we had ever practised (and I have never used again). To further protect against potential damage, the engines were stopped and raised. We used the swell rolling in towards the cliff to ease ourselves underneath the climbers by feeding out the anchor warp and using the boat's paddles to give us a little control over direction – and to fend us off the cliff.

46. *Cliff Rescue training over water.*

While we were establishing that the lifeboat could be positioned under the overhang, Cliff Rescue had lowered their own climber down the cliff.

But the physical challenges were not the only ones requiring innovative solutions. Tomas Kåberger:

> Another was the frustration, [at] how the two climbers, though exhausted and confused, repeatedly interfered with how they were going to be rescued. At one stage I communicated with Erik in Scandinavian languages so the climbers could not understand. We got a formal complaint from Barry Coastguard afterwards because we did not follow 'radio procedure' – but also a clear indication of understanding.

Meanwhile a separate negotiation was going on between the climbers and the ILB below. The second climber on the cliff face, Julian Jones, remembers taking the decision to lower the injured climber into the boat below despite the rough sea:

> I can't give the sequence of events, but when I looked down the ILB was virtually underneath me and Eric was up to my right. He was communicating with people at the top of the cliff, I don't know whether he was doing that by radio or verbally, but I couldn't see the people at the top, so had indirect communication via Eric.
>
> We had to decide whether to take them up over the overhang or to lower them into the ILB. I decided to lower at least one of them into the boat because of its proximity. It just seemed so much easier than raising him to the top.

From the water Colin Harrison and the crew of the ILB watched the manoeuvre while trying to ensure the boat was in the right place at the right time:

> It was an unusual sight, to say the least, to have Julian Jones dangling in mid-air above us; he somehow managed to get control of the injured climber's ropes so that the casualty could be lowered into the boat. The technical difficulty was timing the lowering of the casualty to coincide with when the boat was under him – we were swept in on a wave but sucked back out again as it rebounded off the cliff face.
>
> Julian lowered the casualty part of the way, we got the boat under him and shouted for him to be released the rest of the way. At that moment a wave swept under us and the deck rose to meet the casualty as he was lowered on to it, landing with a bit of a thud but safely aboard.
>
> At that point Ian Paley (I think), who had been controlling the anchor warp, started to haul us out. I prepared to start our engines but realised that as we moved away from the cliff Julian, still dangling in mid-air, was being

pulled with us. What we hadn't realised was Julian's climbing ropes and the casualty's climbing ropes had become tangled underwater. Swiftly the casualty's ropes were unclipped and dumped overboard.

Julian's were not the only ropes that were tangled. Erik Borg was also struggling with the problem higher up the cliff.

On the way up, I realised that the rope was tangled behind a rock. This would not hinder the rescue but would mean that one of the climbers would experience a small drop as the rope got untangled. I explained to the climber that he would drop a couple of feet on the way up. He seemed to understand, but as the rope untangled, he let out a loud scream. I told him that now he would be pulled up more evenly, and he seemed comforted by my reassurances.

The injured climber in the ILB was carried round to Southerndown:

To avoid moving the casualty too much, the crew in the bow of the boat supported him there against the tube while we drove as smoothly as possible back to Southerndown. There was a little surf but enough clear sand to pick the back of a wave and run the boat straight in and up the beach.

The casualty was handed over to Beach Rescue and Coastguards who were at Southerndown. Beach Rescue helped us haul the boat back in the water and we returned to station. The boat was not damaged and the crew were safe – the only injury being to my wristwatch which had cracked against the cliff face and the workings of which didn't take kindly to the ingress of seawater!

At the top of the cliff, Tomas Kåberger, Julian Jones and Erik Borg were proud of the rescue they had accomplished:

The wet and cold climbers were eventually pulled to safety and we realised that we had completed one of our most important rescue missions. Had we come much later, the climbers would have been submerged by the incoming tide. Cliff Rescue ruled the day that April afternoon in 1979.

Tomas Kåberger also claims it as a cliff rescue: 'I remember the enthusiasm from our ILB colleagues on the prospects of lowering one to an ILB, and that we did so even if it may not have been necessary. Good people on the ILB. It was simply a nice show.' He adds, 'Though I think they had some trouble.'

Looking back, Tomas accepts that there was an element of competition between the two services. The college's Cliff Rescue unit had just seen off a challenge from other local Coastguard units and they were pleased to demonstrate their skills.

> By April we were very well trained. Our unit had been challenged by other units along the coast as we were too young, and worst of all, we had girls on the team. In a joint test checked by people from the national Coastguard we had outperformed the other units in South Wales. We knew the drills well, so well that we could improvise as we did by lowering one and taking the other up. This was not necessary, but I can admit now the decision was partly based on an ambition to show off what the college rescue services could do.

Anne Brearley, head of Cliff Rescue, noted in her annual report:

> One especially satisfying and effective rescue was the recovery of two climbers on the 130′ Southerndown/Ogmore cliffs (22 April). One, having fallen, was hanging injured in his safety rope and was lowered by members of the Cliff Rescue unit into the College inshore lifeboat which was anchored close under the cliffs; the second was hauled to the clifftop. The whole operation, carried out in driving rain and under a large cliff overhang, and out of sight of police and others on the clifftop, was entirely in the hands of student members of the rescue teams, who reported at intervals by radio to HM Coastguard.

```
I would like to congratulate everyone concerned on the really
excellent call out performance yesterday afternoon.  It was,
I think, one of the most smoothly and efficiently conducted
rescues the College has ever undertaken.

                        David Sutcliffe

                        _____

                        D.B. Sutcliffe
                        Headmaster

                        23rd April 1979

Cliff Rescue NB
ILB NB
```

47. Ultimate accolade.

* * * * *

Jonathan Lipscomb, who, with a father teaching at the college, had grown up on the Atlantic College campus, finally became a student between 1977 and 1979, and he recalls the intensity of the experience of a successful callout.

> 6 May 1979: This was a Sunday and 'Sunday sea-going' was a voluntary afternoon activity in addition to timetabled service sessions. Having ILBs at sea on these occasions provided escort services for sailing activities. I generally participated and on this occasion was actually in the changing room along with Jeremy Jose and Shushi Kominami, half-dressed when at 13.20 the siren sounded. I well recall Jeremy's gleeful cry, 'OK boys, we're on this one!' since there was no possibility of anyone else reaching the adjacent [RNLI] B-Boat station before us. I remember anyway, taking no chances and securing a coveted RNLI Life Jacket (your ticket to ride) before asking someone to go back to the changing room to recover my footwear.
>
> We understood that a young boy had been cut off by the rising tide between the College and Llantwit Major. As Coxswain, Colin Harrison completed the crew and we launched as soon as a beach party had been

48. A launch using the fixed line to pull the boat clear of the rocks.

49. The beach and caves at Tresilian.

assembled. Given the state of the tide, almost full and with a slight swell, the boat would have been clipped to the line, anchored 100 metres or so out to sea and cast off just as soon as she had floated clear of the trolley by which she was manoeuvred on land.

The continuous ribbons of limestone and shale can make for a dizzying background against which to pick out a casualty but we very quickly located a boy who we estimated to be about eight years old, but according to the official report was thirteen, stranded to the east of Tresilian [see maps, page 27].

After confirming our position and intention with the Coastguard, we beach-landed without difficulty and carried the boy from the cliff face onto which he had climbed, to the boat. He was seated between Colin Harrison and myself and we were instructed to return him to Llantwit Beach. Colin asked him, 'Do you want to go fast?' He nodded his approval but then as Colin recalls, seemed slightly taken aback at the acceleration we were capable of! We took a wide arc back to Llantwit where we beach-landed a second time on the sandy spit to deposit him safely with his mother and the Coastguard before returning to base.

We were experienced by then, capable of working as a team notwithstanding the random nature of crew selection (i.e. Colin Harrison and whoever arrived first).

Breaking the operation down, we had launched and quickly located the casualty despite a distracting backdrop. We had carried out a beach landing on fairly steep shingle which made it easier to protect the engines on approach but harder for the crew to rotate and then hold the boat steady without losing their footing and harder to regain the boat once floating. I struggled myself on this occasion as the official oilskins and life jacket were so much bulkier than our training issue, but it was a team effort and in seconds someone had hauled me in.

We had made a second beach landing, this time on a level base of sand and smooth rock; an entirely different proposition. Holding the boat was easy enough but the approach would have required paddles both for momentum and to probe the water's depth, having lifted the engines to protect the propellers. On leaving we would have paddled clear before lowering the outboards once again and returning to the College, some two miles away. All this and yet the official record shows the boat to have been on service for just 17 minutes.

It was textbook work and with a happy outcome but that was what we had trained for so intensely. At the time I thought little of it and was just happy to have taken part.

I remember being questioned later by someone as to whether I thought

50. Jonathan Lipscomb, Colin Harrison, Jochen Etzel, John Gocek.

we had saved the boy's life. I said, and I remain of the view, that he would probably have been OK if he had stayed put, but if he had attempted to move or a larger than average swell had reached him (it happens) then he might have been lost – but I wasn't keeping score. It just seemed like a nice feel-good 'shout' [callout] to end our tour of duty.

By the time of Jonathan Lipscomb's callout, the rescue services had been going for more than 15 years. Radio contact was taken for granted. But in August 1966, it was still a novelty requiring a series of relays between the castle and a mobile middleman. John de Blocq van Kuffeler was one of those students who always had something to work on at the seafront, and he was there on 20 August 1966 when the klaxon went.

> I was working on a repair on Freya in the early evening when the callout siren sounded. By the time the other crews arrived, I was already in my skinsuit. As Freya was out of service, I went in Mark David's boat and as Captain [of Rescue Boats], I was in charge of the whole operation. We were told there was a boat in trouble at Aberthaw [see maps, page 27].

> After a fast journey we found it quite quickly and it was in some very dangerous currents where the boat was being bashed to pieces in the surf on the rocks. Our boat went in and we managed to get a line aboard secured by the frightened occupants and towed them to the open sea, only to find their boat was sinking.

> With some effort we managed to beach the boat in a safe area and all of us came ashore and with a Herculean effort emptied the seawater out by putting it on its side. It had been holed several times and the engine was beyond repair. We then lifted the boat high up the rocky shore where it was above the tide and ensured the badly shaken crew were collected by relatives.

> On our way back we saw the sun set, my first AC sunset at sea. We arrived back after 9 pm. It was the first time we used radio contact with the shore and we kept in touch with the main receiver in the Mansell Tower and the Land Rover. It worked quite well.

Another early rescue took place when the college boats were on duty for a power boat race off Porthcawl. David Sutcliffe, not yet headmaster, recalled that students saw it as an opportunity to compare the boats they knew so well with the racing competition and were stripping them down to be competitive when Desmond Hoare intervened to remind them they were rescue craft.

And so it proved, later that day in 1968. Gerhard Robbers was on one of the college boats.

51. David Sutcliffe on the slipway.

Our rescue boats were supporting Porthcawl RNLI station in safeguarding a major power boat race off Porthcawl Beach. David Sutcliffe was acting as captain of our boat, I was steering. While patrolling we received a call that one of the power boats had capsized. When we approached that boat after a short while, the boatman was floating alone far away from his boat and drifting out West, dragged by the strong outgoing tide. We picked him up, led by David Sutcliffe, dropped him at Porthcawl beach, where he left us without saying a word. We went out again, secured the capsized boat and towed it into Porthcawl Harbour.

We went back to St Donat's at dawn on a strong, now incoming tide. Halfway, on the [Nash] sandbanks between Porthcawl and St Donat's, we encountered heavy ground swell, capsizing seemed easily possible, but we managed to get through safely.

I still see David Sutcliffe's calm and clear face and his considered instructions of that day.

****

Victims of disaster respond in different ways. The powerboat skipper stomping silently off was one example. Another response to failure, however, is simply to try again – like the hang-glider pilot in this extraordinary story from Tim Haney, a member of the Coastguard team in February 1981:

> I was in the dinner queue when somebody yelled 'callout!' With all the noise in the dining hall I didn't hear the klaxon. I wasn't on callout duty but ran down to the base (Camp Store is what we called it) and helped load radios, etc. into the Land Rover and then stayed on base radio. The message from Swansea Coastguard was that a hang-glider had crashed into the cliffs at Southerndown.

> According to Tellef [Thorleifsson], who went on the callout, what happened was that this guy had been taking off from the beach, running, and then got a bad current of air which brought him into the 250-foot-high cliffs about halfway down. We had been called by 3Llantwit mobile [the Land Rover of Llantwit Major Coastguard] when they received the call from Swansea Coastguard and then Swansea took over the communication with us once we had the Land Rover radio on. By the time our team got there, Llantwit Coastguard had been there for 10 minutes, but they didn't really know how to proceed and didn't even have the right ropes for the job.

> When the guy hit the cliff, he slid down to a point about 100 feet up from the bottom where the cliff angle changes from about 90 degrees to 110 degrees. The nose of the hang-glider had driven itself into the ground. He was just hanging in mid-air knowing that if he moved, the glider would fall. The AC team abseiled down, secured him, lowered him to the ground, and then using a complicated four rope system, lowered the glider down. Tellef jokingly asked the guy if he was going back up again. He replied quite seriously, 'Well, I just have to unbend the nose and it will be OK'. While they were rescuing the one guy, another hang-glider swooped past them.

But most people who need rescuing from life-threatening situations are less sanguine, like this 1974 case of a young boy stranded on a cliff and threatened by an incoming tide – but not responding to calls from rescuers.

Bruce Matheson recalls: 'It was not easy to find the boy in the darkness and also because he did not shout for help. It can be a surprise that people's reactions during these events are not what you would expect when trained to cope.'

Freddie Lloyd-Smith, a Canadian student with a reputation as a swimmer, wrote to her parents soon afterwards:

We had a real callout last Sunday for the first time in ages, Klaxon and all. I was on my way to lunch when it went off so dashed off to the seafront. I got changed into my skinsuit in record time and was fortunate to be chosen as a crew for X-11. The B-Boat (RNLI ILB) went out first and X-11 followed. The electric start didn't work so we started it manually. Took off after the B-boat along the coastline halfway to Llantwit Beach to look for a boy that had been cut off by the tide.

We could see nothing, but there is a large cave in the cliffs there, big enough that canoeists can sometimes get in there if there's not much surf. We got a report from the Coastguard, who of course was in on all this as well, that he was inside the cave but we couldn't see him from the outside, so they and we decided to put a swimmer in to look.

I got into an extra life jacket, two helmets and finally the swimming belt (I was the strongest swimmer), all over my rather bulky life jacket and set off boldly through the surf. I almost missed the entrance because of the masses of white water swilling around the entrance but a few bruises later, stood up and waded all the way in. I peered around and saw nothing, called and heard nothing, looked in every nook and cranny and then began to look for any traces at all. Saw nothing so signalled to be pulled back to the boat. Quite an experience being pulled the wrong way through large surf – one I won't forget for a long while.

I got to the boat and we pulled up anchor and got out of the surf when we heard that the boy was outside the cave, about 10 feet above the water on a ledge. We looked and looked and didn't see anything so Andy, who was manoeuvring X-11, went inside the surf line to get a closer look. Just as he saw him, our engine cut for some reason and just wouldn't start again. It's the kind of situation we always have nightmares about. We tried frantically to paddle out of the surf line but we were broadside to the waves so couldn't. We were swept to the shore and jumped out onto the rocks to hold the boat off them. We got it turned around bow into the waves then Joe and I jumped in and started to paddle while Andy kept us straight, then he jumped in and paddled as well. We made it safely out and eventually X-12 came and towed us out further so we could anchor and see if we could start it.

From this point, we viewed the Coastguard in their Land Rover rescue the poor kid. They dropped their rope ladder over and sent a guy down to put a belt on him and he climbed up with the rescue behind him. Our Cliff Rescue dropped a man down the cliff (not literally) to offer assistance, but it wasn't necessary. A Beach Rescuer that had been brought out in case it was needed was cramped up because of the cold water and was dumped in X-11 so I

52. X-11 with her distinctive tube markings making a textbook landing.

massaged him till I felt sick with exhaustion as we watched the procedure. We traipsed back to the college, X-11 in tow, landed and stayed talking and fixing X-11. I still don't know what happened to it because it has been fine ever since and was fine the day before the incident. Took a long time to unwind from all this excitement. Mr Sutcliffe complimented me on my swim.

Bruce Matheson commented, 'I was never convinced that we were doing line swims in the best way, as the life jackets made it hard to breathe and swim at the same time.'

More than 30 years later, the same technique was used in a rescue where Eleuthera du Breuil was the RNLI helm.

In July 2006, at the age of 19 I had been a helm for the RNLI for a year and a half. I had already done a few callouts both as crew and as helm. I was working as a summer instructor for the AC Extra Mural Centre along with Alex Evans, Ffion Llewelyn and Allan Steynor who had all been my first year. Alex was also a helm.

We were already out on the water exercising when we were tasked to [help] two men who had been walking along the beach and were cut off by the returning tide under Nash Point. On our arrival on scene, we assessed the situation and talked to both Swansea Coastguard MCA (Marine and Coastguard Agency which deals with all shipping traffic and search and rescue operations in UK waters) and Llantwit Major Coastguard (local cliff rescue). The location of the men was a particularly difficult one. The cliff at that point overhangs and therefore the Cliff Rescue team would have been descending into the water if they had attempted a rescue. We asked Swansea Coastguard whether the RAF helicopter was available but it was on another call so we were the only resource that could assist.

The conditions were rough with a lot of surf so the normal protocol would have been to anchor the boat and veer in (reversing on the anchor line so that its inherent elasticity can pull you nose first (very important) through the waves if a big one threatens the boat). However, in this location the beach is made of huge rock shelves with no place for the anchor to hold. With a rapidly rising tide, we decided that the only way of managing the situation was by one of us swimming in, with life jackets, tied to the tow line so that they could be pulled back through the surf. I decided that since Alex was also a helm, he should take over the command of the boat and that I would swim in.

I swam in towards the two men and as I hit the surf line, I felt like I was in a washing machine, being tumbled about uncontrollably. I had to work very hard on keeping the rope from wrapping itself around my legs so I could use them and being able to breathe. At one point I was thrown against a large rock with some force. I felt my shoulder pop. I believe it was dislocated but it popped back in, so I continued, I didn't really have much choice.

I got onto the shore and at that point I discovered that one of the two men couldn't swim. I put the survivor life jackets on both of them and told the chap that could swim that we would be back for him and that if the water reached his waist before we got back, he should swim out towards the boat. After that I attached my harness line to the first man so I wouldn't lose him in the water and signalled the boat that we were coming out. Going back out to the boat was much easier than swimming in because they towed us through the surf and then they pulled us in while I tried to keep the casualty calm. He was increasingly panicky, but we managed to get him on board without mishap. I was extremely tired by this point and my shoulder was hurting me so Alex volunteered to swim and I took over the very difficult job of holding the boat steady so that he wouldn't be pulled away from the beach by the rope. He had been performing that job excellently for me, so I had big boots to fill.

As he arrived in the surf line, exactly the same thing happened to him, but he managed to get the second casualty and we pulled them both into the boat.

When we returned to the station with them, we all felt elation at having rescued the two men and it was only afterwards that it hit us how close they had been to death and the fact that it had only been us standing between them and certain drowning, at least for one of them. It is quite a thought for a 19-year-old.

The RNLI was impressed (BBC news report, 'Lifeboat'). Speaking after the rescue, John Jones, the RNLI's divisional manager said: 'This was a difficult rescue, which epitomised the courage and commitment of the RNLI's volunteer lifeboat crews.'

* * * * *

Some callouts were relatively simple, like this one Bruce Matheson was also on early in his second year:

The first callout was early in August (1973) with a call from the Coastguard to say a boy had fallen from the cliff opposite a hotel in Ogmore-by-Sea. We didn't know quite where this was so DBS [David Sutcliffe] came along with us. The boy had been taking eggs from seagull nests then fallen maybe 15 m into the water. He then climbed back onto the lower part of the cliff but was stuck there. DBS persuaded him to jump back into the sea and we were able to nose in and pick him up. We probably dropped him off on Southerndown Beach for the ambulance to look after but I am not sure of this. He had been lucky that the tide was high.

Not many boys falling from the cliffs were so lucky. Bruce and Freddie were both on another callout the following year – Bruce rescuing the rescuers to start with:

A similar but grim callout was in May 1974 when again a boy fell from the cliffs. This time it was east of Llantwit and the tide was out [see maps, page 27]. Bruce Cowger took B508 [the official RNLI boat] but could only start one outboard (the Evinrude was prone to flooding). We could see that it could not get on the plane [the optimal position of the hull in the water for maximum speed] so I took another boat out after it. When we caught up, Bruce Cowger took this onward while I stopped B508 and got both outboards started. The ambulance crew had walked along the foreshore from near Aberthaw and reached the boy. By the time both our boats arrived they had him on a stretcher. He was quite a mess as the impact had broken his feet off. We helped carry the stretcher to B508 and took them

East along the coast to where there was road access for the ambulance. Later that year he came to see us on crutches having suffered knee, hip and back injuries as well.

Freddie has a much more detailed recollection, for the callout coincided with the students' last big night of their two years at AC.

The date is anchored because as I recollect, right after returning from picking up this severely injured boy, transporting him on an ILB to a beach with road access so we could deliver him to a waiting ambulance, we were to get dressed up for our end of two years Banquet. The contrast between this life-threatening trauma to a young fellow, the physical and emotional impact of effecting a rescue, and a dorm full of women getting made up and putting on their finest was sobering to say the least. And I was supposed to do the same …

There must have been a klaxon sounding on this nice May afternoon, the rush to get into skinsuits, the decision as to which boats would go out. I was captain of X-11 so I think that was the boat I was in and not the B-Boat (RNLI ILB). We went east of the college where apparently a boy had been going after seagull eggs and fell onto the rocks below. I can't remember who found him, who else might have been on the beach or whether it was two crews but find him we did, breathing, unresponsive, one leg virtually severed (I vividly remember it was only jeans material keeping this leg with the boy) and the other leg almost severed as well. We loaded him onto a stretcher and took him back to an ILB waiting for us just offshore. I believe I supported his legs. He was laid on the deck of the ILB and I stayed watching him, trying to listen to him breathing as I remember, it being somewhat noisy but regular, and we headed east, perhaps to Llantwit Beach to meet the ambulance. I remember the stumbling over the rocks and boulders as we carried him. It was hard work and we had no idea if he would survive.

I imagine we were all somewhat in shock after this event and I remember feeling pretty sober during the banquet. I believe Mr Sutcliffe and perhaps others made some reference to our important role in rescuing this fellow. I recall feeling more sober or stunned than anything else about this recognition. I don't recall how I slept that night.

The following day was my birthday and again, the previous day's experience cast a pall, a real time to reflect on the fragility of life, how things can change so very quickly. A week or so after our rescue, a few of us were permitted to go to Bridgend hospital I believe, to visit the boy who miraculously was alive and who had had one leg reattached, the other was not salvageable. That was amazing and unforgettable. Then a year or so later I was told that he and his family visited our ILB station to thank the college and the people who had rescued him. Most of us were perhaps no longer there but some effort was made to tell us of this which I very much appreciated.

*****

There is a recurring experience for all rescue services: the need to rescue would-be rescuers. This rescue, narrated by Rob Steynor, took place later in 1974.

The klaxon sounded and I raced to the seafront. We launched B-508 and I headed down the Bristol Channel to the rescue area – a beach somewhere between Witches Point and Ogmore-by-Sea. We were in radio contact with a land-based crew. [See maps, page 27.]

A fisherman who had been fishing from the rocks was swept overboard by the rough sea and waves. A policeman, who was at the beach or nearby, after seeing the fisherman in the rough seas decided to strip down to his underclothes and swim out to save the fisherman.

The fisherman was able to get himself ashore and it was the policeman who ended up in trouble in the rough seas.

B-508 arrived on site and we were able to rescue the policeman who was suffering from hypothermia. We placed the policeman in a special thermal bag and I believe one of the crew went in the bag with him to warm him up slowly.

Even at that point, everything could still have gone terribly wrong:

Still in radio contact with the land crew and with an ambulance at the site, I attempted to land B-508 on the beach. However, as I was approaching the beach and trying to pick the best sea/wave condition to land the boat safely on the beach, I looked over my right shoulder and noted this huge wave coming into the beach.

Without hesitation, I turned B-508 around as quickly as possible and headed away from the beach into the wave.

After further assessment of the sea condition, I decided that it was safer to take the policeman to Porthcawl Harbour and we met the ambulance there.

A few months after the rescue, the policeman visited Atlantic College to thank the ILB team for saving his life.

Often the nature of the combined operation of cliff and boat rescue was highly efficient. Matthew Goodman (1976–78) remembers one particular example from 1977:

> We launched into very heavy seas to participate in an inter-service rescue of a man who had fallen off the cliffs west of St Donat's while free-climbing. I was radio man.
>
> Nick [on the helm] was a bit over-eager and went to full throttle as we pulled away from the slipway, as a result of which we soared straight up over a huge breaker, went virtually perpendicular – and the twin Evinrudes cavitated. Fortunately, we fell forward with a thump and not backward, or I wouldn't be here to tell the tale.
>
> Back to the story: When we got to the site where the climber had fallen, we saw him lying at the bottom of the cliffs on a small patch of rocky beach. As I recall, he was conscious but had some broken bones and couldn't get up. The tide was coming in fast and the seas were too rough for us to land. Through radio communication with the Coastguard and the College, we decided it was best for the Cliff Rescue team to rappel down the cliffs, put the man on a stretcher, and winch him up the cliff face. With good sight lines a few hundred feet offshore, we in the B-Boat guided the Cliff Rescue team, and after a couple of tricky hours, they successfully got him up to the top. That was definitely a life saved.

53. A quiet day on the water. David Sutcliffe in the bow

54. Cliff Rescue.

I believe it was that occasion when we were heading back to the College and I got a call on the radio that someone had reported a small craft going down in the Bristol Channel near our location. We spent nearly an hour searching before one of us realized that it was WE who were the 'missing' craft! Someone on the cliffs must have lost sight of us behind a wave and reported us missing. Even at the time, I recall finding that rather amusing …

Dave Nockels went on one callout that ended up changing his career choices:

'Cut-off by the tide' was one of the most frequent types of rescue in AC's patch, due to the extreme tidal range, the unwary could be rapidly cut off and at real risk of drowning or being forced to climb the cliffs.

On this occasion, we attended, and the conditions were not good. There was a substantial confused sea and wind with an early breaking surf onto a shelving rock seabed. A feature of the seabed on the South Wales coast is that the layers of rocks do not shelve progressively but drop down in large unpredictable steps. In one place there would be plenty of water depth for a RIB, but a metre or two closer to the shore, the hull or outboard could strike the rocks and be seriously damaged.

55. Low tide exposing the unpredictable seabed.

It was also getting dark. We were exploring the options for recovery to our IRB (line swimmer, veering-in etc.) and none of them looked at all good. As we ran through the options, a canary yellow military SAR [Search and Rescue] helicopter appeared out of the gloom, and within minutes had winched the casualties to safety. I found it remarkable, almost magical, at the way that the helicopter was able to resolve a dangerous situation so effectively. That event had a significant effect on the rest of my life, starting some 20 years later, when I became a professional helicopter pilot.

The long line of high cliffs on the South Wales coast of the Bristol Channel have always been a terrible lure to the suicidally depressed. One early February day in 1981, Tim Haney was called out on an unusual mission, as he wrote later to his parents.

This was a man threatening to jump off the cliff at Aberthaw. I was sitting in my Russian class discussing Chekhov's *The Three Sisters*, when Ivar [Lund Mathiesen] and John David came in saying I was needed for a callout. We left in the Land Rover about 1 ½ minutes later. On the team was Ivar [Lund Mathiesen] driving, John Lawrenson, Snowy [Hugh Lloyd Davies], Megan [Hardwick], Dawn [Ramsbottom] and myself. Aberthaw is where you can see the smokestacks along the beach about 4 miles East of AC.

We arrived in about six minutes and the place was already swarming with police. They allowed Megan, an attractive British [Welsh, I think] girl to talk to the guy who was sitting on about 4 inches of ground with both legs over the cliff's edge. Griff, the Llantwit Coastguard [station chief], ordered John, Snowy, Dawn and I to go down to the bottom of the cliff to prepare first aid equipment in case he did jump. [I recall John Lawrenson had the idea that we might try to use the first aid blanket to try to break his fall and improve his chance of survival].

We were in communication by a Dymar radio on channel zero with Griff at the top. Sometimes I couldn't get through because of interference from the cliff and had to relay the messages via Atlantic College base radio, which has its antenna on top of the castle. We were instructed to stay as close as possible to the cliff base so as not to be seen by the man and possibly disturb him further. Ivar took off his helmet and uniform, hid one of our radios in his vest, and walked out to the sea pretending to be a beach walker. From far away he advised us on our position relative to the man above. Finally, after over an hour and a half of just waiting we were ordered to come out front and confront the man. We moved out to where we could see him clearly and he us. I began talking to him on the megaphone. I really didn't know what to say at first. All we knew was that his name was

John [I think we later learned this was probably not his real name but just something to address him by] and he was about 55.

I talked to him about his family, friends, my philosophy of life, etc. I was pretty worried that I might say just the wrong thing and it would provoke him into jumping. He made little response to what I said. I couldn't hear well with the sea in the background and the distance between us. I had binoculars and I knew I was getting through to him because he'd wince when I mentioned his family. This went on for about an hour and I was running out of things to say when I saw Ivar, who had gone back up by then, creeping up behind him. I kept talking on the megaphone and Griff radioed telling me to just keep going to at least distract him and Ivar would try to grab him.

Suddenly Ivar jumped forward, grabbed him around the chest and flung him back away from the edge. [I learned later that Ivar had been wearing a harness and was belayed by a fireman.] We cheered from the bottom and Ivar signalled for us to come back up. I don't think I've ever felt so relieved as in that moment when Ivar pulled him back. When we arrived back at AC, we received word from Cardiff Royal Infirmary that the man was doing OK. The doctor said he'd never seen anyone so depressed. John Lawrenson told me I should be a preacher after hearing the sermon I gave the guy!

Ivar Lund Mathiesen later recalled that as he was preparing to snatch the potential cliff-jumper, a local policeman who was present very helpfully warned him that if the rescue attempt did not end well, Ivar could be accused of manslaughter.

*****

Callouts could come at any time of the day or night, so training exercises were carried out at all hours too. All the same, it was unusually early one morning in March 1983, when Swansea Coastguard received a mayday call from a fishing boat, the Dorothy E, in trouble off Aberthaw. Moments later, the callout went to St Donat's.

Morgyn Warner (1983–85) was one of the crew selected to go out in the big surf in the total darkness:

I happened to be on call when the Atlantic college lifeboat was called out to a serious emergency in March 1985. A fishing boat named the Dorothy E. had sent out a distress call and had sunk, with five fishermen in jeopardy. It was the early hours of the morning and there was no klaxon call. It was half term break and there were fewer than normal students and staff on campus.

I was awoken by one of the teachers in the early hours of the morning and ran in the pitch dark down to the seafront.

It seemed harder than usual to put on the gear, still wet from the day before. Our crew consisted of Malcolm Ellis (coxswain), Scott Barney, Dezsö Horvath, a teacher David Hobson and myself. We used the winch to launch the boat; the tide was quite high and the surf rough, so the launch was tricky. I remember sitting on the tube near the engines under the flashing blue light as the boat sped towards the sight and focusing on my thoughts that this would be the time to do what we had been trained for.

Dezsö Horvath also remembers being woken in the small hours: 'It was a night callout during spring break around the mock exams. Glyn Harbor woke me up in my room at around 3 am. A small fishing vessel with five people had sent out a Mayday call before sinking near the power station.'

Two Search and Rescue helicopters as well as Barry lifeboat were already hunting for the five men who had abandoned ship. 'Soon the loudspeaker [for the radio] got wet and we did not hear the radio communication anymore.'

Morgyn Warner remembers the search in rough and difficult conditions:

We were given coordinates to search for the men overboard. The Porthcawl lifeboat had found one person and helped him into our boat and transferred him to the larger boat. We found a second person and pulled them into our boat. He was not breathing, and as the first-aider, I began resuscitation until we reached the larger lifeboat and crew members from that boat. Unfortunately, he had been in the water for too long and didn't survive.

Dezsö Horvath:

By the time we reached the site, two people had been saved. Soon we were called to help lift a casualty from the water to a larger rescue boat. Sometime later we spotted the fourth casualty together with a fishing boat, we lifted him into our boat and transferred him to the larger rescue boat. We were then informed that it was too late, he could not be resuscitated. The search continued until it was cancelled at around 5–6 am, when we were informed that the fifth person had swum ashore.

But it was not the end of the expedition. The boat and its crew still had to land safely, as Morgyn Warner recalls:

Landing the boat in the dark in a big surf was also challenging. The coxswain drives the boat towards the trolley and crew members wait for him to yell 'cut' then lift the engines to avoid them hitting the trolley or slipway. Then we all have to jump out of the boat into the water, hold onto the boat and the trolley and guide it back to shore. In a large surf, you have to ride a wave in and time the engine cut just right then make sure you don't get swept off your feet and that the boat doesn't get dragged back out to sea. Fortunately, the landing went OK, though another AC lifeboat launched later managed to lose a propeller on landing.

The callout had been both a failure – a man died – but also a success: there were four survivors, and the college had made a long, challenging journey by night, navigating accurately and returning safely, after playing a small but important part in the rescue.

Certainly the survivors thought they had played their parts well, as Dezsö remembers.

> I know that the four survivors later came to the college to thank our work, Deon Glover told them that we did what we had to. So I myself was happy that I did not have to meet them in person, I wouldn't have known what to say.

Many of the callouts in July and August were crewed by students who had recently left the college, but gave up their summer holidays to train the next generation, and stand by for rescue 'shouts'. Rosie Allen, the daughter of Pelham Allen (one of the coxswains in the Tusker Rock rescue in 1968 described in the next chapter) was one of those, in 2003.

> My most memorable service call was on 29 July 2003, whilst I was working as an Summer Activities Instructor for the Extra Mural Centre at AC. I'm pretty sure we were on pagers during the summer, so no siren went off in the castle (that was always exciting, hey? Although when I was a student it always seemed to go off when I was in the shower in one of the furthest away houses!).
>
> I can't remember where I was or what I was doing. I can't remember the launch, but I can remember being on the boat. We had been called to 'two children with bicycles on the beach between Llantwit Major and Boverton'. It was a pretty grey day and [the wind was] a SW 3–4. Saul Mendelssohn, as helm, immediately took us to Llantwit Major Beach where we saw persons on shore, presuming them to be the casualties. Saul knew we needed more information and decided to put Will Rees, my crewmate, ashore. Will was the obvious choice to be the swimmer as it was not the calmest of conditions (and he was just a tad fitter than I was!) and I remember

watching Will in awe swim through the surf to get to the beach, too far away to send him on a swim line. It turned out that they were relatives of the boys that were stranded and were in contact via mobile, so we recovered Will and headed to east of Stout Point where the casualties were visualised.

By this time there were three of them as one of the boys' dads had scrambled down the cliff to be with them. We considered veering down but looking at the tidal state and checking via radio, Saul considered it too dangerous, especially since the boys were scared and reported to be weak swimmers.

The decision was taken to beach land and I remember standing in the water holding on to the boat as it bounced around in the waves trying to keep my feet beneath me. The boys and father on-board (but not the bikes!), Saul knew he had to move sharpish, pulling away from the shore as Will and I jumped back on board – I don't think I have ever managed to get on a boat so quickly before or since (and I have a feeling there may have been a helping hand on the back of my life jacket). It was all over so quick. And I remember thinking 'wow, we did it'.

I noticed the boys shivering and set about dressing them in survivor life jackets and thermal headwear. But then the landing … Ideally in the conditions we were in we would have net landed [on the net cage in front of the RNLI tractor]. But we had three casualties on board – the boys in the crew seats, the father in the bow, with Will and I sat on the sponsons. I don't know how Saul did it, but he reverse landed the boat in 1.5 m swell and the tractor swiftly pulled us out. The rest was a blur, but I do remember being taken to the pub for dinner and debrief.

I remember not being scared. I remember trusting Saul and Will and the boat. I remember being proud of myself. I didn't actually know Saul and Will very well at that point, and I'm not even sure I had ever been out training with them. But we were there for the same purpose and we had each other's backs. Something I have felt strongly volunteering with the RNLI since. And I was definitely left with a bit of a crush on my helm and crewmate … .

CHAPTER SIX

Tusker Rock

The stretch of water immediately west of St Donat's is among the most dangerous of any around the coast of Britain. Within a couple of miles there are two notorious threats to shipping, each of which has claimed scores of lives. Immediately to the west, just beyond Nash Point, lie Nash Sands, a string of long banks hidden except at low water. (See maps, page 27.)

To landward lies a narrow channel along which fierce tidal currents of up to 5 knots rip. A nautical mile or so further west sits Tusker Rock. Like Nash Sands, Tusker Rock, named after a Viking chieftain, Tuska, is submerged at high tide. At this time, only the ghosts of its victims – a feature of local stories – can be seen.

56. Nash Sands looking seductive off Nash Point.

57. Wreckage, probably of the Steepholm, on Tusker Rock.

But as the water retreats, its history is exposed. It is strewn with the debris of past shipwrecks. The biggest of these is the rusting hulk of a ship's boiler. Some say it belonged to the Samtampa, wrecked in 1947 on Sker Point a little to the west with the loss of its captain and its 30-strong crew. The attempt to rescue the sailors cost the lives of the entire eight-man crew of the Mumbles lifeboat after it overturned.

Others say that the old boiler is all that remains of the Steepholm.

The British dredger Steepholm, built in 1950, was on a short coastal voyage from Barry to Swansea laden with sand, when she was wrecked in heavy weather on Tusker Rock in 1968. The crew of seven was saved, in a long and complex joint rescue by the Mumbles lifeboat and the Porthcawl ILB, in the early hours of the morning of 3 October.

Within weeks, men were salvaging what they could of the wreck. On 11 November 1968, just as the early winter light was beginning to fade, a callout was received at the college. Four men, intent on taking what they could from the wreck, were reported to be trapped after their dinghy was swept away.

It was nearly dark. The tide was ebbing and there was a big swell running. It was, as David Sutcliffe commented when he wrote up the events in his history of the RIB, the college's most dramatic rescue to date.

Willem de Vogel, an 18-year-old Dutch student, was the IRB captain. His official report gives no hint of the challenge he faced after he raced to the seafront.

'Admiral Hoare came down and gave me the instructions,' he wrote economically, 'and the details required. We drove off immediately.'

But even at a distance of more than 50 years, the sense of pumping adrenalin remains in his memory:

> When the callout siren went off, I ran down with many others to the seafront. Upon getting our instructions from our headmaster the honorary RNLI secretary, Desmond Hoare, our hearts pounded faster and adrenaline rushed. This is what we've been training towards for over a year. This is what we had built X-7 and X-8 for. This is what 18-year-olds dream of doing.

One of his crew, Pelham Allen, also recalls the race to the seafront: 'It was a dark November evening, about 5 o'clock, I think. It was very much the end of afternoon, then the siren went and I remember running across the field [to the seafront] at an enormous pace.'

The problem of unofficial salvage, where men were sent out to a wreck to take everything of value that they could unscrew, was well known. Salvage is legal – as long as what is taken is reported to the official Receiver of Wreck. Admiral Hoare himself once tried to rescue mahogany logs, worth the then mighty sum of £300 each, that had fallen into the sea at Bristol when the barge carrying them capsized. (They found some of the logs, but they were too heavy to tow even when three IRBs were harnessed to them.)

It was never clear whether the four men in trouble on Steepholm had honest intentions, but subsequent events suggested otherwise.

'We knew of the wreck on Tusker Rock, between Porthcawl and Ogmore-on-the-Sea [sic],' Willem wrote.

> A few [weeks] earlier in a terrible storm, the dredging vessel Steepholm could not make it into the current and wind and was pushed backwards onto Tusker Rock and stuck there. The captain and crew abandoned the ship.
>
> A salvage crew, terribly underprepared, motored out from shore in a small inflatable Avon dinghy powered by a Penta outboard, and boarded the wreck in the afternoon of November 11. Not having secured the dinghy properly to the wreck, it broke away in the heavy surf. The four men on the wreck had no radios or flares. They found material with which to start a

fire on the aft deck. This was spotted by someone onshore which led to the callout call to St Donat's.

My boat, X-8, was in the shop. So I joined Goetz [Unger] and Pelham [Allen] in their boat, X-7, which they had built, and which had an experimental foot throttle. This became the lead boat on the mission. In addition to X-7 and X-4, X-5 was launched to act as a radio link to St Donat's and was positioned off Nash Point.

58. X-7. Note the experimental foot throttle.

Pelham Allen was only 16 at the time. In his recollection, he thinks three boats were launched mainly to look out for each other.

> The radios we had at that time were horribly unreliable and uncertain. If batteries were charged at all they would only have five minutes' worth of life, and they were terribly susceptible to getting wet. So the rationale would be to have a second boat within calling or perhaps seeing distance – my guess is they would have been told to stay in visual contact. There was the possibility that X7 would flip. Waves were breaking over Tusker Rock … there was obviously quite a swell. If things had gone horribly wrong we would have wanted someone pretty quickly.

Nor were the teenagers so high on excitement as to lack any sense of the risk of the mission they were undertaking. They were setting out to sea with notoriously unreliable radios, in the gathering dark, on an ebb tide, and that heavy swell which would mean big surf in some places.

Willem de Vogel recalls real, if short-lived, uncertainty. 'As we set off, there was a discussion whether or not we could do this. Soon we overcame any doubts we had.'

His memory is still vivid after 50 years:

> As we approached the wreck, we could see the light from the small fire that had been lit on deck. When we got closer, one of the four men asked if we could recover their dinghy first. Today, I see our acquiescence as a mistake. We should have only focused on getting them off the wreck.
>
> We found the dinghy quickly, turned it over to X-4, and returned to the wreck.

The official report that Willem filed when he returned then says:

> I told X-4 to take care of the dinghy and beach it at the nearest point, which was Ogmore Beach, ¾ of a mile away. We (X-7) then returned to the wreck to take off the four men. A very big breaking surf was turning near the wreck and I estimate that the biggest waves were between 6 to 8 feet. At that moment it was just after low tide. We waited for a calm spell and then came alongside very quickly to pick up the four men.

That was the official version. The real story was a good deal more perilous:

> We told the men we would take 2 of them off at a time. Our concern was obvious. X-7, with a crew of 3, would not be as agile in the surf with 4 more

people as it would be with only 2 more. We thought that by shouting to the men we had made ourselves clear.

It was important for us to select the right moment to effect the pick-up of the men since the waves were 6–8 feet high at times. So with me at the wheel, we approached the wreck, timing our arrival to match a calm spell in the surf. However, I came in too fast because I did not handle the foot throttle well. So we went around to try again, Goetz took the wheel and made a perfect approach. But to our dismay, all four men came down a stairway of the vessel at the same time, and three jumped into X-7, the fourth one missing X-7 and falling in the water between the wreck and X-7. That was the moment, if there ever was one, where the concept of rigid-inflatable was validated 1000%. We bumped into the man but did not crush him and it was easy to pull him into X-7 over the wet tube.

The truth of this statement had been demonstrated during the rescue of the original crew in a month earlier. The ship's master had nearly been lost when the lifeboat had been smashed against the hull of the dredger by a wave.

Goetz drove us away with skill. Goetz was an accomplished surfer. He knew surf and waves. He used his knowledge to help us get away from the wreck, using the waves coming from behind us to gain some speed.

Soon we got to X-4, and I transferred to it to make X-7 lighter and slightly more agile for Goetz to land the rescued four men through the small surf at the Ogmore Beach. Before leaving X-7, I asked for the men's names. They refused to give them to me.

'We do not wish to be charged by the police for this.'

During all this time, X-7 had maintained radio contact with an AC Land Rover near Ogmore.

On the way back, we met our radio link, X-5 at Nash Point.

Here the official account gives more of a hint of the dangers of the journey home:

West of Nash we met X-5, our radio link with the College. It was very poorly visible with its present colours, whereas they could see X-7 clearly. I decided that X-7 would go first through the Nash [tidal] race and that the others should follow us.

The perils of the Nash race, and the reasons for it, were later set out in Desmond Hoare's training manual for AC RNLI crew members:

More often than not trains of waves going in one direction are mixed with sets going in another, whether caused by an old wind or by tidal water movement over an uneven sea bottom. To small boats, the latter provides particularly dangerous conditions of tidal races, in which the waves seem to rise up almost perpendicularly with foaming crests, and unpredictably collapse into steep hollows. There are few tidal races which can give much trouble to a ship 200 or more feet long, and few which are *not* [my italics] dangerous to a boat 20 or less feet long in wind situations above Force 4.

But it was not only the sea conditions that the Rescue Boats had to contend with. Maintaining an accurate course between the cliffs and the rocky foreshore and the sandbank itself was also critical. The Nash Lighthouse had been newly equipped with a lighting system where night-time sea traffic was guided onto a safe course by a white beam. Veering off course put one in either green or, that night in November 1968, red sectors of the lighthouse light, a warning to make a swift course adjustment. The returning rescuers were undaunted.

> One moment we came into the red sector of the Nash Lighthouse, but we could very easily adjust ourselves. When we passed through Nash, the Land Rover caught us with its big search light from the cliffs.
>
> When we came in sight of the Castle lights, we established radio contact again to arrange the beach party which was very easy to see in their flame-orange anoraks.
>
> Once all the boats were in safely, I reported to Admiral Hoare that we had saved four men from the Chepstow Transport Company, whose foreman was Mr Phelps.

Again, Willem's memory is more colourful than his official account:

> When we landed back on the slipway at St Donat's, it was in complete darkness, through the 4-foot surf on the rising mid-tide swell.
>
> Someone later claimed we risked our lives. I dispute this. I think the biggest risk we ran was capsizing X-7 in the big waves battering the wreck. But we had neoprene wetsuits, life vests and two more IRBs nearby. Plus, if X-7 had actually capsized, she would not have sunk and we could hold on to her floating upside down.

And once again, landing the IRBs in the dark and with surf breaking felt to some, like Pelham Allen, as dangerous as any other moment in the rescue.

> I think we were closest to death on the foreshore, being crushed by boats

59. A night-time landing.

coming back … that to my mind was the narrow escape. Something like the rescue – I was probably the least experienced of the crew, but I was pretty confident that I could handle it.

It would have been nearly dark, and there was no floodlighting, just torches.

Pelham remembers, adding wryly, 'Willem was always very imperious in these situations.'

Willem felt the rescue had been a justification for the whole Atlantic College experiment, one of particular significance for a teenager whose mother had been a resistance fighter in the war.

For me, the Tusker Rock rescue was the perfect example of Kurt Hahn's philosophy. Here you had a Brit, a German and a Dutchman working in a difficult and challenging environment using all of their acquired skills to rescue four men who might have been in danger of losing their lives.

As a final note,1968 seems like a long time after 1945. But I was raised by a mother who fought in the Dutch underground and spent time imprisoned by the Germans. The one time my mother took us by train to Switzerland through Germany, we brought our own water and sandwiches because

Mother did not want to spend a dime in Germany. As the foregoing account testified, Goetz and I worked together all the same, like real pros.

There was a grim sequel to the Tusker Rock rescue, as Willem recalls.

> Although no one died that evening, all did not end well. Unfortunately, the four rescued men and one companion returned to the wreck the following week. Again in a small dinghy. This time, the dinghy overturned in the heavy swell. Four of the men managed to scramble aboard again. However, sadly, a fifth man drowned before an alarm could be raised. He was one of the four who had been rescued the previous week, and the father of three children.

Willem, Pelham and Goetz were subsequently each awarded a letter of appreciation from the RNLI for their part in the rescue of the men on the Steepholm The RNLI's Secretary wrote:

> The rescue of these men in the heavy surf around the wreck required good judgement and teamwork and I send you an expression of the Institution's appreciation of the seamanship displayed by you on this occasion. I also send you my personal congratulations on the excellent manner in which this operation was performed.

Wrecks and wreckage are widely recognised as inshore hazards. Martin Cannon (1969–71) had an odd and frightening experience on an unsuccessful callout in 1970. In a twist in the tale, the experience itself provoked another lifesaving experiment.

> In the time I participated as a coxswain (I think that was our classification) I recall one callout that occurred off (I think) Southerndown Beach. It was summer.
>
> Our boats were already in the area and the call related to two missing girls (sub-teens as I recall) feared blown out to sea on some flotation device they'd been playing around on in a few feet of water.
>
> The day had begun sunny, the beaches were crowded. As the afternoon wore on clouds gathered and the wind intensified. We (there were at least two, maybe three boats involved) searched across a sort of grid to cover as much sea as possible, one of us standing on as elevated a platform as possible, including for as long as the wind and turbulence allowed, standing on the bench behind the helmsman.
>
> We covered a great deal of space methodically and experienced that subtle

inexorable slow shift from eager alertness to the realization that we were participating in a failing effort. The condition of the sea progressed to a point that made it hard if not impossible to believe young kids could have stayed connected to a flimsy inflatable object of the kind described to us. Toward the end of our effort, we paused for a moment in the by now huge swell and right next to us, maybe 20 feet away, as the boat descended into a trough the sharp rusted bow of a wreck rose beside us, like a skeleton emerging from the ground – eerie, and portentous.

Eventually the effort was abandoned, and I have no recollection of our being informed whether the girls had been found onshore or at sea. The whole episode feels in this recollection to have consumed at least a long hour or more.

As I reflect on this effort to recapture details of the episode, I can only confidently vouch for the following: That a search for missing children did occur off a crowded beach; it began in bright and benign conditions which deteriorated sharply; it followed a call received when we were already out to sea; it involved multiple boats; we had an uncomfortable near-miss with that rusted hulk in the severe swell; it was unsuccessful.

Angus Matthews was on the same callout.

I do recall the eerie experience of seeing the ship's skeleton that Martin reports. It was in late August or early September 1970 on one of the rare occasions when we had four boats at sea. When we received the radio call three boats (likely X8, X9, X11) were assigned to run a search grid and X12 was designated to provide radio relay off Nash Point. My recollection is the RNLI Porthcawl lifeboat made the rescue of the girls further to the west of the area we were searching. The ebb current had carried the kids on the raft further than we expected.

As the tide turned, the surf came up and we were headed back to St Donat's, planning to run on the inside of Nash Sands as usual. On the western tip of Nash Sands Martin's boat (X11?) passed very close to a hulk of rusted steel ribs that appeared out of nowhere in the surf on the tip of the sands. We all stopped to get a glimpse of what appeared to be a 60-ft plus vessel of some kind. In moments, as the surf grew and the sands submerged, the ghost went with it.

We went back with two boats a few days later and could find no trace of what we had seen. I do recall us beaching the boats on the sands, and actually walking on the mysterious sandbar. As the tide rose, the firm sand disintegrated into a waterborne cloud of sand that would not support our weight. We pulled ourselves back into the boats before they drifted off.

This search effort of course gave Admiral Hoare and David Sutcliffe an idea. The admiral designed a series of different buoys that we would deploy and track on various tides and sea conditions. David applied his mathematical skills to devise a drift algorithm of sorts for use in future rescues. This has of course become an essential part of modern-day searches and oil spill recovery planning. We ended up losing all the buoys, which didn't bode well for the success of future searches.

All the same, the use of marker buoys in such circumstances has become standard practice.

CHAPTER SEVEN

Near Disasters

Many calls were false alarms. Occasionally they were pranks or even malicious, but mostly they were genuine mistakes: the caller might have lost sight of a child, or seen walkers going in one direction and not returning. But every call to the emergency phone was treated with the same seriousness and urgency, as a matter that might involve saving – or losing – life.

Yet there was also, always, the risk that the courageous and often selfless approach of the students might cloud vital judgements. An attempt to save life might result in more lives being lost.

An example of the narrowness of the line came early in the college's experience, in 1965.

On 28 October – a day remembered by those who knew of it as 'Black Thursday' – the crews of at least one of the Zodiac dinghies then on loan from the RNLI for trials, and four of the college's Fireballs, came close to disaster. According to a memorandum written later by Hoare when submitting an official report to the RNLI, two of the RNLI Zodiacs and the four dinghies went out at 2 pm 'on exercise'. This was despite the shipping forecast warning that the Force 4 westerly which was already blowing was expected to get up to Force 5–6 before the afternoon was out. Force 6 is a very brisk wind even for Fireballs, whose designers boasted that they were still racing when everyone else had gone home.

Just as the wind freshened, the tide turned. It was now rising, and what Hoare described as 'a large swell' arose. Soon a dinghy was in difficulties. This is how he went on to describe the episode:

> Aphrodite [a college-built boat] went into assistance and, endeavouring to take a tow, stalled the engine. On attempting to restart, the starting cord came out of its handle and vanished into the rewind assembly. Aphrodite immediately anchored and was recovered in breaking surf by Zodiac no.38 at about 15.15 and was towed to base in about 15 minutes. All dinghies were by now in severe difficulties, drifting capsized to the east with the flood tide and wind, being uprighted for only short periods. Sea Rover no.33 entered the surf a mile to the east in an attempt to recover one at 15.30 and was flooded by a breaking wave which stalled the engine. Breaking water continued to come aboard. Atlantic College Bacchus was launched

from base at 15.30 and recovered one dinghy well out to sea. Zodiac no.38 ordered the anchoring of two dinghies at sea and took off the crews of three each and returned them to base. They returned to Sea Rover no.33 by 16.15 and took off the crew of three, avoiding flooding with as much luck as good judgement. The sea on return was very high with breaking water on the crest of nearly every wave.

In the Beaufort Scale of wind strength, breaking water on every crest indicates a wind of at least Force 6.

The following day, all the craft, bar one sailing dinghy, were recovered, some badly damaged. But no one was hurt. The RNLI decided no follow-up action was called for.

Reflecting on the experience many years later, David Sutcliffe commented:

It was the nearest the College ever came to real disaster, a severe reminder of the fatefully narrow dividing line between sound adventurous activity and unforeseen tragedy. The official return submitted by the College to RNLI Head Office recorded nine lives saved. Desmond Hoare, no doubt strengthened by years of professional naval experience, held his nerve in a manner that no civilian colleague could have done. Life went on as before (*Hahn* 57).

Hoare's and later Sutcliffe's confidence about sending crews out in challenging, sometimes dangerous, conditions was born from the certainty that they had been trained to be safe in the most treacherous of conditions.

In his training guide, Hoare says:

If one believes that swimming ability is a survival factor as we do, then clothing suitable for swimming should be worn … We in the Atlantic College believe that survival is best ensured by swim-ability, that this has great rescue importance in some circumstances and we have, therefore, adopted the neoprene wetsuit as standard ILB wear …

No one was allowed out in a boat without a wetsuit: in Hoare's opinion, it could be more important for survival than a life jacket. 'The life-jacketed man in the water in the best conventional clothing will die from exposure in a few hours, much less in winter. He would survive much longer in a skin suit.'

Dagfinn Paust, a Norwegian student at Atlantic College from 1970 to 1972, was unquestionably a strong swimmer. In his second year he was student captain of the rescue boat service, or ILBs. He met all the admiral's personal requirements. But on 3 October 1971, he came perilously close to disaster. This is his story:

> After a long afternoon at sea, followed by an uneventful search 3–4 nautical miles southwest of AC as a result of a reported sighting of a flare across the channel, we landed around 5 pm. The callout siren sounded again not two hours later just after dinner and everyone ran down to the seafront, where the Beach Rescue and Rescue Boat (ILB) teams pulled on their wetsuits and prepared their equipment. We were told by Mr Sutcliffe that a man and his ten-year-old nephew had been reported missing after going for a walk to the beach by Nash Point [see maps, page 27]. It was suggested that they might be trapped in one of the bays by the rising tide, which had already become fairly high by that time. The typical high tide at the Point is more than 8 metres above low tide, and the sea is infamous for its strong currents. While the distance from the water's edge at low tide to the cliff face is deceptively long, often 100 metres, at high tide the waves often wash up the rocky wall sometimes spraying over the top which is more than 20 metres high.

> Initially, two ILBs were launched, some ten minutes after the callout sounded: X9 with Dagfinn at the helm, accompanied by captain of X9 John Ward (Bermudian) and coxswain Geoff Launchbury (Welsh). A second boat, X11 also launched with coxswain Jeff Dowell (Canadian) and crew, including Frances Tomkins (British).

60. Dagfinn Paust with Frances Tomkins, driving X-11 full throttle.

61. An illustration by Apolline Royer of the rescue.

Beach Rescue sent vans with a team of experienced canoeists and their kayaks by road to Nash Point in order to attempt a launch from the gap between the cliffs there. When the tide is out and the water is calm, one can access the sea there from a beautiful rocky beach. At high tide with crashing waves, however, this was not an ideal place from which to launch the kayaks. [See photo, page 142.]

By the time the ILBs arrived offshore at the location off Nash Point, it had gotten quite dark and the narrow strip of almost dry land between the bottom of the cliffs and the rising water's edge was in the shadow of the cliff above. Thus, it was hard to see, but we could make out two figures standing on a rock and presumed them to be the missing persons. Since the surf was fairly heavy, landing on the beach was deemed impossible as it consisted of rock outcroppings between patches of boulders the size of small bowling balls. The ILBs anchored a few hundred yards from the shore.

This is textbook procedure. Hoare's instructions state: 'If the sea is completely calm, one can just drive in to the rescue, watching of course for propeller damage … if there is a considerable breaking swell and rescue is unlikely to be effected from the clifftop down, then an ILB swimmer must go in on the line …'. This was the course Dagfinn now pursued.

The boats were equipped with a long lifeline on a reel. As Captain, I decided

62. The advantage of wetsuits. Note the awkward high collars on the life jackets.

that I should swim in with the lifeline attached to a harness to have the ILB crew (as per procedure) haul me out again later with one of the two missing persons. This was reported over the boat's radio back to the College and possibly to HM Coastguard. There was little debate among the crew, if any, about the best course of action.

In his training manual, the Admiral had also written: 'Life jackets are sometimes discussed as though they were always the determining factor in survival. They are always important, but exposure is of more importance to the good swimmer in many inshore situations from which he can swim out in a skin suit, with or without a life jacket, occasionally better without it.'

This is exactly the thinking Dagfinn followed. He left his life jacket on board, fearing that on the long swim, the cumbersome flotation device would hamper his movements.

Owing to the heavy surf and strong currents typical of Nash Point, I struggled on my way in to the shore as I was pulled off course considerably, but eventually I managed.

I found the two missing persons, who by then had climbed further up inside a cave-like rock formation, nearly surrounded by water. Although the crew never determined at what time the tide actually peaked that evening, the boy and his uncle were judged to be in imminent danger as the sea seemed to be rising further still and the cave might then get flooded. (In the Hon. Sec's subsequent report to the RNLI, it said that the tide was 'near full'. It was full moon the following evening, thus the tide would have been higher than normal).

Hoare's manual, rather ambitiously, states, 'When the "call-out" hooter goes there is no time to look up tide tables. One's own safety as well as one's competence to rescue demands, in an area like the Bristol Channel, that the tidal situation is always on call in one's mind.'

At this point, the rescue became truly dangerous.

> The boy's uncle and I agreed to evacuate the boy by hauling him out through the waves with the lifeline as the crew had trained for.
>
> I waded out into the water with the boy, signalling by hand to the crew of X9 to begin hauling. I had no flashlight or radio with which to signal. The visibility was poor, and the light was fading fast. I did not know at the time if the boat crew saw my signalling. It seemed that they might not see me by the water's edge over the breaking waves, but afterwards I was told that they did and had seen me signalling to be hauled out. Due to the waves pulling on the lifeline, I was also unable to ascertain if the crew actually had begun to haul.
>
> What I didn't realise was that the lifeline had been trapped in the constantly moving boulders on the beach when I had first come ashore from the boat, and a lot of rope had been let out from the reel. Therefore, the crew were not able to pull me in. It is unclear if this was because the line was stuck or if they were afraid that the line was too short.
>
> Sometime later, the crew cut the line.

Back on the boat, John Ward, captain of X9, takes up the story:

> We began hauling but the line was taut, jammed in the rocks somewhere underneath the surf! At this point exactly, what was left of the evening light faded and we could see nothing. We pulled and pulled, afraid of snapping the rope, but to no avail. Our boat's searchlight, a very bright one, was switched on but failed to pick out any activity on the shore or in the waves. With the high seas running ashore as surf, we could not risk trying to take the boat (X9) in closer to the shore; in any case, we still had the swimmer's line in our hand and could not manoeuvre without letting it go.

John and his crewmate Geoff Launchbury decided they had only one option left:

We had no choice but to radio our base station with the news that one of our crew and one other person might be lost in the surf. We requested a search of the nearby beaches by Beach Rescue and additional lights from the Coastguard. The tide was now beginning to go out and we found ourselves in the receding surf line, with waves breaking over the boat. As the engine had been idling all this time, we put it into gear and began moving offshore, simultaneously raising the anchor and paying out the swimmer's line.

In response John Lipscomb, the staff member who was in charge back at AC, launched two more boats, X8 with coxswain Simon Lagoe (British) and crew, and X12 with coxswain Alan Buttigieg (Maltese) and a crew that included Dick Malpas (Brazilian). In what must have been an indication of the alarm on shore, David Sutcliffe, came out on X12.

Meanwhile, with no support, Dagfinn was still trying to get back out to the boat with the boy:

> As I swam out through the waves anyway, with a firm grip on the boy and hoping to feel the crew pull on the lifeline, the stoutly built boy panicked and managed to break free. Then I lost him in the waves and got tangled in the swim line in the swirling surf. After a while, I managed to release the harness and free myself from the swim line.

> When I was able to save myself and crawl back up onto the beach, I saw the boy floating face down in the water. His uncle and I dragged the boy up on land to a ledge.

At this point, Dagfinn, despite his own near-death experience, turned the situation around through his own hard-learned skills. 'Artificial resuscitation ability is an absolute requirement for all ILB crews', says Hoare's training manual. 'They must also be able to deal with heart stoppage by chest manipulation.'

In the relative safety of the ledge, now in almost total darkness, Dagfinn set to work:

> Here, I was able to resuscitate the boy after some time, fortunately, using a combination of chest compressions and mouth-to-mouth. This was a huge relief for an 18-year-old who had realised that he was out of his depth.

> It then became clear that the planned rescue method was unrealistic. Also, after I while I saw that the sea had clearly started to recede. Thus, the best plan of action was to wait it out.

Meanwhile, John Ward and Geoff Launchbury, waiting for the reinforcements they had requested, were still desperately hoping to see Dagfinn's head bobbing up alongside the boat.

> We re-anchored just outside the surf line. Still the swimmer's line would not come free, and we had no idea if Daffy [Dagfinn] was still on the end of the line. Finally, X-8 and X-12 arrived. Before long, a huge rocket whooshed into the sky and a white parachute flare lit the scene for perhaps half a minute. We could not see anyone. A few other flares followed. With the surf retreating seawards, we kept re-anchoring further out. The unhesitating reliability of the Mercury outboard engine was most reassuring in these conditions. At one point, a light like a bomber searchlight came on from a Coastguard vehicle on the cliffs above. They had collected this from their stores some distance away. It lit the scene up like daylight and we felt that now we could discover where everyone was. However, as quickly as it came on it went out, never to be relit.

> By now we could not move any further offshore without cutting loose the swimmer's line, which had been run out to its full limit. A heated discussion ensued in darkness, with waves breaking onto the boat. We did not have many alternative actions from which to choose. However, Geoff Launchbury was adamant that we could not throw overboard a line that might have Daffy and someone else at the other end, even though an hour or two had passed. Further waves over us decided the point but we agreed to tie on the boat's inflated cushion (used to protect the forward crew from the hard deck) so that if they did swim out on the line, they would have something to hold onto.

Further out at sea, the lack of communication was total. Richard Malpas was on X12: 'Exactly what was happening was far from clear. Someone on the lead boat swam towards shore with a rope harness, but what happened then, we could not tell. On our boat we kept our spirits up by singing. I cannot remember more about the details.'

Simon Lagoe remembers: 'X8 and X12 were standing by further out to sea, listening to the Coastguard radio in the dark'. Simon also recalls the boats 'later heading back towards the college and coming round the corner from Nash Point into sight of the road down from Marcross which was full of vehicles with blue flashing lights and realising what a big incident this was.'

Dagfinn was now trying to work out what his next step should be:

After some time, suddenly, out of the darkness at the water's edge emerged a smiling Phil Lloyd, the Canadian Beach Rescue Instructor. He had either surfed in on his kayak, or body-surfed in after leaving his kayak offshore.

It turned out that Phil had managed to launch a small team of Beach Rescue canoeists in kayaks, from the rocky beach by Nash Point. Among them were Walter Erdelitsch from Austria and Amlyn Parry from Wales. They were meant to try to go out through the waves and then come in further west to where the missing persons were. Launching kayaks from the rocks in this way required exact timing of the wave sets and was a harrowing experience. There was a considerable risk that the kayaks would crash and break up on the rocks. Eventually, out beyond the breakers, the canoeists abandoned the idea of landing as planned, and together with their kayaks were pulled aboard the ILBs instead and later brought back to the college by boat.

Meanwhile, on the beach there was little Phil could do except to help keep our spirits up.

Then, from the darkness above a sound was heard of crashing cliff rubble, and down climbed the lighthouse keeper, a very accomplished rock climber.

The Nash Point lighthouse was the last manned lighthouse in Wales. Although it had been electrified in 1968, it only lost its keeper when it was fully automated 30 years later.

He told everyone that since the tide was receding, we should soon be able to get out safely along a rocky ledge to the beach by the opening in the cliffs, where a path led to the clifftop and the lighthouse.

Thus, sometime later our group emerged carrying the boy to the beach at Nash Cwm, the valley where the Marcross stream comes out to the sea. There, the police and coastguardsmen were gathered, with their emergency vehicles at the Nash Car Park. The boy, who was hypothermic, was sent to the local hospital in Bridgend along with his uncle and the lighthouse keeper to be treated for exposure.

I then hitched a ride back to the college in one of the Coastguard Land Rovers and walked down to the sea area. By then, it was 9.30 pm, some 2 1/2 hours since the boats were launched. Seeing that there were people in the water with a boat trolley preparing to land a rescue boat, I walked into the water to assist. There was David Sutcliffe, the college principal [headmaster], who was quite relieved to see me. The ILB that landed, the X9, had my roommate Walter and his Beach Rescue kayak onboard. Forty-eight years later, when asked about this story, Walter's comment to me was: 'I still remember seeing that you had the boy's vomit in your hair!'

In John's words:

> Sometime later, we returned to the college, not knowing what had happened
> to our crew member and the two people who had been cut off by the tide.
> As we came ashore, Daffy walked down the slipway to meet us. After we
> had thrown ourselves at him in joy, he told us what had happened once he
> realised that he was not being hauled out on the swimming line and how he
> and the boy had ended up ashore where, with the boy's uncle, they awaited
> further developments. Some of the girls at the college wept when they saw
> us, for they had heard that it was us who had been lost in the surf.

Dagfinn has no recollection of a debrief after the incident. But then he recently
found a memo from David Sutcliffe, dated 5 October 1971, two days after
the callout, where he called for a meeting to be held to 'consider procedure,
equipment, and future recommendations resulting from the Call-Out on the
Sunday evening October 3rd 1971.' The following were invited and believed to
have been in attendance: 'all staff coaches and Captains of the Rescue Services,
together with material witnesses as nominated by the respective Rescue Services'.
It appears no minutes survive. However, some students initiated an additional
first-aid programme later that autumn, and John Ward also remembers changes:

> The debrief (or inquiry) resulted in an improved approach to certain events
> and the use of floating swimmers' lines was thereafter promoted. Many
> members of the College's sea - and shore-based rescue services later learned
> Morse code so that they could communicate by means of light signals.
> Morse signalling was used thereafter on one or two occasions in the same
> academic year (1971–72) but not in any emergency situations.

Three years later Desmond Hoare's written training manual for the rescue boat
crews was published from notes compiled since 1963. There was never any post-
traumatic stress counselling where the 17–18-year-old crew members discussed
their experience.

On a historical note, in later years, the RNLI removed the swim line reel from the
ILBs and crew members swimming in to retrieve people was no longer Standard
Operating Procedure. Crew members who all the same volunteer to go into the
water (contrary to SOP) to help someone now have to use the tow rope or
anchor line. When Eleuthera du Breuil elected to swim in on the rescue she
recounts above (page 130) she used the tow rope.

Dagfinn finished writing up this account of that night on 11 November 2019, the
day that David Sutcliffe died and dedicates it to his memory. He reflects on the
events of nearly 50 years ago:

In retrospect, it may be argued that this event at Nash Point was a callout that went wrong, but where no lives were lost in the end, fortunately. The rescue attempt got some negative press in the local newspaper, but this was countered by a member of the public in a letter to the editor relating his own story of how he was once rescued by youngsters from the College under somewhat less dramatic circumstances.

Although there were in fact lesson-learning sessions following incidents like this one, the fact such inquests do not loom large in most participants' memories might reflect the college ambition not to stifle the students' spirit of adventure.

Thus, Dimitrios Sotiropoulos recalls no inquiry into his accidental encounter between an ILB and a Fireball. Nor it seems was there an investigation when Ken Wilson came perilously close to disaster right on the St Donat's foreshore, a story told by Auke Koopal:

> We all went out on the foreshore one afternoon in pretty rough conditions, with strong onshore wind of maybe force 6, if I remember well, and 5-foot swells. These conditions were OK for regular kayaks and for most of the Beach Rescue lifeguards, but not for surf kayaks ('surfyaks') with their very limited buoyancy in the back. [The surfyaks – also known as 'surfshoes' or 'bats' – were a cross between a shortened kayak and a surf ski.] Ken took out the surfyak. When his spray cover came off water got in and he had to get out and try to get back to shore swimming with the surfyak.

63. Torbjörn Swartling (AC 1977–79) in a surfyak.

According to Ken:

> The only thing I can remember about my little problem on the foreshore is coming in, swimming.
>
> A huge wave had crashed my double spray cover in and swamped me. I vaguely remember holding one of the lanyards in my hand and it was attached to the remains of the cockpit rim.
>
> The last thing I recall was staggering over the rocks and a couple of people were walking towards me, I guess I was waist deep. Then I saw them stop about 5 metres from the sea, on the beach and I noted they were not looking at me but past me. I do remember one of them had his/her mouth open and seemed either surprised or shouting. The next thing I recall was up in the little bedroom in the castle first aid hospital place. Apparently, some sort of ginormous wave crashed down on me and swept me over the rocks.

Auke:

> We had noticed that Ken had gotten out of his surfyak. That was about straight out from the launch area on the foreshore. And then he started to drift eastward toward Tresilian Bay. All in all, he must have been in the water for 20 minutes or so.
>
> When Ken finally reached the shore, he was exhausted from the effort to get there. Thus, he was easily swept off his feet by the heavy shore break.

64. Surf breaking on the foreshore. Note the loose kayak.

When he was pulled on shore, he was suffering from hypothermia as he had lost a lot of body heat. Luckily there were some Beach Rescue girls who volunteered to give him mouth-to-mouth. We brought him up to sick bay (the school's medical facility) where Sister Stanley took over, gave Ken a small glass of brandy and covered him in blankets. Not sure if the brandy is the right thing to do?

Anyway, Ken recovered quickly and went on to fail his IB [exam] but was accepted in Med school anyway in Liverpool (they had no experience with IB and IB grades), and became a Psychiatry professor, retired two years ago, but went back to work for the NHS for three days a week.

What we learned: 1) don't use surfyaks on rocky shores where there are a lot of (rip) currents and in conditions of strong winds, 2) Make sure to use top condition wetsuits, we remember that Ken's wetsuit had open seams in many places, 3) undertake these activities only after proper meals; Ken had not eaten much lunch.

There is no mistaking the trust that was placed in the students, although it was not invariably unconditional. In 1965, perhaps when the ground rules were still being set, there was a bruising encounter between student and teacher. Jim Buckheit was the student and he filed two versions of his account. This is the first:

A Sunday afternoon in April 1965: a man scrambling on the cliffs near Tresilian Bay, east of St Donat's, had fallen and was injured. Cliff Rescue was dispatched by Land Rover, and we launched two rescue boats from the school. I drove the lead boat with my crewman Assam Farouki and Stephen Cox, head of the newly established First Aid Corps, on board. We reached the victim first, finding that he had a compound fracture of the forearm, which Stephen immediately began treating. By the time he had finished, the Cliff Rescue unit had their gear set up and had a crew on the beach. We assumed the victim would be hauled up by winch to the top of the cliff where an ambulance had been summoned. At that point, Mr Blackburn (administrator on duty that weekend) insisted that we carry the stretcher over the rock ledges along the beach to a point at the head of the bay where the ambulance could get close. It took us almost a half hour to get the victim to the ambulance.

And this is the second, after he had seen the contemporaneous records:

The event is seared in my memory, because I got in considerable trouble. Following the callout, I wrote a letter to the headmaster complaining about

Mr Blackburn's departure from the standard protocols for such an incident, which resulted (I believed) in the risk of having the victim go into shock as we scrambled over the rock shelves with his stretcher. I'm quite sure that the operation took longer than the time indicated on the record sheet. I was called before the faculty committee and dressed down for being disrespectful to Mr Blackburn and required to apologise. I don't think I had actually been disrespectful in person, but I had been quite pointed in my letter to the headmaster (keep in mind he had appointed me Captain of the Corps the previous spring) about what looked like not trusting our Cliff Rescue unit.

He and I had grown close over the two years, and I was sorry to have this issue affect our final weeks. But I see in that incident a theme that had to have been a growing problem at AC over the years, and one that I only appreciated more fully once I became a school head: the tension between authenticity and liability in any kind of service activities, but especially with rescue services.

CHAPTER EIGHT

The Losses

If the students were to be involved in trying to save lives, they were also likely to encounter death. There are no records to show how, if at all, the consequences of this were considered, although it was tacitly acknowledged. But it did, intermittently, become a great challenge for the rescue services.

In late September 1966, a man fishing from a rock lost his footing as a wave hit him, and he was swept into the sea. The beach was at Monknash Cwm (valley), about five miles by road from the college. Both Rescue Boats and Beach Rescue were scrambled.

David Riley was at the start of his second year when the siren sounded.

> It was a summer's evening with a high tide beginning to fall. A lone middle-aged fisherman was reported missing off the promontory cliff ledge at Cwm Nash [the valley where the Nash Brook comes out into the sea]. The sea was flat calm, there was no wind and it was a warm evening.

The IRBs already had an established formula for sea searches, dividing the area to be searched into a grid.

> Beach Rescue went to the site via Monknash and two IRBs [ILBs] were dispatched. One searched the zone close to the cliffs and we ranged more widely across the triangular area between the shore and the Nash Sands, in case the fisherman had drifted south westwards with the falling tide.
>
> After about an hour we learnt the Beach Rescue team (paddling through the now waist-deep water below the ledge) had found his body at the foot of the rocks immediately below where he had fallen in. The man wore full body waders with heavy integral boots, which had held him down below the surface.
>
> The man was lifted into the other, slightly longer, IRB and we returned to St Donat's where his body was laid out alongside the workshop for an ambulance to recover.
>
> What struck me most at the time was how a calm sea and a balmy, innocent summer's evening had ended in death. A life ended and family devastated when nature was seemingly at its most benign. My respect for the sea, water and safety training owes much to that evening.

John van Kuffeler was also on a rescue boat. But he was deep in his books when the callout sounded.

> I was studying for my Cambridge entrance exam on Sunday evening when the callout siren went. We put out two boats at quarter past six to look for a fisherman who had disappeared off some rocks. I was the cox of Freya with Roger van Eeghen and one other crew member. When we arrived at the scene there were two police who confirmed the story. The fishing rod and equipment were there but the fisherman was missing.
>
> The sea was flat calm with mist and about half a mile of vision. In the background was the constant booming of the Nash Point foghorn. With the two boats we did several sweeps to seaward each about 5 miles long to see if we could find him. By this time we were joined by a number of AC canoes, including Wim van Lynden – so there were three Dutchmen on the rescue.
>
> One of the canoeists then stepped on an object in waist-deep water which turned out to be the fisherman when brought to the surface. He appeared to be lifeless. In order to get medical help, we immediately loaded him into Freya and while Roger gave him mouth-to-mouth resuscitation in the bottom of the boat as we sped back to AC and a waiting doctor.

It was instilled into the students as part of the compulsory first aid training that they were not qualified to pronounce someone dead. They had to persist in attempting resuscitation until a properly qualified person could assess the victim. Occasionally, this was a deeply traumatising instruction.

> We unloaded him [from the boat] and a few minutes later the doctor declared him dead by drowning – probably an hour before. The fisherman was a local with no direct family.
>
> By chance the next morning, HRH Prince Bernhard of the Netherlands arrived to visit AC. The visit was closely followed by the press and Roger, Wim and I ended up giving a half-hour press conference after lunch attended by eight British and Dutch newspapers in which the 'rescue' was extensively covered.

According to the *Western Mail*, Prince Bernhard congratulated John de Blocq van Kuffeler, 'the son of the Royal Netherlands Navy Commander', for his part in the rescue and met three other Dutch students involved in it – Jean-Jacques Debrot, Rudolph van Lynden and Roger van Eeghen. The dead man came from Llandow, near Cowbridge.

The newest intake of students (1966–68) had only just arrived at St Donat's. One of them, John Grey-Davies, who went on to become captain of Rescue Boats, remembers the body being brought ashore and loaded into the ambulance more vividly than any of the rescues he was involved in later. It was a hard lesson in the reality of the undertaking to which they had committed the next two years of their lives.

It was not only the students who experienced the dark side of operating a rescue service that afternoon. Andrew Maclehose, less than ten years older than many of the students, had just joined the staff as a canoeist who could also teach economics and history.

> The rescue vans had a blue light in those days. We loaded canoes onto the trailer and raced off down the narrow lanes past the Plough and Harrow pub and down to the last house on the road, inhabited by two elderly sisters, where we parked the van. There was still half a mile to carry the canoes down to sea.

> The tide had recently turned. We launched the canoes and I took a group of canoeists westward [out to sea, with the tide] to look for the body. As the tide retreated David Sutcliffe and other students methodically canoed along the shoreline. After a time, they found a dead body. They tried to resuscitate him.

> The body had been taken away by the time my team returned to shore. It was not the first time I had seen a body in the water. But it made me realise that this was for real. A few days later, I went with David Sutcliffe to try to find a quicker way down to the beach, across the fields. We were apprehended by a very angry farmer who accused us of trespassing until David said, icily, 'I am not accustomed to be spoken to in that manner.' After that he calmed down and the college always had good relations with him, I believe. It was a fruitless mission though. The [inshore rescue] boats were always going to be quicker than a van loaded with canoes.

More than 50 years later, in his eulogy to David Sutcliffe in 2019, Maclehose recalled the trauma:

> Foremost among the qualities which made David a great school leader was that he did not just talk about the UWC mission – he lived it; the first time I witnessed this myself, less than two weeks after I joined Atlantic College, was his own desperate but vain effort to revive a fisherman who had fallen from a rock into the sea off Monknash Cwm, after his body was found by the College's student rescuers who abandoned their canoes and waded in the sea as the tide went out.

*****

The decline of the experience of death has become one of the watersheds between the first and second halves of the 20th century, at least in the global north. Few students at Atlantic College, all born after the end of the Second World War, would ever have seen a dead body. Few would have had the experience of sudden bereavement, or of sharing the trauma of the victim's family. Training covered a multitude of eventualities, but the aftermath of a catastrophe was not among them. There was no official guidance.

Weeks after the recovery of the fisherman's body, many AC students were involved in a terrible national disaster that claimed the lives of 144 people, 116 of them primary school children.

On the morning of 21 October 1966, a coal slurry tip above the mining village of Aberfan slid down in a devastating avalanche that entirely smothered much of the village and, most terribly, its junior school. The village was less than 40 miles inland from St Donat's and volunteers raced to the scene from the moment they first heard of it. One teacher, John Grant-Wood, recalls driving straight from afternoon activities training Cliff Rescue to organising the periphery of the rescue site, directing traffic. Another, John Lipscomb, was put on watch against the danger of a second avalanche. It was, he remembers, a coming of age for the AC Cliff Rescue squad.

> At around 9.15 am on 21 October 1966, the most significant rescue event involving AC staff and students took place when a mining spoil tip at the village of Aberfan collapsed. It created a landslide of mud and slurry down from the tip straight into the top end of the village crushing the Junior school and part of a row of houses.
>
> The news took time to filter out but at lunchtime the College immediately sent a party from Cliff Rescue to give assistance. This was followed by a second group who followed in the early evening when the first party returned to St Donat's. These two parties joined a widely assembled gathering of volunteers digging to recover some of the bodies of the 144 dead (28 adults, 116 children) from the crushed site of the Pantglas Junior School.
>
> On arrival in the dark of that early evening, with this second group, we walked down the village street down into the Aberfan Colliery where we were issued with mining lamps and then were sent out to climb the mass of mud and fallen stones. By this stage all hope of finding survivors had been given up. I was chosen to take a klaxon and directed to a point just above the school on the track followed by the avalanche before it reached the school and the street of houses.

65. Rescuers at Aberfan.

The path it had cleared must have been some 50–100 yards wide at the point where it had impacted into the village, just missing a farmhouse which escaped. I took over as the safety watchman ready to sound the alarm as a warning for those digging in the rubble and ruins below in the valley. I was told to stay there until replaced and be alert to any sign of further land movement from above which would have taken more lives. I had no instructions what to do after sounding the alarm if movement occurred, but I doubt if I could have got off the trail of the slide had there been further movement.

I was very relieved when replaced at first light, mercifully having had to do nothing but keep watch over the remains of the tip behind me and those working below me who had been steadily recovering the crushed bodies of victims. We gathered the Cliff Rescue members and returned in the van to AC. As far as I know, no written record was kept of who had attended and what else students had experienced. I do recall that students in the van I was driving mentioned finding bodies during that night as we drove back to the College.

Among the students who responded to the callout was Howard Newby. He later wrote an account for the student magazine in the form of a letter home that illustrates the transformation from adrenalin rush to reality.

Dear Mum and Dad,

We've just got back from Aberfan. They asked for volunteers to sign up on Friday and we've been on standby over the weekend. The callout alarm went at about half-past six when most of us were in Cardiff, but they awoke the second shift at half-past one in the night.

It seemed quite good fun at first. It was a kind of adventure going out at two o'clock in the morning. It was exhilarating, tearing through the middle of Pontypridd with the siren going full blast and that orange light flashing. Weaving in and out of the traffic with a motor-cycle escort. [Editor's note: Newby acknowledges a degree of poetic licence in his account].

You can get some idea of what it's like from the papers and the television, but the vague, distant pity you feel is nothing like being there.

Someone gives you a shovel and you start digging. At first you are inspired by the self-righteous sense of 'doing something to help'. But soon you settle into a rhythm and become absorbed in what you're doing and the world around takes a few paces back. You just dig and dig. And your back starts to ache and your hands get sore, but you just dig and dig on. You forget why you are digging – it's just a battle with that thick, heavy, slimy black mound. It seems as though you're trying to empty the sea with a bucket. And you dig on.

Then you find a body.

A leg appears. Beyond, a twisted body. It's a little girl of six or seven – or maybe a little boy. You daren't look twice to check. Your guts contort and your eyes warm. What a waste. One moment she was a happy seven-year-old, surrounded by a world of dolls and hopscotch and helping Mummy. Now she's another slim heap under a blanket, retrieved from under two million tons of black mess.

You just dig on and on. Stabbing that stinking, black filth with every thrust. Then you realize the meaning of the 'cold light of dawn'. People drift aimlessly out of their houses, having snatched an hour's anguished respite. You can see more clearly those gaunt faces and glazed eyes. Numb. Dazed. Puzzled. You look away – it's too painful. And all of the time at the end of your shovel, that sea of mesmerised faces.

The workers are marvellous. The spirit dates back twenty years. It's the air-raids all over again. Tea. Soup. Cigarettes. And on and on you dig. And always those faces.

We packed up at nine. I found muscles I never knew existed. I don't know which was worse – working or stopping, allowing your muscles to get stiff and start throbbing. A cramped ride back in the rear of the Land Rover. No excitement this time. Just exhaustion and futility.

And sickness …

According to David Sutcliffe, the college recovered two bodies, of the 118 children and 26 adults who died (Sutcliffe and Philips 92).

* * * * *

Students responded to their encounters with death in very personal ways. Simon Daman Willems (1974–76) twice had to go through the experience.

> The most poignant was the tragic death of a young fellow lifesaver from the neighbouring beaches at Ogmore. The beaches there are beautiful; however, the immense tidal range of the Bristol Channel and the shape of the coastline can create notorious and unseen rip currents which will drag a swimmer out to sea or underwater faster than a fit adult can swim. Human reflex is to fight the current trying to reach the receding beach until exhaustion drowns you, rather than conserve energy and await rescue. The trained lifesaver, a local man, was on patrol there and spotted a swimmer in distress. He notified his colleagues and went to give aid. Somehow, he and the swimmer in distress did not link up. The distressed swimmer luckily reached the beach unaided. The lifesaver was lost from sight, and his concerned colleagues contacted the Coastguard for assistance. We were called out in B-508 and must have been at the location in maybe 20 minutes. We searched in a grid pattern and along the beach for several hours, I think until the light was fading and fuel running low, sadly unsuccessfully.

> Once we landed, still hoping that by some miracle the lifesaver had landed on another beach, one of the staff said quietly, 'In a few days to a week we will find him where he drowned,' which struck me as an odd remark at the time.

> Indeed, almost a week later we were called by the Coastguard. An object had been seen floating near where we searched. We launched and found a floating body, which was later confirmed as the lost lifesaver. It was a quiet and subdued crew that landed that day.

> Later in life I have sadly been witness to a few drownings and recall people's slightly odd reaction when without thinking I said: 'The body will float up here in about a week.' How did I know that, they asked? Experience, sadly.

For many of those involved, bringing the body ashore was not the end that they wanted or needed. Students reacted in different ways. Simon Daman Willems and his crewmates decided to make a public gesture of solidarity with the dead man and his family.

> A memorial service was held for the lifesaver a few weeks after the recovery. I can't recall if we asked the family and lifesaving club if we could attend, or that they asked us, it matters not, we did. As the lifeboat crew we knew no one there, we were in many ways intruders. Still, we stood with the family, seeing their despair, grief and could feel them clearly struggling to understand what had happened. I hope our presence gave some solace. We saw our fellow lifesavers from the club struggling both with the loss, and with 'what more could I have done?'. Myself, I felt a mixture of sadness, as well as anger that despite all our equipment and training the lifesaver had been lost. Oh, and the realisation that he was only slightly older than us, doing what we were routinely doing, and doing it without hesitation for his own safety. Did it change our attitude to launching in future? No, though it was a stark and tragic reminder that despite all that gear the sea is unforgiving.

*****

Unusually Simon Daman Willems, having done one recovery of a drowning victim, then was involved in a second callout also involving drowning victims.

> We launched to search for what the Coastguard euphemistically called 'Objects in water'. A short search found two bodies floating near each other which had been in the water about a week. The human body after a week in the sea floats very low on the surface and is heavy, stiff and slippery as well as being disfigured by water and fish. None of us had ever had to deal with this or trained for it. We had large plastic 'body bags', never thinking we would use them. How do we get the casualties over the quite high gunwales [sponsons or air tubes] of an Atlantic 21 lifeboat with dignity? You are caught between what you know you need to do, and too many horror movies of dark waters with bodies rising out.

> We couldn't just grab a boathook or tie a line around them and pull for fear of disfiguring or worse, dismembering them. One of the crew, I believe it was a Malaysian, Fahmi Salehuddin, volunteered to enter the water. He gently wrapped each corpse in turn, giving the crew something to lift. He also stayed in the water to lift from below. Incredibly brave, and his way of showing respect to the casualties.

> Once the boat was landed, in a very quiet Sea Area, the casualties were lifted onto stretchers to carry to the waiting ambulances. There was a final

moment for me of coming to terms with casualties. The stretchers had been placed across the boat so we could lift them over the bows. I was on the starboard side and another crew to port. At the moment of lifting, he lifted faster and higher than I did and the casualty came sliding out of the body bag feet first into my face.

To drop the stretcher or stand away would leave the casualty to slide off, naked, onto the ground. I lifted as hard as I could and slightly higher as the casualty slid back enough to stay on the stretcher and out of my face. We lifted over the bow, then pulled the bag to cover the casualty and handed over to the ambulance crews. That evening my girlfriend remarked I was very quiet and I mumbled something about never eating fish again, I was still dealing with the day.

* * * * *

Many of the recoveries were of suicide victims. Sometimes, though, they were tragic accidents. Wayne Brommell, a New Zealand student between 1975 and 1977 who was on the Coastguard squad, was involved in one tragedy where the rescuers knew before they left the college that their job was to be the recovery of bodies. An elderly couple had driven their car over the cliff.

I remember the callout well. It was on a weekend, a Sunday I think, but at Nash Point rather than Southerndown.

Anne Brearley [Coastguard instructor] drove us there in the Cliff Rescue Land Rover.

Four of us made our way with a stretcher round to the base of the cliff where the vehicle was lying on its roof. There were two occupants inside, an elderly man and a woman, and both were very obviously dead when we arrived.

Eventually it was decided that as the tide was low, it would be better to transport the bodies back to AC via ILB rather than stretcher to the top of the cliffs. So, someone had to remove the bodies from the car and place them in the stretcher.

Kiwis [common NZ slang for a New Zealander] are generally fairly practical, matter of fact people, so I stepped forward and so did Sally [a fellow New Zealander]. I was also the Vice-Captain of Cliff Rescue, so felt it was my responsibility to take a lead in this. Between the two of us, we managed to extract the bodies from the car, place them in stretchers, then assist the ILB crew to carry them out to the waiting boat.

Then it was back to college.

Later that evening, Graham Howells, my housemaster, made a point of checking how I was feeling, with the offer of a chat if I ever felt the need. I think Sister Stanley [school nurse] also approached me in the following days with a similar offer, although I didn't feel the need to take up their offers.

This may sound callous, but the experience didn't really affect me that much, or not that I know. When we came upon the casualties, it was very evident to me that they were dead – their souls had departed their bodies, and in that sense they were not really 'people' anymore. They really had passed on, so what had to be done was to deal with what remained. I remember thinking at the time the best thing I could do was to save someone else the unpleasant task before us by doing it myself, and to treat the bodies with as much dignity and respect as we could while doing it.

The way the rescue services were run and the ethos behind them at the time conveyed the understanding that in joining a rescue service, it was our job to deal with things like this when they occurred. This is what we'd signed up and practised for, so you just had to get on and do it.

Sally is one of the inspirations for this collection of accounts. David Sutcliffe always remembered her response to the tragedy of two old people apparently accidentally driving off a cliff after muddling the gears. She shaved off her hair and sat at the front of assembly until it grew again.

Students reacted very differently to their encounters with death. Like Simon Daman Willems, in a callout in 1988, Richard Thompson had to go in search of a body that had been in the sea for days.

I absolutely loved my time at Atlantic College. People sometimes ask me 'What was the best thing about it?' Getting to know people from around the world was wonderful, obviously, but being part of the ILB unit was something truly very special. Driving an Atlantic 21 inshore lifeboat in big seas easily ranks as the biggest adrenalin rush that I have ever had. It was like piloting your own rollercoaster. Knowing that your friends' lives were in your hands, just added to the experience. I am nearly 50 and I still miss it hugely!

By the end of my August period, I knew the B-boat manual inside out. Without fail, I signed up for weekend callout duty. I knew the exact time when the staff member was going to pin up the rota sheet on the Friday morning, and having checked the tide tables to calculate the time of the highest probability of a callout, would sign up for the premium slot. As a responsible crew member, I abstained from alcohol. Throughout the week, I always had one ear cocked for the wail of the callout siren in order to steal a march on everyone else sprinting down to the seafront. I could run from the top lawn to the lifeboat station, taking the steps four at a time, in well under a minute. I even practised. I even secretly hoped (half-hoped?!) that members of the public would get into trouble so that I could be involved in rescuing them.

The first callout I went on was on 23 October 1988. I had been waiting for the opportunity since I joined the ILB unit over a year earlier. I was confident in my abilities and this was the chance to demonstrate my professionalism to staff and my fellow students. It was also infinitely more fun being aboard an expensive, fast, inshore lifeboat with three of my mates than attending lessons!

Our job was to stand by while a team of Barry Coastguards retrieved a body that had been washed up on Porthkerry Beach a few miles east of Llantwit Major. It was high tide when we arrived. I rather suspect that the wily and experienced Coastguard unit decided that they would rather stay in their van than get their feet wet just in order to deal with a corpse.

We beach-landed the boat and, while Andy and Jan held it in shallow water, Mark and I headed off rather nervously along the beach in search of a body. Unsurprisingly, neither of us had ever done anything like this before. I recall gingerly prodding at large rocks with my foot wondering if they were parts of a dismembered corpse. After a while we spotted, and smelt, what we were searching for. We tried not to look, as the poor chap had clearly been in the water for more than a few days. That had not left him looking his best.

We unzipped the body bag length ways, placed it over the deceased and then rolled him into the bag. Zipping up the bag proved a challenge as his arm was sticking out at an angle. I tried to use the bag to manoeuvre his arm as we had not thought to bring any gloves and I really wanted to avoid touching him. Unfortunately, nerves got the better of me. My hand slipped and I inadvertently ended up putting my fingers into a large open wound on his arm. This was too much and I remember yelling out loudly in shock.

Mark was great. He quickly calmed me down and we got on with the task in hand – zipping up the bag. Our next problem was that he was too tall. So, with his legs dangling out the bag, we carried the corpse for 300 m along a rocky beach. We quickly learnt the significance of the phrase 'dead weight'. However, we managed. By the time we got to the boat, we had regained our confidence and showed scant sympathy for Jan and Andy who were quite shocked at the sight of two visible limbs.

Somehow, we finally managed to zip up the bag. We floated it out to the boat and rather unceremoniously pushed it on board. Three of us walked the boat to deeper water while Andy started the engines. We then hauled ourselves aboard and I managed to land on top of the body. The resulting squelch was not a pleasant sound. However, I am pleased to report that, this time, I avoided yelling out loud. And that was that. We checked in with Swansea Coastguard, sped back to college and landed the boat. Our staff members were rather concerned about our psychological well-being as I don't think they had actually expected us to have to do what we did. They repeatedly asked us if we were OK and told us that they were available if we ever needed to talk.

I saw Mark at lunch the next day. Both of us had been affected in a similar way. When we had woken up that morning, both of us had felt really ill. But both of us had forced ourselves to get up, go for breakfast and get on with the day. After that, I was fine.

The training we had received from the staff and our second years had been really first rate and this ensured we were able to respond in the way we did. I recall being really proud of what we had done. We hadn't saved the man but at least his family could now give him a decent burial. It is more difficult to remember how, or if, this callout affected me subsequently. I think I was already pretty confident but perhaps it made me realise I was more than capable of coping with challenging situations with the help of my friends.

Lorenz Breitfeld was at AC from 1991 to 1993. He was captain of Rescue Boats in his second year, and he came back for three more years to work at the Extra Mural Centre over the summer. He went on to train as a doctor and from 2008 to 2018 was a crew member on Austria's helicopter emergency medical service – both career decisions shaped by his experience at St Donat's. But despite his extensive experience since, he still vividly remembers a callout in June 1993, just after they had finished their final exams.

It was a hot morning – it must have been the weekend, as we had late breakfast. The siren went off at about 8.20 and we ran down to the seafront. On the way down from the castle one of the boat crew members (Jane Heaton or Annie Berube) met a man, wandering in the gardens. He did not belong to the College and was obviously exhausted, wet and not clearly orientated. He said something about that he was 'looking for his mates'. We did not connect him with the present callout at once. Only later, it became clear that he was one of the casualties. I don't know who initiated the search for the people and set off the callout in the first place. [According to David Cope, the distressed survivor appeared just as the Coastguard called with news of a sighting and was able to tell them what to look for.]

CHAPTER EIGHT: THE LOSSES

We were told that a small fishing vessel, called Emma Louise, which was out fishing overnight, had been stranded at Nash Sands. There were four people on board. It turned out that the boat was poorly equipped with lifesaving equipment and short of life jackets. The men had to leave the boat and swim for the shore. In retrospect, I am not sure whether all were able to swim. As we heard, one of the shipwrecked, the man in the garden, managed to get ashore at St Donat's. It is possible that the alarm was sounded as a result of his telling someone at the College about the shipwreck.

We launched the boat at about 8.30 [one of the strengths of the AC RNLI station was that the crew lived on the station which meant speedy response times]. I was coxswain, on board was also John Barr, Mathematics teacher, houseparent and member of staff, as well as fellow ex-students Annie Berube (she was vice captain of the year 1992–93) and Jane Heaton (also ILBs from 1991 to 1993).

The sea was calm, no wind, clear sky. A perfect summer day!

The tide was [coming] in and we started our search East of the College. Halfway between Llantwit Spit and St Donat's we saw a casualty floating. He showed signs of life and we got him aboard. We had been informed that there was an ambulance near Llantwit Major waiting at the beach and we dropped the heavily hypothermic person ashore and handed him over to the paramedics. He had drifted far. Nash Sands are between 8 and 10 nautical miles west of where we picked him up!

He and the other men must have been in the water for 4–6 hours, drifting with the tide. The water temperature was maybe 12°C, with a significant wind chill factor. [Predicted survival time in such cold water would be six hours at the very most.]

In the meantime, we heard a Coastguard helicopter also searching nearby. We continued our search and found a second body afloat. He wore a life jacket, [but] it was not put on properly – it must have been too small. We got him aboard and started with CPR. We informed the helicopter via radio and the casualty soon thereafter got winched up to the helicopter in a stretcher.

A few days, or maybe a week after the incident, two of the casualties came to the College to say thank you. They also informed us that one of their mates, the person we had picked up by the lifeboat and started CPR, sadly did not survive in the end. It was a very moving moment, to meet these two survivors and to be able to speak to them about their tragic accident.

The following month, the story appeared in the prestigious specialist paper, the *Times Educational Supplement*, with photographs and interviews with the two female crew members, Annie Berube and Jane Heaton. 'At 16,' the report began, 'Jane Heaton couldn't swim five lengths of a swimming pool. Two years later she played a crucial role in an air-sea rescue of three fishermen in the Bristol Channel.'

It was Jane Heaton who had tried to resuscitate the second casualty they pulled from the water, the one who failed to regain consciousness. Like other students, she found it a very difficult experience. But the impact of trying so hard to save life, and only partially succeeding, really hit home after two of the survivors came to the college a few days later.

> When I was told that the man I had tried to save was dead, I had cried. It was a way of letting it out. But it really hits you after. It was not just the fact of seeing them [at the college] but of realising what you have done.

The crew were each awarded a letter of commendation for their part in the rescue, with special mention of the standard of first aid.

* * * * *

The encounters with death, that experience of mortality and the understanding that life is fragile and precious often had a powerful and enduring impact on the students involved.

Eboo Versi, a student in Beach Rescue from 1969 to 1971, has never forgotten his first encounter with a fatality:

> It was early in my first year when we were called out to go to Southerndown Beach to participate in a rescue. It was exciting, we had had rudimentary training in resuscitation and the use of a kayak. Naively, I felt fully prepared to meet the challenge as I unloaded my canoe, actually technically a kayak, and carried it on my shoulder to the water.
>
> Apparently, a young boy, a teenager, had been trying to steal eggs from the nest of a protected bird on one the cliff to the west of the beach and had fallen. Our rescue boats had launched from the College seafront but it was thought that perhaps Beach Rescue should use kayaks to try to help.
>
> The only thing that was on my mind, as I walked barefooted over the stone beach to the water's edge, was how painful it was. Just eight years earlier I had been running barefooted around the streets of Zanzibar with my gang of young boys without it being an issue. I remember when I first came to

England, when challenged to a road race, I'd first remove my shoes. Now less than a decade later, the soles of my feet had become Westernised.

Before I got to the water's edge, one of our inflatable rescue boats had come close to shore and unloaded the injured boy onto a stretcher. A small party of students was carrying the unfortunate boy towards the awaiting ambulance. As they passed me, I saw that half of his head was missing but his face was intact, he was still alive. The scream started in my brain and then was vocalised. 'Why are you not giving him mouth-to-mouth resuscitation?' I followed the stretcher repeating this and becoming more hysterical and tearful until one of the teachers put his arm around my shoulders and said, 'It's too late.'

Of course it was too late, but I had never seen such a sight before. We were lucky. At that same time six and a half thousand miles away, boys of my age were seeing much worse in Vietnam. Did I suffer PTSD? No. I'd like to think in my second year I would have been more professional but despite being a part of many subsequent rescues, I never saw anything like that again. A decade later, as a doctor, I had patients die under me during a crash call on the ward or in the operating room with my hands in their belly but by that time I had learned to control my emotions and only let the anguish get to me when alone in the changing room of the operating theatre or in my on-call room.

Unlike a callout where a victim was rescued, perhaps badly injured but still alive, seeing death close up seems to have diminished ego and placed the rescuer in a broader context. Meeting death is not only their own subjective experience. It also belongs to the dead person and their family. Part of the rescuer's experience is the grief and loss that the bereaved suffer.

Richard Naylor, a student at the college from 1993 to 1995, then an instructor at the Extra Mural Centre, and finally on the AC staff, training coastguard and boat crews, found many students capable of great maturity and sensitivity. 'It's not true that all [later] students were less capable, or mature,' he says, 'there were some who would never have been in charge but others who were outstanding.'

The burden of the experience made some staff wary of involving students, and it sometimes put a strain on the idea of 'trained and trusted'. As an instructor, Richard Naylor was involved in one particular recovery of a suicide that stayed in his memory:

> My most significant 'shout' [callout] was in early January 2001, when I went out on a rescue boat callout to retrieve the body of a suicide. It turned out to be the body of the local TV news reader.

The inquest in June 2001 was told he had taken sleeping pills but left no note, although he had talked to a colleague on the phone earlier and told her he was suicidal [BBC news report 'Newsman']. Whether he intended to kill himself or not, his body had been found by a walker on the beach near Llantwit Major, where he lived.

An unusual aspect of the recovery was that the dead man's wife worked on campus as a Nursery School teacher.

When it came to going ashore, Richard went on his own to assess the situation. The two students who were also on the crew were instructed to stay put. 'One of the students expressed his disappointment. The other staff members thought it was just being gung-ho, macabre. I disagreed. We could have gone in together.'

* * * * *

Almost exactly 20 years earlier, in January 1981, Tim Haney had been faced with an even more deeply traumatic episode. The Coastguard Auxiliary were called out to a potential suicide off the cliffs at Nash Point. The rescue Land Rover was able to take advantage of low tide to drive to the foot of the cliffs. At that point there is no beach, only a pavement of flat rock. The clifftop, with the lighthouse, was 75 feet above them.

On the ground lay a young man. He was not breathing, and he was lying in a contorted position. But his forehead was still warm. They decided that they should attempt mouth-to-mouth resuscitation.

> Blood was coming out of both ears, nose and mouth. The face was really bad. I just gritted my teeth and started on the respiration. Snowy [Huw Lloyd Jones] was doing the compressions. I'd do one breath, he'd do five compressions. It went on like that. It seemed like ages because I was fighting sickness every minute. After a while I got used to it though, and it didn't bother me. They wanted to know whether someone else should do it and if I was getting tired or not. I just thought, if anyone else has to go through those first few minutes … it was horrible.
>
> We weren't getting anything. We had one person checking the pulse and I was watching the breathing after each breath to see if he was responding. No response. We went on and on. One of the times I came up, I asked a man standing by: 'Do you know him?' He said, 'I'm his father.' That really struck me. That made me just want to try so hard to bring him back to life.

66. The lighthouse on Nash Point.

After several minutes an ambulance arrived. The body was getting blue and cold. But Tim was reluctant to give up hope before the boy had been declared dead by a doctor.

> Then we just stopped. The other people told me, 'Cliff Rescue, you've done all you can.' We put the body on the stretcher and carried it up and put it into the ambulance. Terry, my friend, had his arm around the father and was trying to comfort him.
>
> It was a shocking experience, but it didn't shock me at that time. I couldn't think about it. I came back to the college and the whole call team went for a swim, which was kind of a crazy thing to do at a time like that. We went to evening class that night.

Tim Haney's life-changing experience was reported in a magazine called *Highwire*. There was a quote from an unnamed staff member, 'No matter how we see them as students, we stand in awe of them at times like this.'

The Coastguard concurred. In a letter to John David a few days later, the District Controller of the Coastguard LJ Kent wrote to praise his 'sterling efforts.'

> Mr Haney's efforts, under the conditions that existed, earned him the admiration of all present. Perhaps you would convey the appreciation of HM Coastguard to Mr Haney on my behalf and also to all who took part in the incident for the very efficient manner in which it was handled. Unfortunately on this occasion to no avail.

As a postscript, Jim Buckheit, the student from 1963 to 1965 who fell out with a teacher over how to conduct a rescue and who went on to spend his whole life in education, visited Kurt Hahn's first school Salem, in south-west Germany, in 2002, soon after students had been involved in the grim task of retrieving bodies from the scene of a plane crash.

> Part of the genius of the original AC model was our engagement in real work, which required real engagement with each other. There weren't many callouts, but the preparation was deadly serious, and the RNLI affiliation added credibility to the demands.

> I had an opportunity to observe directly a wonderful example of that Kurt Hahn tradition when I attended a Round Square conference at Schule Schloss Salem in 2002, just months after a mid-air collision over Lake Constance that took many lives, including those of 52 Russian children and teenagers.

> Many of the students in Salem's international college (the eldest two years) were members of the local volunteer fire brigade, who spent the night of the accident fighting fires and the following day recovering bodies from the lake.

> The school then offered its assembly hall as a mortuary, with students serving as hosts to the Russian parents who arrived to claim their children. I had the opportunity to talk with several of those students and was deeply impressed by the maturity of their reflections, in particular their appreciation for their training and for the responsibility entrusted to them.

> The recurrent lesson for me, dating back to our days at St Donat's, is the importance of getting students to take themselves seriously. That, of course, starts with the adults taking them seriously – our gift from Dr Hahn and Admiral Hoare. Not always comfortable, but definitely educative.

CHAPTER NINE

The Child

Beach Rescue could sometimes feel like a Cinderella service: it was not often needed on a callout to provide emergency help, like the Cliff Rescuers who were on the Coastguard squad, or the Inshore Rescue Boats, part of the RNLI. But lifeguarding is at least as much preventative as reactive, and it had an exceptional lifesaving record. However, its members too encountered death.

Paul Belcher ran Beach Rescue, or Lifeguards as he rebranded it in the 1980s, for 20 years.

> Several cases of Beach Rescue (renamed Lifeguard Service by me when I was chief coach), helping people in severe difficulties in the water, were because we happened to be in the right place at the right time. This happened with a regular kayak paddle when a boy was found in problems in the water off Llantwit Beach. On two different occasions a kayak trip finishing at Manobier in West Wales found swimmers in severe difficulties due to a rip current and were able to solve the problem. In the second case it was a family group of children and recognising the characteristics of people in trouble in the water greatly assisted.

67. Paul Belcher teaching kayak rolling.

The main service to the community that Beach Rescue provided was to run Lifeguard Patrols so that the public could use beaches and go in the water in a safe environment. Every afternoon during August Period a swimming area was set up on Southerndown Beach with a student captain in charge. The first aid hut was also manned. The aim was to keep it as a safe beach rather than have to do lots of rescues.

The main work was to provide advice, keep swimmers away from surfers and provide first aid. I am pleased that we never had a water fatality during all the combined hours that we looked after the beach. We had lost children to deal with, which came in two varieties, one where you had the child who had lost their parents and two (more worryingly) when you had the parents, but the child was lost. One problem was that you could never predict what the British weather was going to do and the patrol rota had to be set up beforehand. So some days the beach and thus the students were extremely busy whereas on others it was pouring with rain and there was hardly anyone there.

Other local beaches e.g. Llantwit and Ogmore, were patrolled at times when we had requests from the Surf Lifesaving clubs responsible for those beaches. Atlantic College was the first Surf Lifesaving club in Wales and was instrumental in the foundation of many of the others.

Beach Rescue never was a front-line callout service in the same way that ILBs and Cliff Rescue were. When the siren went, we did rush to the seafront in wetsuits and start tying kayaks onto the trailer. In many cases we then stood down as the boat was going to get there much quicker or the problem was halfway down a cliff. We were used in search situations with the boats out at sea and Cliff Rescue on top of the cliffs and us filling in on the foreshore on foot and next to the surf-line with kayaks. There were also occasions when we had to help recover bodies, often sadly due to suicides.

One of those occasions arose one day in early May 1978, in the neighbouring village of Llantwit Major where Stephan Barker and Phil Green, both at AC from 1976 to 1978, were two of the team. Phil Green tells his story:

Saturday May 6, 1978. 16:28. Callout to the cliffs near Llantwit Major.

I was in my room at Glover House when I heard the callout siren. I put on enough of my wetsuit that I could run, flew across the stile over the barbed-wire fence surrounding the field that was part of the college farm, and ran at full speed to the seafront while trying to get my arms into the wetsuit and zip it up.

At the seafront Alan Glanville, one of the teachers who led the Beach Rescue unit, had already pointed the van and trailer towards the road so we could dash out. As students in wetsuits showed up, he pointed a finger at the six students he wanted on the callout and said 'you' to each. We lashed our kayaks to the trailer, grabbed our life jackets, helmets, spray skirts and paddles and threw them into the back of the van, and climbed in.

As soon as we were underway Mr Glanville, normally upbeat and bright, told us nervously that a boy had fallen off the cliffs near Llantwit Major while collecting bird eggs. We listened in silence, our attention focused by the adrenaline running through our veins. Mr Belcher drove us through Llantwit, down Colhugh Street where a depression in the cliffs brought us right to the water's edge, and where a few people were assembled, looking east.

It was sunny, the tide was out and the sea was calm. We could see a small group of people a few hundred metres east of us at the foot of the cliff and were told by someone that that was where the boy was. With the tide out we had no need of our canoes, and we could walk there over the rocky shore with our stretcher.

We had had training exercises where other students played the role of victims. They were told how to act, had bloody make-up and plastic wounds applied to them, and lay amongst the jumbled rocks at the college seafront to mimic a disaster of some sort. When the 'victims' were ready, we had to run out and deal with them, while instructors watched how we performed. It was exciting, challenging and fun.

That was no preparation for seeing a young boy lying still, silent and distorted at the foot of the cliffs. A bit of blood had trickled from his ear but had stopped before it got far. The sight of him brought us all to a standstill, with the sound of the wind, waves and gulls in the background. We had been trained to patch up and rescue the living, not recover the dead. The medical doctor who had given us part of our first aid training told us we were not allowed to make a determination of life or death. It was obvious to us though there was no point in using our first aid training. After a short pause and moment of contemplation, we lifted the body onto the stretcher. We turned west and saw that an ambulance and a few more people had arrived.

As we walked along the shore towards the landing, I heard a man wailing. He was wearing a grey coat. He was looking up at the sky and crying in anguish, then bending over, head nearly between his knees, and sobbing, then looking up to the sky again, over and over. We continued walking towards the ambulance not knowing how to respond to this intense demonstration of grief. Stephan Barker, one of the students on the callout, said 'take off your helmets as a sign of respect, and stand at attention.' We instantly complied with his order, standing 50 feet or so from the father. We

68. An illustration by Thierry Green of his father Phil's experience,

then continued to the ambulance, helmets tucked under our free arms, to deliver the body to the ambulance.

I learned an immense amount about Stephan with that simple, sensitive gesture. We became lifelong friends and have called each other on almost a monthly basis across the Atlantic ever since (he lives in Munich and I near Toronto). We have paddled together in a variety of locations, including but not limited to the Hebrides and the Canadian Arctic. I frequently seek his advice on sensitive matters, as sensitivity to others has never been one of my strengths.

By the time we were back at the college and showered, it was dinner time. The siren ensures everyone knows there was a callout. By then they also knew who was on it. When I sat down among other students at one of the long benches in the dining hall, they asked me about the boy. 'He definitely showed signs of absence of life,' I answered, prompting a chuckle from them. These were the words the medical doctor had told us to use when a victim was obviously dead but we weren't allowed to say so. Nobody thought any of us would ever say them. We spoke about the incident from beginning to end. I didn't realise it at the time but being able to speak right away with peers who had been trained the same way I had, with whom I had practiced and paddled and swam in the ocean for nearly two years, was comforting. I suspect it would have been much harder to go home, alone, without anyone to talk, to joke with, and with whom to contemplate the callout and what we had been through. I remember that conversation, and the eagerness with which my peers engaged with me about it.

The image and cries of the anguished father have stuck with me all my life.

This is Stephan Barker's account of the same event:

These are my recollections of an incident in which I, as a member and instructor in the College's Beach Rescue, was involved. After so much time, many smaller details have now lapsed from my memory, but I have tried to remember what I can, in particular the strong impressions that remain of that sad day.

On a cool and cloudy Saturday in early May 1978, I had spent the afternoon preparing for the imminent IB Higher English examination paper. I remember having spent the afternoon working on my own in the small English department library in the AC languages blocks. I recall that I had been trying to memorise short passages from *Hamlet*, and late on in that exercise I studied the lines from the final scene of Act V where Hamlet says,

'… We defy augury. There's a special providence in the fall of a sparrow. If it be now, 'tis not to come. If it be not now, yet will it come. The readiness is all.'

It was late afternoon and I was packing up my books, when suddenly the callout siren sounded. I dropped everything and ran to the seafront where to my surprise it was Beach Rescue that were being mustered, not the 'usual' callout for ILBs. A huddle of the BR staff and student-instructors formed and I remember our head-of-service Alan Glanville announcing that a group was being formed for a callout to Llantwit Beach and him selecting the group. As with the others, he looked me straight in the eye, pointed his forefinger directly at me and called out, 'you!'

A short while later the members of our group were in a van pulling on wetsuits, training shoes and helmets.

I can't remember at what point it was made plain to us that there had been a fatality and we were going to recover a body. This was to be no rescue. As the van drove down towards the beach from Llantwit Major there was a thoughtful quiet in the group.

On arrival at the car park, we were told to take a stretcher and we set off to the west picking our way for some 300 or 400 metres over the polished limestone rocks of the rock beach. (These rocks are roughly the size of large watermelons or pumpkins.) We headed towards a small group of adults collected at the foot of the cliff at the west side of Llantwit Beach. As we drew nearer, I could see that among the group of adults there was a small figure lying on the ground near the base of the cliff. A boy of around 12 had been out searching for gull eggs at the top of the cliff and had fallen to his death. My gaze fixed on the boy. Slim, with longish fair hair, his face was devoid of life and his body appeared limp. The boy's body lying before us reminded me of the dummy on which we practised mouth-to-mouth resuscitation.

There was a wait of several minutes. I vaguely recall looking into the faces of fellow BR members trying to find solace in the eyes of others. But hardly a word was spoken by our BR group. In later years, Philip Green, my old friend and then housemate, asked me if I could remember the bitter sobbing of the boy's father who the men present were trying to comfort. I could not. My memories of that moment were filled with the lifeless features of the boy.

After a while, the boy's body was lifted carefully onto the stretcher and covered. Our BR group was then directed to carry the stretcher to the waiting ambulance adjacent the car park. We made our way back over the rocks. When it was my turn to take one of the handles of the stretcher, I remember how light the load felt and how carefully I looked at where I trod, fearful of slipping on the sea-polished rocks. We arrived at the ambulance and handed over the stretcher. A stunned silence prevailed for the journey back to College. For most of us it had been the first time we had seen a dead body, let alone that of a child.

After changing back out of my wetsuit, I headed down to the castle from my house as we had been informed that supper had been left out for us in the Dining Hall. It was by this time evening and the milky-grey light was darkening. I saw, approaching me from the castle, David Sutcliffe, the headmaster. He greeted and stopped me and asked how I was feeling. I answered something along the lines that I felt 'OK' and, in what I now see as an attempt to distance myself from what I had witnessed, I expressed the view that 'at least' things must have happened so quickly that the poor lad could not have known much about it. David paused. And then he gently but clearly said that the real point was the profound pain and loss that was being felt by the parents of the boy and his family now and for their whole lives to come.

It had been a day of events and impressions that I would never forget.

****

The encounter with death and loss and grief must have been all the more traumatic for its distance from normal Beach Rescue activities.

From the start, the local sea conditions had shaped Beach Rescue as much as they had the IRBs and Coastguard services. The surf, the tides and the currents made the waters both potentially treacherous and exhilarating for everyone who could get out on the water. Surfing in kayaks, on surf skis and in the surfboat Cabbage Tree II, which had arrived at the college from Australia in 1968, were all part of afternoon activities, a mix of rescue service and sport.

In the earliest days, as Rhodri Bradley-Jones explained, heavy and cumbersome wooden kayaks were the only available Beach Rescue craft. They needed both skill and strength to roll and were vulnerable on the rocky shoreline. By 1967, fibreglass kayaks had replaced them, and within a few years many students were making their own. Kayak lifeguarding was an important part of Beach Rescue until the late 1980s.

69. Kayak classic: the pop-out – an unforgettable experience.

In 1973, Assia Brandrup-Lukanow was very happy indeed when a kayak turned up as she tried to bring a stranded holidaymaker safely ashore at Southerndown.

When we had to choose our service, I had taken Beach Rescue as a service, not because I was a champion swimmer or kayaker, but more to overcome my own fears of being upside down in the water and things like that … and I did love the water and swimming, and I did not particularly like motorboats, so it would not be ILBs.

So, in the first year, we were trained by our second years – by Auke Koopal (from Holland) and Frants Bernstorff (from Denmark), and the teachers Alan Glanville and John Hemery. We had good first aid rescue training with trained actors making emergencies look really real, and we had also started giving swimming and kayaking lessons to children with physical/mental handicap, and children from disadvantaged families. (I actually think these were the best and most sustainable rescue operations we did, but that is another story …).

In any case, in August 1973, we were to be ready to patrol the beach at Southerndown, and to provide the life rescue services and beach supervision there.

It was the holiday period and weekend, and lovely weather, so the beach was really crowded, and there were about eight of us out there. One in the Lifeguard's seat, two in the middle of the beach, two out to the sides, and three out in kayaks.

Southerndown Beach had very big differences between high tide and low tide, so one of our main tasks was to walk to the edges of the beach and tell people to move back before the tide started turning, also because there were parts of the beach that were connected at low tide, but disconnected or even flooded at high tide.

We shared out the tasks, and I was to walk down the right side of the beach and warn people there to come in. When I had reached the end of the beach and had talked to everyone, and was about to turn back, a group of three people in their 30s to 40s approached me and said they had been having a picnic on a piece of higher land about five minutes away, and the husband of one of the ladies had not believed that the tide was coming in and had wanted to stay there. They asked me if I could go and convince him, as they were worried because he could not swim. I agreed and waved back to the Lifeguard's seat that I was going on in that direction and received an OK sign back (I don't remember who was in the seat then).

So, I walked on alone, and walked and walked – it was much further than five minutes. The tide had turned and was beginning to come in. Finally,

I found a man in his 30s, sitting calmly on a piece of little cliff, eating his picnic.

'We have to go,' I said, 'the water will soon surround this part here.' He was a bit scared and it took me a long time to convince him. Finally, he stood up and came along. By this time the water had risen higher, and we hurried along. But then we got stuck and could go no further, the water had come up, we had to swim along the cliff.

He was terrified. 'I can't swim,' he said. He was a big man, not light. I remembered all I could about rescue swimming, putting him on my side, and how to knock him out if he struggled too much against being towed. So, we agreed how to do this, I swam on my side and pulled him/held him as we had learned, but the waves were coming in with quite some power and kept pushing us against the cliff.

I could feel that I was beginning to get exhausted and of course this man was getting more and more frightened. I told myself not to panic, but I was dead scared. I hoped so much someone would come for us. Finally, I saw a kayak in the distance, it was Daniel Meyer, patrolling by kayak, maybe sent out to find us. I managed to wave. Daniel approached, and threw the line to tow us in.

We landed safely on the beach. Both my 'rescuee' and I were trembling with exhaustion. I think if Daniel had not found us in that moment or a few minutes later, we could have drowned both of us.

I remain ever grateful to Daniel for saving me/us, and to Alan, John, Frants and Auke for the great training that helped us survive.

What shocked me most was that the man then told us he was a sports teacher but had just never learned swimming.

The core of the service's role was the summer beach patrols at Southerndown and Ogmore. This was a job that required a completely different mindset to the high-adrenalin, fast-moving callouts that usually only involved the Rescue Boats, although on occasion it could be both. With a tower from which a member of the patrol scanned the sea, and flags marking the safe swimming area, away from the rips and from any other water activity, the beaches should have been safe. But, particularly because conditions could change with the tides, or the afternoon offshore wind, holidaymakers were often caught out.

Andrew Verrinder (1976–78) had a Southerndown experience that illustrates the varied challenges that lifeguarding entails, as well as shedding light on the contest between the services.

70. The beach at Southerndown at low water.

If you are not familiar with Atlantic College's Beach Rescue ('BR') unit then it's important to understand the significance to the BR teams of the August period patrols on Southerndown Beach. Choosing BR as a service brought with it the challenge that virtually all of the emergency incident callouts the College would ever experience would land on the ILB teams, with meagre pickings for Cliff and Beach Rescue. That didn't stop BR teams training as if the next thing to happen would be a boatload of surfers in difficulty, or – better still in our imagination – rescuing a boatload of ILBers after their boat capsizes in the surf!

One differentiator for BR was our role providing lifeguard services for the local authority at the very popular Southerndown Beach, a few miles down the coast from the College. BR recruitment was also undoubtedly boosted by the cool lifeguard shorts and the opportunity to wear mirror shades while we hung out around the lifeguard tower. Years before Baywatch, of course, but you get the picture.

The reality of the lifeguard patrols was mostly very un-Baywatch-like. The incident log in our lifeguard station at the head of the beach was rarely dusted off. When it was, it was mainly for bee stings, temporarily lost children and/or parents and unfortunately for clogs in the public bathroom.

CHAPTER NINE: THE CHILD

Occasionally there was real beach drama and, for those of you who know me, there'll be some incredulity that my name should be featured in a 'real' Beach Rescue incident. This is because I am not a natural swimmer, so I joined BR patrols as a trained first aider and was expected to stay dry. That meant I hung out mostly in the lifeguard station (handling the bee stings) while the real swimmers looked cool – and did their job – from the lifeguard tower further down the beach. So low down the lifeguard totem pole was I, that – on this day – even one of our team with a full plaster cast on one (broken) arm ranked ahead of me as far as the tower was concerned.

Southerndown is a large beach, and that makes it popular and attracts crowds. With the Bristol Channel's huge tidefall, and the beach's long and gradual slope into Dunraven Bay, most of the time there's a lot of easy-to-access shallow water beach and good surf. The tidefall, however, is a big deal – at the head of the beach there's a mass of large boulders which are reached, and sometimes covered, at high tide.

On this particular day, the tide had turned and the shallow grade of the beach deceived many beachgoers as the water raced up. It even caught our lifeguards on the hop, so they struggled to get the tower moved back up the beach. Back at the station, as the tide started to swirl around the first part of the rocks near us, I and a colleague noticed many beachgoers struggling nearby. Amongst them was a young boy – around 11 years old – who was manfully assisting his grandmother up and out of the water to safety.

To our consternation, having successfully done that, he turned around and waded back fifty meters to rescue the deckchairs, beach balls and other essential British beach paraphernalia that he'd left behind while wisely opting to save grandma first. Heavily laden, he started to struggle under his burden as the water rose quickly to his shoulders and beyond.

Having signalled to my colleague, I then blew my lifeguard whistle (for what purpose, I still don't know), grabbed a torpedo buoy and splashed into the waves in the general direction of the struggling lad. If you've ever tried to run over two-foot boulders submerged under three feet of swirling surf, you'll understand the challenge – and the risk. Eventually I reached the lad and spent an ineffective moment trying to encourage him to let go of his collected beach goods, all while we were being buffeted by the rising surf.

Evidently his grandma was a bit of a dragon, since he appeared to prefer drowning over letting her prize deckchair go. So I grabbed him, separated him from the deckchair, and wrestled our way back through the waves and eventually up to dry land. Having ensured he was fine, and reunited him with his grandma, they were excited when I was able to retrieve the deckchair as it washed up close by. I went back to assisting others and we eventually returned to the lifeguard station. There I found my colleague writing up the 'rescue' in the incident book. By her analysis – and she was, after all, a star witness – the rescue involved a 200-meter free swim on my part. Despite my protests, that's what ended up in the incident log. Thankfully those logs are lost to time. It would generally take me a week to swim 200 meters.

It does not take ace kayaking skills to save lives. Andrew Verrinder took some wider lessons away with him too:

> At the time, the amusement of my colleagues rather masked my thoughts. Nevertheless, what's stuck with me are a few truths: most importantly the power of the sea, even in shallow water a few meters from land. For that reason, we taught our daughter to swim as soon as we could. From the age of three she's been a fish, unlike me, and I'm happy about that. Also, deckchairs and the like aren't important when compared to things like grandmas and lads.
>
> Remember also that the first thing I did was to tell my colleague what I was doing. That was drilled into us – going into (three-foot deep rocky waters!) danger on your own just means two people at risk not just the original one in trouble. I've found that to be a good guide for everything. You don't see many lone lifeguards, and if you are planning a long life, shouldering every burden alone is a recipe for stress and failure.
>
> Oh, and – perhaps especially relevant in today's times of instant and often fake social media news – when it comes to incident logs or anything for that matter, don't always believe what you read.

Part of the skill of the good beach guard was to understand when swimmers were in, or soon to be in, trouble – perhaps before they did themselves. In the summer of 1974, Sten Hammarlund was on patrol. This is his laconic account of events that afternoon:

> I saved two small boys caught by the tidal current at the beach of Southerndown.
>
> That was during the August period in 1974. I was in Beach Rescue and standing guard at the east end of the beach. The current was to the east, so the tide was coming in. The boys were not so far out, so the whole thing went rather quickly. The mother was very happy.
>
> I was happy too, especially that I saw what was coming.
>
> It could easily have been missed, with rather different consequences.

Phil Green had a similar experience a couple of years later. This is from a letter he wrote home shortly after the event on 3 August 1977.

> Dear Everybody,
>
> Even though I haven't written before, I only have time for a small note – I'm just so incredibly busy. On Wednesday I saved 5 lives. At first 3 people were caught by the current and were being carried around a rocky point – I swam to them and pulled the mother around and talked her two children over. Then I helped them over the point and saw that two more people were caught by the tide. I swam out (with a torpedo buoy). A boy about 11 was swept onto the rocks by the waves and was badly scratched. I towed him off without myself being bashed by the surf and talked his sister to safety. Then I had to do first aid on the kid … 5 people saved – got one thank you from the mother of the boy who had gone on the rocks: 'that's his job.' When I was doing first aid on that kid another guy was caught by the tide and another AC student saved him. What a day that was!

Even 43 years later, Phil can still recall many of the details:

> I had been patrolling at the Eastern side of Southerndown Beach when I saw the mother and her two children. It was low tide, and it had just turned, so there was a current from west to east. The water was calm with a small swell. On the eastern edge of the beach is a promontory with a rocky outcropping called Witch's Point [see photo, page 65].
>
> The current came on suddenly, catching them by surprise and pushing them towards the outcropping. They weren't screaming or waving, I saw only the classic signs of swimmers in trouble – swimming hard but not well, not making any progress, heads low in the water.
>
> When we were on patrol, we carried flags and whistles to communicate with other Beach Rescue students who were also patrolling the beach, to ask for help and direct efforts. Before I rushed into the water, I raised one flag and moved it in a circle above my head, pointed the other in the direction of the swimmers, and blew my whistle. The student in the portable tower saw me, and with similar signals instructed a third student to paddle over in her kayak to give me support. As I swam I saw that the paddler could not find me and had turned back to the centre of the beach. I was on my own.
>
> When I towed or talked them to safety, I took them to the eastern side of the outcropping, and then helped them scamper over it and back to the beach.
>
> It seemed to me that there had been a major failing in our rescue. There

were many students on the beach, but I was left to rescue them on my own. I did not want to point fingers at anyone so I kept my silence, but I had hoped that there would be some kind of debriefing. There wasn't. The day after, Alan Glanville, the teacher in charge of Beach Rescue, bumped into me somewhere on the college grounds and said simply, 'I'm glad you were on patrol at Southerndown yesterday, Phil.'

CHAPTER TEN

Reflections

There is no real test for Kurt Hahn's belief that some kind of muscular morality could be imparted by the practical experience of being on a team that was helping others at some personal risk. Thankfully, few AC graduates have returned to countries run by genocidal demagogues, although many have had much harder experiences than getting scared, cold and wet in the Bristol Channel.

Often, when people look back on their time at school, it is individual teachers who stand out as important influences. This was surely as much the case at Atlantic College as anywhere else. But the AC experience was unique, and for some people what happened in those two impressionable years somewhere on the journey between adolescence and early adulthood had a powerful impact.

Dagfinn Paust, for example, who had to fight to save the life of a boy in terrible conditions of Nash Point, found it a formative experience:

> I kept in touch with David Sutcliffe on an irregular basis over the years – remembering when DBS as college principal had been preparing himself for having to inform this student's parents that he was missing at sea.

> I was honoured when my old headmaster and Rescue Boat chief asked me to help write this book, shortly before he died.

> To wind down after the harrowing experience at Nash Point after we got back to our dormitory, Walter [his roommate and part of the Beach Rescue team that night] and I sat up talking all night till the early hours, still in our rubber wetsuits. After that, the evening's events were hardly discussed more than once or twice over the following forty years, until Walter came up from Austria to my home in Norway for dinner with my wife and two grown sons. Then the whole story was revisited. My wife had been aware of the general story the whole time, because one of the first things I did when I first met her (boating in Norway), one year after Atlantic College, was to take her to the college and to the cliffs at Nash Point to tell her about this remarkable event.

> The training was possibly a reason for our ability to deal with the events in retrospect. We were trained, a bit like firefighters living above the fire station. Thus, to us, what we did was only natural. This attitude, like the Boy Scouts' motto 'Be Prepared', was not drilled into us, but absorbed as if through osmosis.

Everyone just got on with their lives – probably feeling that they had tried to do their best in a difficult situation for which they had been trained, adequately or not.

One aspect of this should not be underestimated, and that is the close bond that developed between students, rescue service leaders and their staff coaches, as David Sutcliffe alluded to above. Although I hardly spoke with him about the events at Nash Point over the ensuing decades, except in very general terms, the two of us shared both the experience and the relief that David did not have to telephone my parents with bad news. While probably not many students received a hug from their headmaster, I did that night on the landing trolley!

Andreas Schwerdtfeger was one of the very first intake of students, in 1962. He does not recall the broader ambition of the rescue services. But it turned out that they were an important preparation for his career.

I was among the first generation of AC students in this completely novel experiment of teenager education. Under Admiral Hoare as Headmaster and his staff, there was then (at least in my memory) very little talk of 'international understanding' of 'leadership' and 'teamwork' – we were trimmed more towards practical doing instead of theoretical discussion in the field of the College's activities. This is not meant as a judgement. I mention it more to illustrate that we never really thought much about our joining in these activities as a step towards certain qualities in later life.

For us it was necessary and much wanted physical exercise as a counterweight to the academic side of the College; it was for most of us a completely novel experience given the fact that our schools before AC obviously didn't offer such opportunities; and it was a great adventure. I will admit to you that I never thought about 'responsibility' when doing my job as coxswain, I never thought of myself as the 'master' aboard – we were instead a team of friends in happy circumstances and just enjoying the sport. Of course, we were serious about the task we had but we did not lift it to a theoretical ideal.

After AC I joined the German Armed Forces as a career soldier and officer. My experiences from the two AC years were, of course, a good preparation and helped me both physically and mentally in this career. What had been fun and adventure in school times became serious responsibility in my service life. But at the time we were low on theoretical idealism and high on practicalities. If my participation in the boating activities taught me one thing for life then it was that good leadership includes trust and confidence in your team and your subordinates and that 'meddling' in their responsibilities is not a good idea.

I know that after my time, the idealistic course of active representation of the College, both within its walls and towards the outside, as an institution of 'international understanding and co-operation' became more prominent – and, of course, I do not criticise this in any way. But in my time, I believe, we just accepted that as 'obvious' and got on with our business.

Paul Belcher, who worked as Beach Rescue instructor from 1975 to 2018, strongly believes that the nuts and bolts training he did with students would also change the way they looked at the world.

I have always hoped that Lifeguard training would be a training in attitude for life. If an ex-student ever came across others in difficulties in life then I hope that they would step in and do what they could to assist, rather than just be a bystander. We have had numerous cases of feedback from ex-students who have been able to use their training to assist people in dangerous water conditions and to employ their resuscitation skills. Ex-students have set up Lifesaving organisations in their own countries, e.g. Japan, and there have been many examples of initiatives designed to help others.

Another long-serving teacher, Ivar Lund Mathiesen (at AC 1974–1987), also saw practical training as foundational for the students' futures:

I think the most valuable result of the unit's existence for the AC students was the practical training, exciting experiences, the building of self-confidence by tackling difficult situations, and the lasting friendships that developed in and around this amazing group of people at this amazing school.

Assia Brandrup-Lukanow is now a distinguished specialist in tropical diseases and international public health. She drew enduring lessons from her experience of rescuing the holidaymaker from the tide on Southerndown Beach in 1973 when she came close to getting into trouble herself.

First, I never forgot it because it was a near miss.

Second, I learnt that I was stronger physically than I thought I was – and that learning the right techniques/skills to solve a problem helps.

Third, most importantly, I learned that thinking you can manage something alone when in fact you can't do it without others/a team, brings you and others into danger. That goes for physical danger, political danger, psychological danger.

Perhaps that experience contributed to my becoming more of a team player than an individualist, and certainly helped me, when I was in leadership positions, to convince others that it's better to tackle a task together, even if you sometimes think you will be faster alone.

Etienne Grall, who was in Cliff Rescue 1976–78, has also been influenced by the importance of the team, and of shared responsibility:

> A few decades on, what do those years mean? The first word that comes to mind is responsibility. At 16 and 17 we were given responsibilities that I never dreamt of taking before. The style of supervision was very empowering, in stark contrast to my previous academic and hierarchical education experience.
>
> It taught us several key lessons: think straight, take charge, collaborate. But also know how to find the right dosage between trusting your own capabilities and trusting others. Have I always been able to consistently apply those skills? No. Have those lessons stayed with me to date? Absolutely, and I sometimes surprise myself thinking: what would my younger self have done in these circumstances? As if to underline that, at 17, we were developing a form of wisdom that can only come out of exceptional circumstances.

One student from the early years, John de Blocq van Kuffeler, still marvels at the scale of the challenge they faced with such enjoyment:

> Today, I am amazed that at AC I was never daunted at the enormity of the responsibility or phased by rough weather or difficult conditions. Instead it was a skill which I enjoyed applying to difficult situations. As a child, my heroes had been the legendary captains of the Dutch lifeboats which operated from the northern string of islands and I devoured every book and publication about them. So for me, it was a genuine calling and becoming a coxswain will always rank as one of my highest achievements.
>
> Returning after a callout, I was mostly able to return to my studies or other normal activities – though I do remember choosing to go to the AC film night to cheer us up after picking up the dead body, but we were fine by the following morning.

Gerhard Robbers, another Dutch student, found being on a rescue boat in a position of responsibility an important but not a transformative experience.

> I was not one of the cool and in people at the college and certainly not in Rescue Boats. And yet, Rescue Boats were, together and deeply interwoven with the College's international atmosphere, the very heart of my Atlantic

College experience. They have accompanied me all my life, and I am grateful for all this.

Was it useful in my life? Sure. Learning a foreign language, experiencing the equality of people from all those different cultural and political backgrounds, mastering new challenges. But then again: Does it have to be useful, applicable? It is just a part of my life, a wonderful part. During the Six-Day War between Israel and Egypt in 1967, I have seen Israeli and Arab students going out in rescue boats working together saving peoples' lives. I have seen students from different sides of the iron curtain becoming friends.

Being a German I was and I am so grateful to have been welcomed by the Jewish family of a friend from Atlantic College, a family who had suffered from Nazi terror, and I was and I am so grateful to have been welcomed by the Welsh family of a girlfriend whom I found near the College, a ship owner family who had lost their fleet in the First World War and had lost their fleet again in the Second World War.

To me, Atlantic College is friendship, peace, knowledge and challenge – and, mind you, a whole lot of fun. It's just the good side of life.

*****

For others, it was the experience of teamwork under pressure and the weight of responsibility. Richard Thompson and Simon Daman Willems were at AC more than a decade apart, but they took away the same intensity of experience. First Simon:

> Like most of us, apart from the friendships and people, my strongest recollection and the greatest impact on my life from Atlantic College was my time in the Lifeboat corps. The College, led by DBS (as he was usually known in hushed terms), gave us incredible responsibility and trust. I, like many, rue the day that today's Health & Safety Culture took over. We would never have had that opportunity to learn what it really means to balance risk and safety, teamwork and leadership, heroism and good sense without him.

Richard Thompson, who started in 1987, would not have known David Sutcliffe – he left to start the new United World College at Duino in Italy in 1982 – but he had the same sense of a bond with his contemporaries as Simon.

> Last summer, I chatted to some of my fellow ILB-ers at our 30-year reunion. We all had this bond of shared experience. We had all been part of a very close-knit team. We had entrusted each other with our safety and had handled being given a great deal of responsibility at a very young age. That

was our connection. We didn't really speak about it, but the bond was almost tangible. And for us, that was the legacy of being part of the ILB unit.

Part of the strength of the team comes from the shared experience of fear. Matthew Goodman (1976–78) learned that there was such a thing as mortality:

> I'm not sure I can honestly say that the ILB experience 'changed my life.' But it did have a significant impact on me in at least two ways. First, it gave me my first exposure to real physical danger and helped me manage the fear that comes with that. Like all young people, I thought I would live forever when I was 16 but being out in rough seas on a callout was the first time I saw the possibility of my own mortality – or at least I can see that now in hindsight. I also saw a dead body for the first time while on ILB duty. Those experiences helped me begin to cope with fear and death later in life, as one inevitably has to do.

> Second, being on callouts with classmates of all nationalities and backgrounds helped reinforce the UWC mission for me in a very tangible way. When you're working together on a shared objective in a high-stakes situation – as lifesaving surely is – you lose all interest in, or even awareness of, your fellow crew members' backgrounds; all that matters is the task at hand and who is doing what to get it done. I often find myself, even today, citing ILB callouts as a vivid example of what makes the UWC experience unique.

Dezsö Horvath (1983–85) – who was on the night mission to try to save fishermen from a boat that had sunk – calls these 'transferable' experiences now he's looking back from a land-bound chemistry lab. But it was not all about the adventure:

> Ever since I left AC, I have a 'terrestrial' life, yet I have gained a lot from those two years spent at the unit. Looking back, it seems that incredible responsibility and power were given to us at the age of 18. I am happy we did not mess it up.

> Personally, the most important effect came from being a captain of a boat, through which I learned how to lead a small group of people, how to handle their personal problems, how to bring out their best. This has helped me when I was the head of the Chemistry Institute and I hope it will when I start my duties as dean from this July.

> Sea-going often required quick decisions, and the ability to make them comes in handy in our lives. The idea of doing a service did not really come

through in my mind the way I hoped. Signing up for weekend cover did not give the impression that I actually do a service. During that night callout, in the end we only 'recovered a body' as the log said, I did not feel the success of the service. So at first I myself thought that I got more out of that adventure than I actually put it in return. Now I believe that being ready and handing on the knowledge to the next generation were also part of the service.

Morgyn Warner was on the same callout, and also found it revealing.

I remember being nervous and full of adrenaline when running down to the boat in the early hours of that morning, worried that I would forget something or wouldn't get something right. But once in the midst of the callout, there was no time to worry and we were all focused on finding the sailors.

While my memories of this event have faded somewhat now, it was something I thought about and relived for many years. I wondered at the time if there was anything we could have done to save the man we picked up. Years later, once I trained as a doctor and had to resuscitate others, I realised that there was nothing we could have done to change the outcome in this case. All of us who were on the callout were very proud to have had the chance to participate in a rescue and put our training to use and prove our capabilities.

Looking back now, it is amazing to think that we, as 18 and 19 year olds, were given such responsibility and I am glad that we were. I think the preparation to be an ILB crew member taught me resilience, tolerance of physical discomfort, teamwork and in the context and spirit of Atlantic College, brought people of very different backgrounds together to focus on a task [with] the secondary benefit of letting people get to know others they might not ordinarily have met.

My time at Atlantic College was an amazing experience and being part of ILBs was for me an important part of that and this callout was an event I will never forget.

Other people also found that the whole experience confirmed or exposed something about themselves that they were able to draw on later, like 'Freddie', Winifred Ann Lloyd-Smith, the Canadian swimmer involved in two demanding ILB callouts in 1973–74. She became an anaesthetist.

I think the rescue consolidated my ability and passion for rescue and using skills to cope and resolve emergencies, proving I had the 'stomach' and poise to do this kind of work. I went on to view anaesthetists as the ultimate rescuer/resuscitator plus it was portable so this all ties in at least in my mind. Interestingly with this COVID-19 situation, I find myself once again revisiting my 'rescue' instinct: anaesthetists are considered the airway experts and tend to be at the forefront of intubating patients, the mantra being that the most experienced practitioner should be doing these most risky procedures. While many of my anaesthesia group (I am Chief and Medical Director of Anaesthesia at my hospital) have been reluctant to expose themselves to this risk, I have wanted to be directly involved, doing my thing, doing what I have always wanted to do! I have decided rescue and/or adrenaline rush is in my DNA and is just part of my fabric and will always be there it seems.

Phil Green (1976–78) also took home with him the traumatic experience of the death of a child and the devastation of a parent, in a way that he perhaps would have preferred to avoid.

About five years [after leaving AC], I took up a position at Dalhousie University in Halifax, Nova Scotia. I had learned to scuba dive at Atlantic College and immediately joined the Dalhousie scuba club on my arrival. My first – and last – dive with the club ended in catastrophe.

I became separated from my dive partner in the murky water and surfaced. A few dozen metres away was another couple of divers, one of them screaming, the other immobile. I ditched my dive gear and swam over to them. 'Danielle is not breathing,' she screamed, as she hopelessly tried to stuff her scuba mouthpiece in Danielle's mouth. I immediately started mouth-to-mouth in the water and pulled her closer to shore as I did so. By then the lady minding the tender, a small rubber inflatable, heard the commotion. She motored over and we lifted Danielle into it. I performed CPR while she drove us to the village where we were able to call for an ambulance. Danielle did not make it, she died of a massive air embolism.

A few days later a man knocked on the door of my Dalhousie office. It was Danielle's father. He spoke to me in heavily accented English; I recognized he was from Quebec and responded in French in which I am fluent. He wanted to see where his daughter had died. I dropped everything and agreed to accompany him there, a 40-minute drive. We hiked to a hill overlooking the bay where she had died. He looked over the bay for a few minutes, said 'merci', and turned back. We exchanged contact information. My wife was pregnant at the time. When our daughter was born a few months later, we gave her the middle name Danielle so that her name would live on. Every year for 30 years, on the anniversary of the accident, I sent Danielle's father a card and photo of our daughter and continued with email. He always responded, and sometimes sent small gifts to her. I believe that my experience on that rocky Llantwit Beach had moved me to do whatever I could to assuage Danielle's father's – and mother's – grief.

The question of how the AC experience can be carried into the future has many answers. But the one that is perhaps closest to mirroring the original Hahn and Hoare ideals is Atlantic Pacific, a sea rescue project that uses RIBs and some of the same rescue techniques that were developed over half a century at St Donat's.

Eleuthera du Breuil (2001–03), one of the youngest ever RNLI helms and still an active RNLI volunteer, also works with Atlantic Pacific.

> Being on call for the 2nd year of AC gave me a sense of duty and a certain amount of nervousness, I think. At first, I could never fully relax knowing that at any moment I could be called to go out into conditions that most people wouldn't dream about.
>
> After a while, after I became more confident of my abilities and the abilities of my fellow crewmates, through continuous training, I relaxed and felt more secure in knowing that we could deal with most things. It never left the back of my mind though.
>
> I think that amount of responsibility at such a young age can mature a person quicker than normal. That might be beneficial to some people and detrimental to others. I found I flourished with the responsibility, as Hahn had intended. I relished the opportunity not only to serve my community but also to be able to pass on the excellent training to my first years that I had received.

71. Ella du Breuil at the helm with an all-female crew.

Everyone grew up fairly quickly at AC, the atmosphere and the academic challenges and social situation saw to that. Not every ILB member was chosen to be part of the RNLI crew but those that weren't were given the opportunity to still serve their community by training the first years and doing safety boat cover for the sailing activity. I felt that those of us on the lifeboat crew and in the other rescue services grew up a little quicker, at least once they had figured out the risks and responsibilities that they faced.

I have been involved in the RNLI since my 17th birthday and am still an active crew member on the Chiswick lifeboat. In addition to that I have volunteered with a charity acting as a search and rescue asset on the north shore of the Greek island of Lesvos, providing safety for migrants crossing in dangerously flimsy and overloaded boats from Turkey to the EU. I am also the chief instructor for Atlantic Pacific, a charity started to provide lifeboats where there are none and to provide training for crew going out to act as search and rescue operatives in the Aegean and Central Mediterranean migrant situations.

My time at AC definitely instilled in me the concept of service. Service to your community, and to humanity. Not only that, I feel it instilled in me a knowledge that I could do pretty much whatever I put my mind to. That feeling gave me a confidence to face the rest of life that I am not sure I would have had if I had not first discovered it when cold, wet, scared and loving every moment of my time on the treacherous Bristol Channel.

Merel van Slageren, one of Ella du Breuil's contemporaries, has found the experience of learning how to do inherently dangerous tasks as safely as possible shaped her in ways she did not at first understand.

The ILBs/RNLI at AC – where to begin? Looking back, I think it taught me things that I have only recently started to realise I learned. Very broadly speaking they are related to self-confidence and self-knowledge, and I have an anecdote for both.

Regarding self-confidence, I vividly remember being out on a B-Boat training session with my houseparent Graham [Smith], who was a helm. I'd come on to the helm in order to park into the trailer. It was a bit choppy but nothing serious, nevertheless: Graham kept giving instructions about what I was to do and I kept messing it up. After a few attempts and in slight panicked frustration – it was after all one of the more precarious moments of training, Paul [Dowling, the RNLI mechanic and instructor in charge of the lifeboat house] was watching from the trailer tractor and the rest of the crew were having to wait until I'd managed to get this done – I edgily told Graham to 'just … let me do this. I can do this, let me try by myself.' 'Fine.' And he sat down on the sponson and said nothing more. I approached again and much as I could see him frowning from the corner of my eye I parked safely, smoothly and in one go. I learned that although my ways might be somewhat unorthodox at times, if I believe I can do something and I have the confidence to request the space to do it, my way is no worse than any other.

Self-knowledge took a bit longer to come by, but it has influenced decisions I have made since then. I think in August period, the then second years chose a Captain, a Head of ILBs, a Head of Maintenance, etc. I had my heart set on Captain, for various reasons. I was elected Head of Maintenance, and in brutal truthfulness: I was disappointed. In hindsight my peers knew me better than I knew myself; over the years I have ended up, and in some cases fought for, a maintenance role, notably on the committee for the student rowing club I was part of. The safety and longevity of equipment is essential, whether in sport or in rescue, although admittedly the latter has higher stakes of course. The importance of replacing a seal on a drysuit perfectly had as much to do with working to the highest possible standard as it did with the safety of the crew member who was wearing it, in replacing or fixing engine parts precision was paramount. As I said, self-knowledge about how my approach could make a difference came later, but I think perhaps in this fastidiousness my crewmates saw a safety – no small importance, in a rescue service – that I was maybe not always as aware of at the time.

Being part of the ILBs definitely changed me, and it is sometimes good to reflect on that. Having a pager made me feel responsible but showed me I do well in positions of responsibility. Consequently, I see I have taken on more positions of responsibility and leadership that I would otherwise have done. Being part of a crew showed me I don't always have to be captain to still fulfil an important role, and I see I have taken on supporting roles as well that play to my strengths sooner than taking a leading role that would have left me out of my depth. Finally, knowing there is more than one way to do something right has given me the confidence to suggest a squiggly line when the straight one keeps encountering an obstacle. I am still uncovering the value of the lessons I learned then for my life now.

Dave Nockels, who was at AC between 1969 and 1971, also found it a life-changing experience. Despite having grown up landlocked in central England, he became one of the most competent boat handlers of his generation.

My time at AC was probably the most significant two years in my life. Looking back now, I can see that what I learnt and experienced at AC had a major effect on what and how I did many things subsequently.

My career took two paths: working as a risk management engineer/ inspector in high hazard industries such as chemical plants, offshore oil and gas; and subsequently as a professional helicopter pilot working for the UK emergency services.

The way I approached risk management was quite different from many safety professionals. In my experience, much of 'health and safety' involves trying to stop and restrict things. This contrasts with risk management which is focused on managing the risk: a different perspective.

Working as a pilot for the emergency services had some obvious similarities with rescue-boating, with the same fundamental rewards of helping to save people's lives. Rather to my surprise, I have found the most satisfying part of flying proved to be instruction. As at AC, one of the best aspects was training the 'first years'.

The lessons I learnt at AC have been used countless times in what followed.

CHAPTER ELEVEN

Fifty Years On

The rescue services ideal was at the heart of Atlantic College. The mission was to offer arduous, exacting training that would prepare ordinary young men and women to do extraordinary things – to take responsibility for saving human life, and to judge when to risk their own. It was this that had inspired Kurt Hahn, Desmond Hoare and David Sutcliffe, and the teachers and students that they attracted to the college from its inception. For 50 years, from 1963, when lifeguarding began on neighbouring beaches and the RNLI first invited Atlantic College to take part in its experiment with inshore rescue stations, to 2013 when the RNLI station – the last of the rescue services to survive – finally closed, the ideal endured. And then, although some lifeguarding duties continue, it was over.

So how did it happen, this apparent rupture between the Hahn belief that 'the passion of rescue releases the highest dynamics of the human soul' and the College it had founded? Because the evidence of that first iteration of it has gone, it is easy to think the ethos has gone too. But perhaps it has not ended at all, merely adapted and evolved to re-emerge in a form that meets the needs of students in the 2020s.

The story of AC's rescue services falls into three time periods: 20 astonishing years of growth and innovation; another spell of consolidation and professionalisation; and finally, the slow decline as most of the obligations of the Beach Rescue service were ended, then the Coastguard station closed, and finally the RNLI inshore lifeboat station itself was shut down.

The first two decades were years of strong and committed leadership and energetic engagement, at a time when the coastal rescue ecology was in its infancy. The times were ideal for the pioneering integrated services that Atlantic College aspired to provide. Yet it was always a dynamic, changing environment. Nothing was fixed, and three particular developments were already leading to the evolution of the college's ambitions.

The first was its own success in spreading the idea of training young, local people to provide lifeguards on busy beaches. As early as 1969, a Welsh national training centre that had begun in the Extra Mural Centre at AC was established at Aberavon, advancing Desmond Hoare's ambition to develop a national service that would offer school leavers and pre-university students opportunities similar to Voluntary Service Overseas and the US Peace Corps. But its success removed AC from its centre.

The second development was the steadily increasing demands of academic work. The International Baccalaureate, which was introduced in 1972, had attracted Admiral Hoare's ire from the start. He always believed that character and practical skills were as much a part of the developed individual as academic qualifications and he feared that, whatever its merits for an international sixth form college that was in the business of educating pre-university teenagers from all over the world, the IB would simply demand too much of the students' time.

That was clearly not true: for years after its introduction, students who were committed to the rescue services continued to find many hours a week to devote to training and various forms of boat and kayak building and maintenance on top of their studying. But academic performance can be measured, and alongside the demands of the IB, the entrance standards for the best universities steadily rose – together with parents' expectations of and involvement in their children's education. In an ever more competitive world, the results of these exams slowly but inexorably came to be taken as the measure of success. The impact of the services and their role in developing rounded human beings with a robust sense of right and wrong is much harder to estimate, and there was no comparator against which it might be assessed.

The third development was the unintended consequence of a change that appeared to be entirely for good: the culture of safety. Safety was something about which Hoare cared greatly and thought deeply (contrary to the impression left by some of his decisions on some of his students). In 1966 he had prepared a long paper for the Chairman of the Outward Bound movement with what David Sutcliffe described, in his portrait of the Admiral, as a 'comprehensive review and critique' of accident investigation for sports casualties and near misses. In 1969 his authority was recognised when he was invited to join the RNLI management committee. It is obvious from his time as headmaster of Atlantic College that he was not interested in stopping students engaging in risky behaviour. Only think of what became known as 'Black Thursday', the 1965 incident involving several sailing dinghies and the college rescue boats (see Chapter 2). But he did not think safety was a matter of chance. Rather, independent investigation of accidents and national standards of safety were the foundations for the successful management of risk.

Clearly that did not preclude what nowadays looks like a dangerously high level of risk tolerance, with no evidence of a corresponding level of accident investigation. Yet the culture did change, as two near disasters, 20 years apart, may illustrate.

In the 1969 promotional film, *A Place in the World*, which opens with the emergency call to the college described earlier, the centrepiece is a mock-up of a rescue of a rock-climbing accident victim. The film shows glamorous images of rescue boats soaring over the Bristol Channel waves, while the Cliff Rescue Land Rover races to the top of the cliff below which the 'accident' had taken place. Peter Jolley's elaborate tripod and crane is swiftly erected and two rescuers descend the rock face while the boats stand to off shore. The 'casualty' was a Swedish first-year student called Anna Dixelius. This is her story:

> I started at Atlantic College in the fall of 1968. I was 16 years old and did not speak English well.
>
> Approximately six weeks later, I arrived for a regular Cliff Rescue session and found a film crew there. They were preparing to stage and film a mock rescue that afternoon. I had never seen a rescue and heard nothing about a film until then.
>
> When I arrived, someone said, 'Why don't you play the victim? We need someone slender. You're slender, would you do that?' I agreed. It all happened very fast.
>
> They put some bloody make-up on me and positioned me at the bottom of a cliff. The Cliff Rescue crew set up the crane at the top of the cliff, while being filmed. Two students abseiled down and secured me to a stretcher, with a helmet on my head. Then we started up, one student on either side of the stretcher, which faced away from the cliff. When we were partway up the cliff, I heard a call from above 'rocks falling.' Normally in this situation the climber would flatten herself against the cliff, hoping the rocks would fall over and past her. Of course, I could not do this. A rock hit me, knocking me out. I woke briefly in the ambulance on the way to the Bridgend hospital.
>
> My 5th, 6th and 7th vertebrae had been compressed by the force of the falling rock. I also had a small vertebra fracture. I stayed in hospital for a few weeks, perhaps a month. I was in a lot of pain, and on strong medication. I was in a contraption designed to separate the vertebrae. I came in and out of awareness. The doctors kept scratching my foot, to see if I could feel anything, and asking me to clench my hands. They told me that I had in effect broken my neck and how lucky I was that I hadn't died or been paralysed.
>
> The college contacted my parents, who did not understand the seriousness

of my condition. After being released from the hospital, I spent a couple of weeks in Sick Bay before going home to Sweden for the Christmas holidays. At that point my parents realised how seriously I'd been injured and sent me to an orthopaedic surgeon.

I returned to AC a couple of weeks late after the Christmas break. Instead of participating in rescue services, I went off to a physiotherapist in Bridgend twice a week. I was still in a lot of pain.

In late April my parents called and said they wanted me to come home and do rehab, so I did. I was in rehab throughout that spring and summer. I returned for second year and completed all my courses successfully. But I wasn't able to participate in the life of the college in the way I would have liked. I was still in pain and I had missed a lot the previous year, so I had to work hard to catch up. I continued to suffer back and arm pain. It was three or four years before it went away altogether.

I got the strong impression that the AC staff felt I should just put on a brave face, leave the incident behind and get on with life. I did put on a brave face and I didn't think too much about it until I was halfway into my second year. Then I started to feel angry and frustrated at the way the College had handled the situation. I never received any apology or any reassurance that the College had learned something and was improving safety procedures as a result.

Atlantic College took great pride in its rescue services and it seemed as if the headmaster and staff did not want to acknowledge the fact that Cliff Rescue had had a near fatal accident. This meant in turn that a substantial part of my own Atlantic College experience was not acknowledged either.

Some of my friends also became angry and frustrated at the College's response – or lack of it. The staff simply did not want to talk about it. The whole incident was swept under the carpet. If the matter was mentioned, they referred to me as a volunteer. This is also the term used by David Sutcliffe in later publications. I think they tried to distance themselves from the incident by dimming the fact that I was a student doing what I was asked to do. I left AC with mixed feelings. The attitude from headmaster and staff made me feel belittled, angry and disappointed. At the same time student contacts were enriching and my world expanded. I also gained new insights about my own abilities.

Neither Anna nor her parents made any move to sue the college, a decision that might have been disastrous for its future. One teacher, Tim Agerbak, who was on the scene as driver and supervisor, thought it was a 'heroic' decision: 'The real heroes were Anna and her parents. In this day and age, the college would have been taken to the cleaners. I have a lot of admiration for what the family did – or didn't do.'

As Anna Dixelius commented, there appears to have been no investigation. Agerbak has no recollection of a post-mortem about the accident. But memory alone is not reliable. Dagfinn Paust, involved in the near-fatal rescue of the boy and his uncle trapped by a rising tide, recalled no debrief. However, he was astonished recently to find a 1971 memo from Sutcliffe instructing all concerned parties to attend one. John Ward, also on the callout, recalls some procedures changing as a result. Other students involved in traumatic or misjudged rescues have no memory of any attempt to sit down and learn lessons.

But as inshore rescue was professionalised, times and emphasis changed. Almost exactly 20 years after Anna Dixelius's injury, in September 1988, a callout went wrong and a group of students had to be lifted off the cliff at Nash Point, west of the seafront, by an RAF Search and Rescue helicopter. Some say the seven students were never in danger, others that they came perilously close to drowning.

Unusually, all three services were involved the initial callout to rescue a group reportedly cut off by the incoming tide between the college and Nash Point. The B-boat, the RNLI boat, was launched with three student crew and a staff member, a reflection of the exceptionally rough sea, described by one observer as 'at the very limit' of the boat's operating capabilities.

The Coastguard vans and crew were also part of the emergency response. They were dispatched by road to Nash Point. And, most unusually, Beach Rescue, rarely involved in this kind of rescue, and with the sea far too rough to risk going out in kayaks, instead ran down to the area where the victims were reportedly trapped below the cliffs, scrambling over the boulders and rock ledges in the direction of Nash Point. Critics of the event believe it was rash for them to go at all, and entirely wrong to go as they did, uncounted and unequipped – in some cases barefoot, all without life jackets, a first aid kit or even a radio. Others say some of those involved simply got carried away and tagged along behind the official party.

The ILB was having a torrid time at sea where the surf was so big the automatic cut-off switches, designed to turn off the engines and stop the propellers if the boat capsized, were triggered at least once by the steepness of the waves. But worse was happening to the beach rescuers, who by now had realised the whole thing was a false alarm.

With hindsight, that was the moment at which they perhaps should have been winched up by the Coastguards, who were above them. But the Coastguard had not set up for a rescue, and there were scrubby bushes and growth on the edge of the cliff. So instead, the Beach Rescue party set off back the way they came. By then it was nearly high tide and huge waves were pounding the foot of the cliffs. Some of the group made it back safely, but seven were unable to get through. They scrambled up the cliff to escape the waves, about 150 m from the safety of the sea wall at St Donat's. Someone had called the RAF Sea King helicopter to come from across the channel in Devon. It successfully lowered a winchman and lifted the seven off, one by one, and then flew the whole group back to the college a few hundred metres away.

The ILB crew decided not even to try to come back and land at St Donat's but instead went west round the bay to the more accessible RNLI slipway at Porthcawl. As one observer put it:

> It was very easy at the time to blame certain staff members involved. The student narrative firmly placed the blame at the feet of one young staff member. With hindsight (and having now spent 30 years in education), I feel that was unfair. The reality is more nuanced. A quick decision by a staff member, a misunderstanding, a lack of established protocols and procedures, youthful enthusiasm and a desire to help, all combined to produce the perfect storm.

Jan Helbing, a second year who watched events unfold, wrote this terse account:

> There have been almost no callouts during our second year at the College – I only remember recovering a dead body that had been spotted on a beach cut off by the tides – and in retrospect this 'lack of action' may explain a lot of what went wrong during the unhappy callout in 1988. When the klaxon sounded on a stormy afternoon, we immediately ran down to the lifeboat station at the seafront. We were told that people had been spotted below the cliffs between St Donat's and Nash Point with the tide moving in very fast.

> Callouts usually involved only the Lifeboats and Cliff Rescue, so I was very surprised to see a group of students from the Beach Rescue unit run down the slipway and towards Nash Point before we had even gotten the lifeboat ready. I remember the ILB [had] to remain on standby for quite some time, and we listened in on the radio conversation with Swansea Coastguard as the situation deteriorated. It was the Beach Rescue students who were now stuck below the cliffs just off the College premises, while the Cliff Rescue unit tried to get to them from above. The people who had caused the alarm had probably already made it to the beach at Nash Point.

> At this stage the ILB was launched in spite of the high waves in order to

help locate the stuck 'rescuers' and to direct Cliff Rescue to the correct spot. Unfortunately, however, the vegetation on the top of the cliffs was too dense for a successful 'in-house' rescue. I think the Coastguard called in the RAF helicopter, when the situation became more and more dangerous.

I was not on the lifeboat myself, but it remained in sight all the time as more and more people gathered at the seafront. I remember that many of us felt angry about the 'irresponsible' or 'pointless' move of the Beach Rescuers who had put themselves into danger. Old clichés and rivalries between the rescue services surfaced. This anger soon turned into deep concern for our friends and fellow students, and I felt both relief and embarrassment when the helicopter came.

Because of the severe weather, the lifeboat could not land at St Donat's that day (quite crazily, landing meant that a group of 6–8 students held a trolley on the slipway in the breaking waves, hoping that the approaching boat would cut its engines on the back of a wave and drop down right in between them, sometimes form 1–2 metres above … strangely enough, it almost always worked!). I was asked to recover the rescue boat from the port of Porthcawl the next morning, together with three other students. We were dropped off at the harbour by a member of staff, got the boat ready and brought it back on our own – no question Atlantic College students could not be trusted, even after such a traumatic event!

Paul Belcher was chief coach of Beach Rescue. This is his account:

We had a call that there were some people in danger of being cut off between AC and Nash. The wind was strong from the west, the tide was rising and there was rough surf. Progress would not have been made west in kayaks. I appointed a team to run along the flats underneath the cliffs to investigate towards Nash. Because this was from the College, after I and the team set off, others decided that this was their chance to be involved in a callout and just followed. Shortly before Nash no one had been found and it was then water across to the cwm [the mouth of a stream]. The group then had to return quickly to the College. This most did, but the last few when they were almost back to the scramble up at the west end of the sea wall decided that instead of taking to the water (our natural environment), to move up the cliff onto a ledge. We were then faced with the difficulty of rescuing our own from this situation. Cliff Rescue went into operation to lift them up from above but setting this up was taking time due to the undergrowth at the top of that section of cliff. This is when a helicopter was used to remove students from the ledge. It is true that I was not best pleased with how this callout had gone and afterwards [but] I do not think that there were any people in danger in the first place.

In college mythology, this is when Beach Rescue became the lifeguards. It stopped being part of the college's integrated emergency callout system and became an entirely proactive operation focused on preventing disaster happening.

There was a full investigation of the whole episode. A report was circulated internally and also sent to the Coastguards and the RNLI. Opinion was strongly divided about what exactly went wrong, and therefore what should be changed to put it right. It was a public embarrassment for the college, and it led to the introduction of a new level of preparation, emergency action plans, drawn up as part of rescue procedure.

This near disaster put more people at risk and exposed flawed operating systems more clearly than Anna Dixelius's accident. It also provoked a proper post-mortem. One reason for that is the cultural transformation that had taken place in the 20 years between the two events.

The Health and Safety Act 1974 is regarded as a watershed in UK law. Before, workers were protected against specific and identifiable risk by a legal system that dated back to the Victorian era. After, a system was introduced that laid only broad obligations about ensuring safety on managers and employers. It was their responsibility to fill in the detail required to keep people safe in their area of operation. In effect, the Act transferred responsibility for safety from a series of situation- or occupation-specific laws, to a general requirement for employers 'to ensure the health and safety, so far as is reasonably practicable, of his employees.'

The employer's duty also extended to ensure the health and safety of anyone who might be affected by the conduct of their undertaking. All sorts of subordinate legislation – often regulations and codes of practice – have subsequently been generated, but all act under that broad overall duty established in 1974.

The effect over the years has been a greatly increased awareness of risk. It was an unforeseen consequence that risk awareness would sometimes become risk aversion and contribute to an environment unsuited to encouraging teenagers to do self-evidently risky activities like launching big heavy rescue boats off a trolley into surf, or going to sea in a self-built kayak, or abseiling down an unstable cliff face.

One former AC student, Richard Thompson (1987–89), who, for six summers after he left, returned to work as an instructor at the Extra Mural Centre, summed up the way he now perceives the risk that he had been happy to accept as a student:

A 17-year-old student is waiting about 150 metres off the slipway aboard a college built half-ton rigid-hulled inflatable lifeboat. The boat is being buffeted by the rough seas in the Bristol Channel. The student is trying to pluck up courage to drive the boat at speed towards a heavy metal trolley, positioned on the back of a wave. And possibly for the first time. Eight of us are standing in freezing cold seawater wearing helmets and our self-made wetsuits, holding the aforementioned trolley in position. The student needs to consider: the timing of the run in; wave selection; the positioning of the boat to allow for substantial drift and a lack of visibility. Having chosen the perfect moment, the throttle is engaged, and the landing procedure begins. When the boat is judged to be directly over the trolley, the red 'cut cord' is pulled. The engine is lifted quickly as the boat drops into the trolley without touching the sides. The crew jumps out and the trolley team hauls the boat out of the water and up the slipway. Easy!

We were well trained by the staff and our second years. However, the brutal fact is that some people, no matter how academically gifted, are not blessed with boat handling ability. I will not be the only student to recall feeling somewhat alarmed, while holding the seaward corner of the boat trolley, as an out-of-control lifeboat came surfing down a wave towards me. If the coxswain was driving too fast, the boat would overshoot the wave. Driving too slowly could result in being caught by the next wave.

Looking back, it was extremely dangerous, and it really is a miracle that no one was ever badly injured, or worse. However, how else were you supposed to train to land an inshore lifeboat on a rocky shore in breaking surf? Submersible tractors and trolleys with a net recovery system were still being developed by the RNLI and were not widely deployed until the 1990s. Even when they did arrive, landings could still go wrong. I witnessed coxswains drive the boat over the net, under the net and even miss the trolley altogether. Landing the boat in surf, whichever method was used, was not easy!

Events beyond the college also influenced what was possible within it. In March 1993, on the south coast of England, four teenagers drowned in a sea kayaking accident during a privately run outdoor education activity day in Lyme Bay. Even more than the Health and Safety Act, this event and the legislative changes that followed had a profound effect on those who managed the activities at Atlantic College.

The Lyme Bay tragedy was caused by incompetence and ignorance. In the criminal trial that followed, the owner of the activity centre was convicted of gross negligence manslaughter and served a two-year prison term. But there were much wider consequences. Self-regulation of outdoor activity centres was replaced with a licensing system under the Adventure Activities Licensing Authority. Although Atlantic College did not have to be licensed as an Adventure Activities centre, the Extra Mural Centre did. Richard Naylor perceived a widening gap between the orderliness and demanding standards that they learned in order to meet their licensing conditions, and the contrasting sense of amateurishness in college activities. In 2007 the Corporate Manslaughter and Corporate Homicide Act made it possible for the first time for companies and organisations, rather than individuals, to be found guilty of corporate manslaughter if serious management failures resulted in a gross breach of a duty of care.

Other factors, not inevitable but hard to avoid, also began to change the character and the culture of the college despite committed efforts to find ways of accommodating the new demands. The age and interests of the staff began to change. In the early years they were young and often uncommitted. When Andrew Maclehose joined AC in the 1960s, he came from teaching at Timbertops in Australia, while a contemporary, Tim Agerbak, and his wife arrived – young, idealistic and internationalist – from working in Africa. It was expected that teachers would do much more than teach their academic discipline. From the start, applicants who saw the advertisements in the *Times Educational Supplement* for staff for the new college could have had no doubt about the importance of non-academic activities, nor the hierarchy that put such activities on at least equal footing with its academic ambitions.

Another recruit to the new college was a young Scot, John Grant-Wood. He was headmaster of a primary school on Shetland when he saw the ad for various jobs at a new international college. Although they weren't recruiting people to teach his subject, geography, he talked his way in, clinching the deal when he offered his wife, Pam, as part of the package. She became Desmond Hoare's secretary.

Those first generations of staff were almost uniformly young and committed to the ideals that Atlantic College was founded to instil. They brought energy and iconoclasm and a level of commitment that meant they devoted far more hours to their non-teaching duties than their contracts required.

Desmond Hoare had an idea that staff, like students, should change frequently so that ideas and attitudes were continually refreshed. But that is a hard act to maintain, and it is not necessarily a successful business model. Against the benefits of continuing innovation has to be set a lack of continuity, and a tendency for each new generation to reinvent the wheel. David Sutcliffe himself provided both the continuity and the drive until 1982 when he left to become headmaster of the new United World College at Duino in Italy. None of his successors quite managed to match his engagement across all the college activities, and few tried to emulate his hands-on involvement in the rescue services. None lasted as long (although it is significant that every principal, until Colin Jenkins retired in 2000, had started at AC in its first decade).

As time went by, newly recruited teachers tended to be a little older and often to have young families. They were sometimes reluctant to make the same investment in after-hours working, and – anecdotally – it seemed to become more of an obligation than an enthusiasm. Long-serving teachers grew older, and, unavoidably, less fit.

Another small, but important episode illustrates the consequences of this slight dulling of commitment. It took place during first year camp early in the 2000s. Initially the camp, for every intake of new students a truly memorable, if sometimes nightmare, experience, was run by the team who organised Cliff Rescue. Sometimes it took place in the Brecon Beacons, sometimes on the West Wales coast when Beach Rescue could contribute while widening their own experience under RNLI supervision on new and different beaches.

On this occasion, the camp was in mid Wales. Two groups were doing a walk in the Black Mountain area from opposite directions. A student had a seizure and in the ensuing panic, no staff could be located where they should have been. The anxious second-year students in charge felt they had no choice but to call in a rescue helicopter.

Happily, there were no lasting consequences for any of the students, but the following year, the Extra Mural Centre took over responsibility for the first year camp. It is telling that what the EMC would see as its higher concern for safety, meant for students a less exciting experience.

David Cope joined the staff at AC in 1983, soon after Cliff Rescue had taken over as the Auxiliary Coastguard station under Ivar Lund Mathiesen. He stayed for more than 20 years. His main job was to run summer programmes for visiting young people at the EMC, attended by between 2,000 and 2,500 a year. But he was also on the Coastguard squad and every summer second years who had reached the Coastguard's exacting standards came and taught the visitors while also manning the Coastguard station. Cope was aware of changing attitudes in their parent organisation.

Atlantic College was an anomaly for HM Coastguards. It had a larger company than any other station and utilised rescue techniques that did not appear in the Coastguard Handbook. Initially this was accepted by those in charge but as time went on and personnel in HMCG changed, our differences became one of the main reasons, along with arguments about insurance and Health & Safety issues, that they closed the station and returned it to Llantwit Major.

Under Ivar [Lund Mathiesen] and up until the Station closed, AC had a very good relationship with the people in Swansea, which is where we were managed from. The Sector Officer who was in charge of us, as well as the Porthcawl and Barrie stations, was called Peter Furlong. He was very understanding in terms of how we operated even though we were a 'bit' different. The College had developed different systems which drew from both mountain rescue systems and Coastguard standard practices. Student training sessions were often witnessed by the Regional Controller at Swansea (Dick Richards) and the District Controller (Leighton Kent) on their monthly visits. They seemed to enjoy visiting and joining the Coastguard students for lunch. When Peter Furlong retired, so did the Regional & District Controllers and so the personnel changed.

The change of personnel at Swansea followed other problems for the college's provision of coastguards that only escalated after Ivar Lund Mathiesen left in 1987. The service was divided into an elite Auxiliary Coastguard and a Cliff Rescue squad, under different heads. John Lawrenson, later deputy headmaster of AC, ran Cliff Rescue and David Cope ran the Coastguard.

The Coastguard has a particular status in the coastal rescue ecology because it is staffed by paid professionals. The college and students were, nominally, paid if they went on a callout, although in fact their earnings went straight into the equipment kitty. The Coastguard's status means it takes the lead at the scene of an emergency. It has authority not only over the RNLI but also, where they are present, the police.

When it came, the closure of AC's Coastguard station was a shock to most of those involved. No one at AC felt that their standards were slipping. Richard Naylor, who was often the senior Coastguard figure during summer callouts, believes the AC station was at least as good as any other. He remembers one particular 'shout' [callout] on a proverbially dark and stormy night:

I can't imagine there was any other Coastguard unit so well drilled. They were on the demonstration cliff or another rockface four times a week for two years. By the time they came to the Extra Mural Centre [immediately after leaving AC at the end of their second year] they were extremely good.

There was one shout in particular that really felt like we 'saved a life' (two lives actually). A couple got cut off by the rising tide at Southerndown and climbed up the face of the cliff to keep out of the waves. The wind blew up to gale/storm force and was so fierce that even though Swansea sent the helicopter from Devon, they wouldn't send the winchman down for fear that he would swing in the wind and knock the couple off the ledge they were clinging on to.

So we had to pick them off with the Cliff Rescue kit. By then it was dark, and although it was summer, the wind was so strong that it made the work difficult, and it was chilling for the casualties, who were only in very light beach attire.

It's a big job, involving enormous cast iron spikes, 5 ft long, that have to be driven into the ground to anchor the winching equipment and all the ropes. The winchman went down and discovered he was 2–3 metres wide of where the victims were. So we had to upsticks and rip up the rig and re-erect it. It's a massive job to rip the stakes out of the ground and I can't imagine any other Coastguard could have done it. We did it in something like ten minutes.

I find it hard to think any other could have done it better.

However, changes were taking place in the world of coastal rescue. In 1998, HM Coastguard was merged with the Marine Safety Agency. Coastguard stations were closing, victims of a combination of cost saving, digital communications and the growing use of helicopters which shrank the time needed to cover any area of operation.

At the same time, new training standards and a new style of training were introduced, 'competency-based': all the 30 or so skills required of a cliff rescuer broken down one by one. With the introduction of the new scheme, all serving Coastguard personnel were obliged to rate themselves. David Cope thought the new regime at Swansea, which ran all the Bristol Channel Coastguard stations was out of sympathy with the special approach of Atlantic College. Richard Naylor thinks perhaps there was a generational difference of approach that the college stalwarts failed to understand, responding to the self-rating request with exaggerated claims of competence. Whatever the reason, in 2002 Swansea told the college it could not reconcile the twin problems of insurance and health and safety, and the station at St Donat's would have to close. It would be relocated back to Llantwit Major, where it remains.

It was a terrible blow for David Cope:

> We had no warning at all. We got a letter to the principal saying, as of
> Thursday next week the Llantwit Major station will be closing – it was still
> called that and we still had three Llantwit Major people who'd stayed with
> the station when it moved to St Donat's (well, two from town plus John
> David who'd left the college but remained as auxiliary Coastguard, with
> George Egan and Les Beckwith). We were called to a meeting with the
> Swansea District Controller and the newly appointed Sector Officer Nicola –
> and were told they were closing stations. They provided spurious arguments
> that we weren't doing the things the way we should be, they talked about
> conformity right the way across the service.

> We put up an appeal, it was rejected. They took everything that was theirs.
> It was quite soul-destroying. Students still trained, but they never did any
> rescuing, so it went back to being more mountaineering and climbing.

There was more to it, however, than the old vs. the new. Training was more
demanding, and assessments and exams more formal. The area of flexibility that
the college had previously enjoyed was getting smaller. And it was becoming
harder to justify the cost of training students who might only have a few months
at peak efficiency, or perhaps a year or two if they came back in their summer
vacations to work at the Extra Mural Centre, when the alternative was to train
local people who would be available all year round, for years to come. As another
instructor and ex-student Julian Jones recalls, 'it was not considered value for
money.' For a time, the college joined the Cardiff and Vale Rescue Association,
which looked for missing people. But it lacked the drama and the demands of a
coastal rescue service. Students soon lost interest.

'Value for money' turned out to be a portent. In Beach Rescue it had been
decided to stop competing in national contests because the division between
the competition squad and those who turned out for August period lifeguarding
duties was viewed as corrosive – a problem Phil Green had been trying to address
as long ago as the late 1970s. Kayaking faded from the seafront. Local government
increasingly took responsibility for providing lifeguards for their local beaches, with
AC surf lifeguards working alongside them. Then, as council budgets became
more squeezed, the RNLI took over the job, as well as the training. Especially in
first aid, it was to a very high standard. But now the August period itself was
shrinking, as the college argued that it was no longer economic to be only half full
for part of the year. Teacher Paul Belcher watched it all diminish:

> Project week activities became more diverse with board surfing replacing
> kayak surfing and Coasteering and Stand-up Paddle Boards being

introduced. There were still kayak and sit-on trips and the desire to find interesting pieces of coastline for rock-hopping.

With the erosion of August Period [which was abandoned altogether in 2018] and being more egalitarian and not going to the SLSA championships, long 'Service weekends' were introduced. Lifeguard Service students went camping in Tenby. This allowed those students who had qualified as Beach Lifeguards to gain more experience, working under the RNLI, on the three busy beaches in Tenby. Others such as the Swimming Instructors did a variety of activities such as board surfing, kayak or sit-on trips and coasteering.

The burden of training to crew the RNLI B-boat had also greatly increased. The college's old coxswain requirement became more strictly enforced, and the training and qualification requirement increased and became more and more stringent and severely limited the number of people who were qualified to captain, or helm, a B-boat on a callout.

Merely to qualify for a place on a helm training course, additional skills were required which would normally take at least two years of experience on the boat. These courses only ran in winter, in order to test candidates in the worst conditions possible. By 2001, it was no longer possible to become a coxswain inside the two academic years at Atlantic College.

Many teachers were keen sailors and would occasionally go out in the rescue boats when these were supporting the sailing activities on weekday afternoons or with the regattas on the weekend. However, before the 1980s, teachers would not normally go to sea on callouts.

With the introduction of the new and costly two-year requirement students could generally only qualify if they committed to work in the Extra Mural Centre in the holidays providing callout coverage when most students were away for vacation. In any one year, it became unusual for more than one former student to attain RNLI approval to launch and helm a B-boat on callouts. The kernel of the rescue service mission – that it was the students themselves who were to be trained and then trusted to do the job – was lost.

By 2004, the RNLI was insisting that potential crew members passed their level two Royal Yachting Association exam for powerboat handling. It was a sign of the times that Eleuthera du Breuil was asked to commit to working at the EMC as a Royal Yachting Association instructor for three consecutive summers in return for the college paying for her training as an RNLI helm. She qualified in January 2005, still only 18.

Another change: in the daily training of the rescue boat crews, sailing had played a key role. The boats' initial purpose had been to protect the sailors. But in 2005, sailing was relocated to the calmer waters of Barry Harbour, half an hour from the college, and the hours of 'bashing the Bristol Channel' that had taught the crews so much, were no longer required.

By 2012, it was becoming clear that the RNLI station at AC was on borrowed time. It was no longer a pioneering force. Its decline was in part a sign of the RNLI's own successful efforts at public education in beach and water safety. But there were other factors.

In Barry, to the east of the College, the RNLI station got a new and faster (25 knot) all-weather lifeboat with a bigger range. At the same time, to the west, Porthcawl had the large Atlantic 85 class boat capable of doing 35 knots. Thus, capacity was expanded on both the eastern and western sides of Atlantic College's traditional area of responsibility. Likewise, across the Bristol Channel in Minehead, where the RNLI station had had an inshore lifeboat for many years, an Atlantic 85 was installed in 2007. In addition to the College's own B-boat, three other neighbouring boats would normally be able to reach an incident in the area within the required 30 minutes. The number of callouts involving the AC station steadily declined. Between 2009 and 2013 the AC boat went out only five times a year on average.

The St Donat's station had one great advantage: the time between 'shout' and launch. Until the advent of the Thames lifeboat in 2002, it was consistently the fastest responder in the country. But this did not give it an edge over larger boats that could cover a bigger area faster and could operate at considerable speed even in fairly rough conditions. The RNLI proposed replacing the current Atlantic 75 class boat at AC with the 1 metre longer model, the Atlantic 85.

But that meant more investment at the seafront, even knocking down parts of the existing concrete and rock sea wall to make a wider opening. The slipway would need widening and the boathouse expanding. It was a huge undertaking. The RNLI had been generous in their backing for the AC station. One reason may have been that it was a useful vehicle for the kind of publicity that would help attract young recruits as well as donations. But it was never a sinecure for AC, as Ray Kipling, then deputy director of the [RNLI] told the *Times Educational Supplement* in 2003.

> If it wasn't working we wouldn't continue with it. We have got to keep to pretty high standards at all our stations. We can't get sentimental about it.

Basically they are a good bunch of young, fit people who take to training very well. There is a genuine need for a lifeboat there. It is a most unusual set-up but it works very well indeed.

They have to be confident enough to do whatever it takes to effect a rescue and to get that information across to the person in trouble.

With hindsight, his words contain more than a hint of a warning of the challenges faced by Atlantic College in maintaining the RNLI station – 'high standards … can't get sentimental … most unusual set up…'.

Bigger boats with a longer range meant fewer stations as well as more formal training, and a new reliance on SOPs (standard operating procedures). In a more litigious society, questions of legal liability became more onerous.

These developments were set against the demands of the International Baccalaureate, parental expectations of academic success, and the outlook of students themselves. With fewer and fewer opportunities to serve in the rescue services, the motivation for committing to the training and the long hours at sea or on the cliff meant fewer students taking part.

In 2013, the RNLI closed the St Donat's inshore rescue station. A memorial given to the college by the RNLI recorded the moment thus:

Atlantic College has played a unique and central role in the development of fast inshore rescue boats for the Royal National Lifeboat Institution. The Atlantic 21, named after the College, made history as the first rigid inflatable lifeboat to be accepted into the RNLI's operational fleet. The Atlantic 21 paved the way for her successors the Atlantic 75 (1993) and 95 (2005).

During a 50 year history, the crews of Atlantic College Lifeboat Station have launched on service 459 times and saved a total of 98 lives.

Their contributions to the innovations of the lifeboat fleet and their dedication to the service over the years have been sincerely appreciated.

A sombre David Sutcliffe made no attempt to disguise his sadness.

In a few moments the Atlantic College lifeboat will travel down the College slipway for the last time. I do not think that the decision taken can be judged either right or wrong. Rather, it is the natural outcome of events and developments in the wider context of lifesaving, all of which are to be welcomed unreservedly.

In the early days of the College, boats whose time had come were often doused in petrol, launched into Bristol Channel, set alight and given a true Viking funeral. Perhaps this evening's crew should bear this in mind if they detect the smell of petrol. But I ask them above all to be aware that they are taking down the slipway with them irreplaceable memories, truly formative experiences, the pride of accomplishment, undeniable evidence of a technological and educational achievement of absolute world class.

It would be presumptuous and absurd to claim that Atlantic College was responsible for all or even most of the advances in lifeguarding and inshore rescue. When challenges arise, like-minded people generally arrive more or less simultaneously at similar conclusions and solutions. But the College was in the vanguard, and the vanguard is a good place to be. Let the College for ever be proud that it was a really serious partner with the RNLI in a common enterprise of great import. Before the College opened in 1962, it was necessary to break a gap in the sea wall to gain access to the Bristol Channel. May that gap never be closed again!

CHAPTER TWELVE

Epilogue

If the rescue services that were invented and honed over 50 years by staff and students in the turbulent inshore waters of the Bristol Channel are no longer an option, can their purpose be reinvented somewhere else? In what other way can the almost universal desire of teenagers to respond to need, their appetite for risk and their enthusiasm for shared experience be answered?

When the official Atlantic College RNLI inshore rescue boat was launched for the final time, it was crewed by the last of the AC students to meet the stringent crewing qualifications, Lily Eckersley-Jones. Also on board was Robin Jenkins, the longest-serving RNLI helm to have qualified at AC. He was a veteran with more than 20 years' experience at St Donat's and also as a volunteer on the Thames RNLI boat in London.

Robin Jenkins grew up at St Donat's. His father, Colin, had come to AC for the first time in 1971 and was headmaster from 1990 to 2000. Robin was a student from 1990 to 1992 and returned many times afterwards to train RNLI crew in the August period and, in the famous saying, to mess about in boats.

For him the closure of the station was a terrible disappointment. But if it was the end of an era, it was not the end of the idea behind it. Through him, a series of otherwise disconnected events were linked up into what has now emerged as a new venture: Atlantic Pacific. All proceeds from the sale of this book will go to Atlantic Pacific

Atlantic Pacific is an NGO that is dedicated to providing training to young people who want to respond to the calls for help they hear from around the world, in all the skills that are useful – boat handling, lifesaving, casualty handling, conventional and psychological first aid for the injured and traumatised, and also fundraising, charity management, organisation and HR obligations.

The sequence of events that led to the founding of AP illustrates the power of AC to connect people. Back in 2011, two seafront enthusiasts and AC alumni, Saul Mendelssohn and Asbjørn Damhus (also a long-time teacher), heard on the grapevine that Barry Yacht Club had discovered deep in their storage containers what they thought was one of AC's earliest RIB designs. They wondered: Did AC want it back, or should they destroy it?

Soon the hull was back at AC. Saul, Robin and the RNLI mechanic Paul Dowling – together with another friend of Robin, and a team of students – were hard at work stripping the hull of what slowly emerged as 'probably' the old rescue boat X6 which was built – perhaps professionally – in the mid-1960s [see John Grey-Davies' story in Chapter 1]. With a hull of Egyptian mahogany ply, it was in remarkably good condition. The boat was carefully restored, then a mould was made, and two more boats built of fibreglass were constructed. A few years later the boat, now called 'X Alpha' by the college, and the whole RIB design developed at AC was awarded the Engineering Heritage Award by the Institution of Mechanical Engineers (IMechE). This plaque hangs on the wall of the old lifeboat house by the college seafront.

74. Engineering Heritage Award.

Event number two was a chance conversation between Robin, who is an architect as well as RNLI helm, and the curator of the De La Warr Pavilion, a gallery in Bexhill-on-Sea, on the south-east coast of England. The curator thought the history of the rigid inflatable would make a great summer exhibition for the seaside town. Robin was duly commissioned to curate the show.

The reason why Robin and friends subsequently decided it would be fun to take the two boats to the exhibition not overland, but by sea – a journey of some 550 miles – is less clear, but it certainly generated great publicity as well as establishing all over again what a seaworthy craft the basic RIB is.

Event number three was the closure of the RNLI station at St Donat's in 2013, which fell between work beginning on restoring X6, and the Bexhill exhibition itself.

Event number four came in the long aftermath of a much greater tragedy: the earthquake and tsunami that devastated northern Japan in 2011. Three years later, Robin, who was now teaching at the Chelsea School of Art in London, was asked by his principal if he would like to go and scope out a community rebuilding project in the small Japanese mining town of Kamaishi which had been badly damaged in the tsunami. While he was there, he heard of the terrible experience endured by survivors, safe on shore while hundreds of their friends and families who had been washed out to sea could be heard offshore crying for help. There was no lifeboat to send to their aid. Japan has no national lifeboat service.

It did not take him long to grasp the serendipity of the rediscovery of X6, and the need for a simple, effective inshore rescue boat that could be delivered in a crisis. Back in the UK, he challenged AC students to come up with a lifeboat design modelled on X6. That August period, he and a team of students worked on a new model, fundamentally the same as but longer than the original. On another visit to Kamaishi, he unveiled the project – only to be presented with the problem of where it would live.

On the long flight back to London, Robin realised that as the rescue boat would need to be shipped out to Japan in a container, the same container could be repurposed to be a basic lifeboat station. Once in London, he acquired one and with the backing of the art school, he set it up in the courtyard beside Tate Britain in central London. With ideas and practical help from his students, he refurbished it.

But before the Japanese project was completed, a parallel series of events began to unfold. It was 2015. In the Mediterranean, the refugee crisis was at a peak. Thousands of desperate people fleeing Syria, Iraq, Afghanistan and parts of Africa were dying at sea. Late that year, a German ex-student Annegret Berne asked Robin if he could help with search and rescue around the island of Lesvos.

Back in South Wales, Robin, helped by Lily Eckersley-Jones, packed one of the new boats into the back of a van and despatched it to the island of Lesvos. They next saw it a week later on a wintry beach on the Mediterranean island. Before they had had time to begin to train volunteers in its use, they were called to the aid of a refugee boat. Training, it turned out, would happen on the job. 'We probably saved more lives in two and a half weeks than any AC boat had done its entire lifespan,' Robin believes.

It was the experience that Robin and Lily had in Lesvos that convinced them that there was an urgent need for a training programme for the thousands of young people who want to be useful in a humanitarian emergency: Atlantic Pacific was born.

Atlantic Pacific is now regularly training AC students and others to work in the Mediterranean. Rune Øster Mortensen is a recent graduate. His first callout was with the NGO, Refugee Rescue which Atlantic Pacific partners with, on 15 August 2019 in the afternoon. They were based in Skala Sykamineas, Lesvos, Greece, and the refugee boats were spotted north-west of there, towards the Turkish naval border.

This is his account of it:

> Yesterday we were about to sit down for lunch when we got a call to assist a refugee boat two miles offshore. As our helm Mary describes below, we had to use the refugees' own boat to bring 31 children and 19 adults to shore on a rocky beach as access was denied to the harbours in the area to avoid disturbing the many summer tourists. My crewmate Rob from England and I had to get in the water to swim the boat the last bit of way from our rescue boat to the shore. Thank you to the volunteers from Lighthouse Relief who were ready to take over from here. Today we were about to sit down for lunch again, when we got a call and assisted another two boats with ~90 refugees to a safe landing.

This is Mary Finn's account. Finn, who is British, attended the UWC Adriatic (one of several other United World Colleges) 2013–15, and is working to help refugees around Europe.

I was overwhelmed by how co-operative and trusting the passengers were on this mission. There were 50 people on board the dinghy: 9 men, 10 women, and 31 children and even though we weren't moving anywhere, and were frustratingly close to the coast, they all remained calm and compliant while we waited. Our team used this time to distribute water, and blankets to protect from the sun, and we were able to assess those on board more closely. I noticed an unusually high number of passengers from Afghanistan had scabies, suggesting that many had been waiting in very poor, cramped conditions prior to taking the trip. A number of the children were also diabetic, with no medication to hand, and there was a young baby on board. Seeing a baby always puts things into perspective for me, reminding me of the risks people take, and how awful the situations they're fleeing from, must be.

We began transferring the group to Agios Dimitrios beach, so as not to disrupt the tourists on Skala and Tsonia. We knew the transfer from water to land was going to be difficult to navigate.

We decided to act quickly and use the dinghy to get the passengers from the authority vessel to land. Two members of our crew bravely hit the water, using all their strength to employ throwlines to draw the dinghy, and those on board, towards the shore. They had to make three, arduous trips back and forth between the [Greek] authority vessel and the land to ensure that everyone made it off safely – an incredibly strenuous and exhausting operation for us, lasting well over an hour. But it was good to see the passengers again.

They kept hugging and thanking us, saying how much they appreciated our kindness. I was struck by how helpful and considerate they had been throughout the whole rescue.

Other missions have seen a number of difficulties, with boats refusing to turn off their engines due to the understandable fear of being deported. But these passengers put all their faith in us, and I was so thankful they did. It aided their safety, and the overall success of the rescue.

Thanks to the team's commitment and dedication, everyone made it safely out of the water and were placed in the care of the Lighthouse Relief team at approximately 17.00.

A great deal of patience and teamwork were the order of the day here to ensure the safety of those who made the crossing. As always, our team delivered. Thank you!

*****

Robin Jenkins believes AP represents one way of reinventing the original ideal of service and adventure for the 21st century, in keeping with the original ambition of designing a boat expressly for inshore rescue.

The Atlantic75 (or lovingly known, B Boat), was a symbol of what could be achieved by a group of young, visionary students. It represented the chance of making a huge impact on humanitarian endeavours. The RIB went on to become the most widely used tool in sea rescue, and probably the most successful boat in seafaring history. The closure of the RNLI station at St Donat's should not be seen as an end to this incredible story, just the end of a chapter. We believe Atlantic Pacific can write the next one.

Researching the history of what had taken place during the early days of AC's industrious seafront, it became clear that what made the RIB a success was that it was a genuine challenge with a clear objective – to develop an asset for the purpose of rescue. The 'process' lay in the creativity it demanded, and the responsibility it devolved on to students. Atlantic Pacific decided to revisit this pioneering methodology and challenge the students once again.

The difference is that while the AC Lifeboat Station served as a resource to help the local community, Atlantic Pacific is challenging the students to consider the whole of humanity. Seven years on from the closure of the RNLI station, Atlantic Pacific is now a growing organisation, with a presence in the Mediterranean refugee crisis and continued work in Japan. There is a new training facility coming online in London in 2021, and there are ongoing developments at AC where we have ambitious plans for the seafront that include new boat building facilities, an enhanced training programme and the resolve to develop the next major innovation in sea rescue.

Kurt Hahn was responsible for a myriad of relevant statements that I could quote here, but I believe the most appropriate one for our ambitions at AC is this one:

'There are three ways of trying to win the young. There is persuasion, there is compulsion and there is attraction. You can preach at them, that is a hook without a worm; you can say "you must volunteer," and that is of the devil; and you can tell them, "you are needed," that appeal hardly ever fails.'

*****

Afterword
Phil Green

Desmond Hoare once wrote, 'The heart of the matter is the need to demonstrate that self-discipline, devotion, imagination, courage and response to challenge can be developed in materially prosperous societies … the instinct to helpfulness is present in every youth; it can either be fostered and flourish or it can be neglected and fade away.'

So the question remains, did AC achieve those aims? The stories clearly answer in the affirmative.

The vehicle of the rescue services was picked to meet the needs of the age in the mid to late 20th century: increased recreational use of the seaside, lack of inshore rescue craft and skills. And in part, because of Atlantic College and those amazing teenagers and teachers, those are no longer the needs of our age. The College introduced disciplined, intensive training, in the classroom (tides, boat maintenance and so on), on shore and at sea. It set up an environment wherein teenagers could find their common humanity – and this shows through in the stories. It taught students to assess and manage risk, to take responsibility, to use their hands (Hoare: 'to instil respect for skill of hand in the academically besotted students'), to become leaders (training first years, becoming a cox, leading a rescue) teamwork, learning to fail, dealing with trauma and mostly importantly learning to trust well-trained peers. Many referred to these ideas in their stories.

So what are the needs of our age today? Clearly there are many. Can teenagers be trained and trusted to tackle those issues? We think they can.

The human need to help remains as vital as ever, and channelling it is still as rewarding.

Atlantic Pacific offers one way of meeting Kurt Hahn and Admiral Hoare's dream all those years ago. There are many other possibilities too. May the courage, the drive and the creativity of the college's founders and the impact they had on generations of students serve as an inspiration to their successors.

David Sutcliffe had asked, referring to the traumatic experiences that students lived through, 'how we in the college coped with such events?' When we started the project, we thought we would hear from students who had suffered from post-traumatic stress disorder (PTSD), unknown at the time most of the stories took place. But we didn't. There may have been students who suffered from PTSD who did not contribute. It seems to me now, after having worked on this project for four years, that the answer was in the unique nature of the community of students and staff that lived at St Donat's. It offered students a chance to act selflessly, thereby building that inner moral law, as Hahn called it. When they did, and ventured out in lifeboats, or in the Land Rover to a cliff edge, or in kayaks, all to face real physical danger to save lives, it was a shared experience. Everyone at the college heard the klaxon. Everyone knew members of their community had put themselves at risk to help others. And that community, as the stories show, offered support when they came back, whether it was over a meal in the dining room, or talking all night in a dormitory room. When I went back to reunions and met fellow AC students, I saw how important that community of people from all over the world truly is to me, and, I am sure, thousands of other AC alumni.

Acknowledgements

Many people provided the stories that constitute this book. The quotes, long and short, are taken from emails, telephone and video calls, conversations and letters exchanged in 2019–2020, unless otherwise indicated. Atlantic College alumni and staff, past and present, responded enthusiastically to the idea of this project and were generous in sharing their memories and reflections.

There may be discrepancies or even inaccuracies in some of the stories; different people remember events differently. We focused on trying to capture the feelings and experiences of callouts, rather than on absolute historical accuracy.

In addition to those on our list of contributors, we'd like to thank Pelham Allen for his assistance retrieving records; Pippi Reader for her assistance in finding contact information for alumni and staff; Gareth Rees for his feedback and insights into ILB history; Michael Sutcliffe for his very valuable efforts in providing access to his father David's records after his death; August Thomas and Geoff Williams for reading and providing helpful feedback on early drafts of the book; Hayley Whiting at the RNLI office for early assistance finding archival records of callouts.

We wish to extend special thanks to Elisabeth Sutcliffe for her support after David's death.

Very special thanks to fellow ex-student, Willem de Vogel, for his generous financial contribution which enabled us to launch the printing and publishing of this book. As a result, all profits from book sales will go directly to Atlantic Pacific.

The authors have attempted to identify and find the photographers of the photos used in this book. This has proved difficult. Many of the photos were taken several decades ago and the photographer is unknown. In some cases, several people sent us the same photo without knowing its origin. In such instances, we have attributed the photos by naming our source. In other cases, we thought we knew who the photographer was but were unable to contact them. Where we have been able to obtain permission, we have credited the image as appropriate. We apologise in advance to anyone we have not credited.

Thank you, also, to everyone at Atlantic College who participated in the rescue services over five decades. Without you, there would be no book.

Contributors

(*staff member)

Tim Agerbak *
Ana Alexander
Pelham Allen
Rosie Allen
Stephan Barker
Paul Belcher *
Joy and Antonin Besse Jr
Erik Borg
Luigi Boscarelli
Rhodri Bradley-Jones
Assia Brandrup-
    Lukanow
Anne Brearley *
Lorenz Breitfeld
Eleuthera du Breuil
Wayne Brommell
Jim Buckheit
Michiel van Lookeren
    Campagne
Martin Cannon
David Cope *
Simon Daman Willems
John David *
Anna Dixelius
Malcom Dixelius
Walter Erdelitsch
Beatrice Cito Filarmino
Mary Finn
Matthew Goodman
Etienne Grall
Philip Green
Thierry Green

John Grey-Davies
Douglas Hamilton
Sten Hammarlund
Tim Haney
Sue Harris (née Parker)
Colin Harrison
Jan Helbing
Dezsö Horváth
Lis Hostvedt McLoughlin
Robin Jenkins
Julian Jones
Lily Eckersley-Jones
Auke Koopal
John van Kuffeler
Tomas Kåberger
Simon Lagoe
Geoff Launchbury
Jonathan Lipscomb
Freddie (Winifred Ann)
    Lloyd-Smith
Ivar Lund Mathiesen *
Andrew Maclehose *
Richard Malpas
Bruce Matheson
Angus Matthews
James Mendelssohn
Saul Mendelssohn
Tim Milligan
Rune Øster Mortensen
Claes Moth
Richard Naylor
Sir Howard Newby

David Nockels
Ian Paley
Amlyn Parry
Neill Patterson
Dagfinn ('Daffy') Paust
David Riley
Gerhard Robbers
David Ross
Apolline Royer
Andreas Schwerdtfeger
Merel van Slageren
John Smalley
Dimitrios Sotiropoulos
Rob Steynor
B St-Onge
Sally Stradling
Anna Margareta
    Sundberg
Michael Sutcliffe
Penny Sutton
Richard Thompson
Götz Unger
Andy Verrinder
Eboo Versi
Willem F P de Vogel
John Ward
Morgyn Warner
Meg Westley
Peter Williamson
Kenneth Wilson
Jurgen Wrede

Works Cited

'Lifeboat crew hurt in sea rescue', news.bbc.co.uk./2/hi/uk_news/wales/south_east/5180980.stm. Accessed 04 February, 2021.

'Newsman drowned inquest told', http://news.bbc.co.uk/2/hi/uk_news/wales/1398901.stm. Accessed 05 February 2021.

Sutcliffe, DB. *Kurt Hahn and the United World Colleges, with Other Founding Figures.* Privately Published, 2013.

Sutcliffe, DB. *The RIB, the Rigid-hulled Inflatable Lifeboat and Its Place of Birth, the Atlantic College.* Granta Editions, 2010.

Sutcliffe, DB., and Glanmor Philips. *The Story of St Donat's Castle and Atlantic College.* Hyperion Books, 1983

The Creative Team

Eleuthera (Ella) du Breuil (AC 2002–04): Ella is half British, half French. She is a paramedic dividing her time between working on ambulances in London and training people with the NGO Atlantic Pacific for humanitarian volunteering, mostly with migrants in the Mediterranean. She also volunteers with the RNLI as a crew member and helm.

Philip Green (AC 1976–78): Phil is Canadian. He never grew out of kayaking after he left Beach Rescue at AC and is now Commodore of the Port Credit Paddling Club in Mississauga, Ontario, where he paddles about 1,000 km every year. He is CEO of First Resource Management Group Inc., a forest management and technology firm. Phil has a Master's in statistics and has written two business books.

David Nockels (AC 1969–71): Dave is British and trained as a naval architect and marine specialist in the North-East of England. He worked as a UK Health and Safety Executive Inspector and then in the offshore oil and gas industry in the field of technical risk management, with a speciality in emergency evacuation, rescue and recovery. Later he became a professional helicopter pilot, working in the UK with the police and air ambulance. He was married to the late Hilary McDermott (AC 1970–72).

Dagfinn Heyerdahl Paust (AC 1970–72): Dagfinn ('Daffy') is Norwegian, and after AC and the ILBs, worked as a boatbuilder and served in the Norwegian Navy before university in Switzerland and USA, where he got his Master's in Business. He has worked in finance there and in Norway, mostly with private equity, but also with maritime safety. Now semi-retired in Oslo, he is Chairman of the Board of Positron Capital and its numerous investment funds.

Anne Perkins (AC 1969–71): Anne is a British political journalist, writer and broadcaster, and holds a first class honours degree in history. Her career has been divided between the BBC and Independent Television News, and *The Guardian* where for 20 years she was a political correspondent, columnist and editorial writer. She is the author of four books: *Red Queen: the authorized biography of Barbara Castle*; *Stanley Baldwin; A Very British Strike* and *The Little Book of Political Ideas*.

Ross Slade (AC 1970–72): Ross is a Canadian national, retired and currently living in Umbria, Italy. Following his rescue boat and building experience at AC, he helped build the first rescue boats for Pearson College (AC's sister college in Canada). He obtained a Master's degree in industrial design and had his own design company, RJS ID Inc. in Ottawa, Canada for many years. Ross has been actively involved in AC alumni activities.

Meg Westley (AC 1970–72): A native of Canada, Meg has a PhD in Drama, and spent her career teaching communications and drama at post-secondary institutions. She has also written two books (fiction and memoir) and held a variety of volunteer positions, including president of Dying with Dignity Canada and chair of the local school board. Retired, she lives in Stratford, Canada.